# MAMMALS
# OF INDIA

## VIVEK MENON

PRINCETON UNIVERSITY PRESS
PRINCETON AND OXFORD

Published in the United States, Canada, and the Philippine Islands by Princeton University Press, 41 William Street, Princeton, New Jersey 08540

nathist.press.princeton.edu

In the United Kingdom and European Union, published 2009 by Christopher Helm, an imprint of A&C Black Publishers Ltd., 36 Soho Square, London W1D 3QY

www.acblack.com

ISBN 978-0-691-14067-4
Library of Congress Control Number
2008938840

First published in India in 2003
by Dorling Kindersley (India) Pvt. Limited
in association with
Penguin Books India (P) Ltd.

Printed in Singapore

1  3  5  7  9  10  8  6  4  2

# CONTENTS

# CATALOGUE

# Author's Introduction

Mammals are the most charismatic of all fauna. Perhaps it is because we belong to the order ourselves that we find them of perennial interest. Majestic big cats fascinate us, gigantic elephants hold us spellbound, and primates with their forward-facing eyes and human-like faces remind us of our own origins. These charismatic mega-fauna serve as flagships for a class that encompasses 4,629 distinct species.

India has about 400 mammals, some of them widely recognized such as the national animal, the tiger, and others such as the tree shrew, enigmatic and evolutionarily unique. Around 65 per cent of the world's wild tigers and Asian Elephants are found in India, as are 85 per cent of its One-horned Rhinos. It is also the only country to have the Asiatic Lion. India teems with antelope and deer, has five species of big cats, four massive wild cattle, 11 wild goat and sheep, and 15 primates. Add to these the numerous bats, rodents, and cetaceans, and you have the most incredible array of wildlife.

While Indian jungles, unlike African savannas, do not offer the visitor dozens of mammal species in close proximity, areas do exist where wildlife may be viewed in abundance. Herds of elephants at the Kabini reservoir in the months of March and April, the bats that swarm into Robber's Cave every evening at Mahabaleswar, or the temporary associations of wild goat and sheep as they shift their altitudinal range in response to the climate, offer unforgettable glimpses into the world of mammals. Wildlife enthusiasts are also guaranteed memorable encounters in the wild with the high density of tigers in reserves such as Ranthambhor, or of One-horned Rhinos in Kaziranga, Gaur in Nagerahole, elephants in Corbett, and Blackbuck in Velavadar.

Ever since it was published in 1948, S.H. Prater's *Book of Indian Animals* has been the standard reference on the subject of Indian mammals, providing detailed accounts of all the

common species. The present book is the first comprehensive guide that attempts to cover all the mammal species of India. It is the product of many years of field observation and personal research, strengthened by the comments and suggestions of over two dozen researchers and scientists, and further polished by the comments of five mammalogists of national repute. It is not meant to be a comprehensive academic treatise on mammals of the region, but a companion in the field for ready identification of species. For this reason, most of the identification tips that accompany the species profiles are visible in the field, and despite a lack of photographs in some cases, care has been taken to see that all animals which look significantly different in the field have been illustrated. Text, identification markers, photographs, and maps, wherever provided, have been designed in close proximity to aid field use. In addition, field behaviour has been used to complement external morphology to help identify species.

It must be kept in mind that while most people might see animals as depicted in the photographs or illustrations in this book, it is possible to see animals that look a little different. This is primarily because animals differ in coat colour, pelage and size, depending on race, geography, and the health of the individual. It is also worth mentioning here that while photographs in the wild were preferred, a number of photos are of captive specimens, taken for identification purposes, and there is always the possibility that the wild animal might look slightly different from the captive one. Among other things, diet in captivity can influence a change in coat colour and texture.

As a recognition guide to the wild mammals of India, this book is intended for the interested lay person. It is hoped that it will also be of use to both the amateur naturalist and the wildlife professional.

# THE WORLD OF MAMMALS

Most of the animals that we encounter in our daily life are mammals. There are over 4,000 species found on land, in the air, and underground, ranging from enormous whales to tiny bats and rodents. Humans are also mammals. Our closest living relative is the Bonobo, or Pygmy Chimpanzee, whose genes and social behaviour are markedly similar to our own.

## MAMMAL CHARACTERISTICS

THREE CHARACTERISTICS set mammals apart from all other living beings. They are warm-blooded; their skin is clothed with fur; and females feed their offspring on milk from their mammary glands. Being warm-blooded means that mammals produce heat from within their bodies and have the ability to regulate a constant internal temperature. In scientific terms, this is known as being endothermic and homeothermic.

Most mammals also have visible fur or hair on the body, which acts as a temperature regulation mechanism. Unlike other living creatures, mammal young feed on mother's milk for several months or years of their life; their dependence on the mother is more than in any other animal group. The mammary glands that give the class its name are specialized sweat glands located either on the chest or the abdomen.

Within this general body plan that characterizes all mammals, myriad variations account for the 4,629 mammal species belonging to 1,135 genera and 136 families. And thus it is that the tiny Pygmy Shrew and the mammoth Blue Whale, the flying insectivorous bats and the fossorial moles are all linked together in the class called Mammalia.

## THE ORIGINS

APPROXIMATELY 300 MILLION years ago, in the Carboniferous period of the Paleozoic era, reptiles ruled the earth. At this time, the first mammal-like reptiles called the synapsids came into being. The first true mammals known as the cynodonts evolved around 100 million years later. They were small nocturnal creatures resembling the tree shrews of today. However, the synapsids and cynodonts were marginalized by the dinosaurs who established themselves supreme over land, water, and air. It was only when dinosaurs became extinct that mammals came into their own and began to diversify.

skin covered
with hair

mammary
glands

BEING MAMMALS
*Rhesus mother and baby display the mammalian characteristics of hairy bodies, mammary glands, and the typical primate feature of forward-facing eyes.*

## MAMMAL GROUPS

ONE OF THE WAYS of classifying mammals is based on the way in which they reproduce. A small group of mammals called monotremes, such as the Duck-billed Platypus and the Spiny Echnida, lay eggs from which the young are hatched. Another group known as the marsupials, have babies that develop in a pouch in the mother's body. Monotremes are restricted to Australia while the marsupials are found in Australia, New Guinea, and South America. All the other mammals in the world, in fact all Indian mammals, are placental mammals – the foetus develops inside the womb and the young are born more or less fully developed. Placental mammals are divided into 19 orders, of which 12 are represented in India. A more detailed taxonomy is presented on p.8–9.

## EVOLUTIONARY ADAPTATIONS

MAMMALS LIVING in different strata evolved in different ways in response to their environment. Such evolution is primarily responsible for the wide variety in the mammalian world.

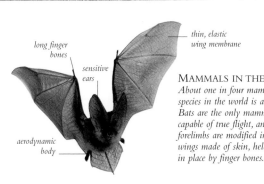

*long finger bones*

*sensitive ears*

*thin, elastic wing membrane*

*aerodynamic body*

### MAMMALS IN THE AIR

*About one in four mammal species in the world is a bat. Bats are the only mammals capable of true flight, and their forelimbs are modified into wings made of skin, held tightly in place by finger bones.*

*blowhole for breathing*

*upright dorsal fin*

*horizontal tail-fluke*

### MAMMALS IN WATER

*Fish-shaped mammals such as whales, dolphins, and porpoises have smooth streamlined bodies that enable them to glide through water. Their forelimbs are modified into flippers and they have powerful tail-flukes to help them swim.*

*flippers*

*streamlined body*

# CLASSIFICATION

TAXONOMIC NORMS of classification have been followed in this book with respect to the arrangement of orders, families, genera and species, though some minor adjustments have been made to keep similar looking animals close to each other, for easy reference. Scientific nomenclature follows Wilson & Reeder (1993), although for certain orders we have departed from this in favour of more recently published work wherever it has been nationally and internationally accepted.

The following listing covers all wild mammals in India, except extinct species. The number of families and species that have confirmed wild populations in India are mentioned first and the number within brackets includes those that are known to stray in from neighbouring territories, or of which there are unconfirmed reports.

However, taxonomy changes constantly – scientific names change when scientists so determine, and common names and local names change even more frequently. To avoid confusion, every species in this book has been titled with the most commonly used English name, and the local names in the languages that occur in the range of the species are also given.

| ODD-TOED HOOFED MAMMALS | | |
|---|---|---|
| ORDER Perissodactyla  FAMILIES 2 | | SPECIES 3 (4) |
| WILD ASSES | | |
| FAMILY Equidae | | SPECIES 2 |
| RHINOCEROS | | |
| FAMILY Rhinocerotidae | | SPECIES 1 (2) |

| ELEPHANT | | |
|---|---|---|
| ORDER Proboscidea  FAMILY 1 | | SPECIES 1 |
| FAMILY Elephantidae | | |

| PRIMATES | | |
|---|---|---|
| ORDER Primates  FAMILIES 3 | | SPECIES 15 (16) |
| PROSIMIANS | | |
| FAMILY Loridae | | SPECIES 2 |
| MONKEYS | | |
| FAMILY Cercopithecidae | | SPECIES 12 (13) |
| GIBBON | | |
| FAMILY Hylobatidae | | SPECIES 1 |

| EVEN-TOED HOOFED MAMMALS | | |
|---|---|---|
| ORDER Artiodactyla  FAMILIES 5 | | SPECIES 30 (34) |
| DEER, MUSK DEER, CHEVROTAINS | | |
| FAMILY Cervidae, Moschidae, Tragulidae  SPECIES 9 (12) | | |
| CATTLE, ANTELOPE, GOAT, SHEEP | | |
| FAMILY Bovidae | | SPECIES 19 (20) |
| PIGS | | |
| FAMILY Suidae | | SPECIES 2 |

## CARNIVORES

| ORDER Carnivora | FAMILIES 7 | SPECIES 58 |

**BEARS, RED PANDA**
FAMILY Ursidae · SPECIES 5

**DOGS**
FAMILY Canidae · SPECIES 6

**HYENAS**
FAMILY Hyaenidae · SPECIES 1

**CATS**
FAMILY Felidae · SPECIES 15

**MUSTELIDS**
FAMILY Mustelidae · SPECIES 16

**CIVETS**
FAMILY Viverridae · SPECIES 9

**MONGOOSES**
FAMILY Herpestidae · SPECIES 6

## PANGOLIN

| ORDER Pholidota | FAMILY 1 | SPECIES 2 |

FAMILY Manidae

## HARES, RABBITS, PIKAS

| ORDER Lagomorpha | FAMILIES 2 | SPECIES 11 |

**HARES, RABBITS**
FAMILY Leporidae · SPECIES 4

**PIKAS**
FAMILY Ochotonidae · SPECIES 7

## INSECTIVORES

| ORDER Insectivora | FAMILIES 3 | SPECIES 30 |

**HEDGEHOGS**
FAMILY Erinaceidae · SPECIES 3

**SHREWS**
FAMILY Soricidae · SPECIES 25

**MOLES**
FAMILY Talpidae · SPECIES 2

## TREE SHREWS

| ORDER Scandentia | FAMILY 1 | SPECIES 3 |

FAMILY Tupaiidae

## RODENTS

| ORDER Rodentia | FAMILIES 4 | SPECIES 101 (102) |

**SQUIRRELS**
FAMILY Sciuridae · SPECIES 27 (28)

**RATS, MICE**
FAMILY Muridae · SPECIES 70

**BIRCH MICE**
FAMILY Dipodidae · SPECIES 1

**PORCUPINES**
FAMILY Hystricidae · SPECIES 3

## BATS

| ORDER Chiroptera | FAMILIES 8 | SPECIES 113 |

**FRUIT BATS**
FAMILY Pteropodidae · SPECIES 13

**MOUSE-TAILED BATS**
FAMILY Rhinopomatidae · SPECIES 2

**TOMB BATS**
FAMILY Emballonuridae · SPECIES 6

**FALSE VAMPIRES**
FAMILY Megadermatidae · SPECIES 2

**HORSESHOE BATS**
FAMILY Rhinolophidae · SPECIES 15

**FREE-TAILED BATS**
FAMILY Molossidae · SPECIES 4

**EVENING BATS**
FAMILY Vespertilionidae · SPECIES 58

**LEAF-NOSED BATS**
FAMILY Hipposideridae · SPECIES 13

## CETACEANS

| ORDER Cetacea | FAMILIES 7 (8) | SPECIES 29 (31) |

**BALEEN WHALES**
SUB-ORDER Mysteceti · FAMILY 1 (2) · SPECIES 6 (7)

**TOOTHED WHALES**
SUB-ORDER Odentoceti · FAMILIES 6 · SPECIES 23 (24)

## DUGONG

| ORDER Sirenia | FAMILY 1 | SPECIES 1 |

FAMILY Dugongidae

# FEEDING

On the basis of diet, most mammals can be grouped into two broad categories: carnivores (that eat flesh) and herbivores (that feed on plants). Omnivores can feed on both. There are also dietary specialists such as insectivores that feed on insects, frugivores that eat fruit and piscivores whose diet consists chiefly of fish. Diet is a major factor that influences physiology, and mammals have developed specialized aids to gather food and feed. The powerful forelimbs of a tiger help it hunt, primates use their opposable thumbs to forage, the large molars of herbivores help them chew, while the complex stomach of leaf-eating species helps in digestion.

## CARNIVORES

The Order Carnivora comprises 271 species of terrestrial meat-eaters with specially adapted carnassial teeth, and over two dozen cetaceans. Cats, dogs, bears, weasels, civets, mongooses and hyenas are terrestrial carnivores. Many of them have powerful and agile bodies designed for running, and jaws that are adapted to capture and tear up prey. Since their diet is high in protein, carnivores do not need to feed as often as herbivores. The word "carnivore" means flesh-eating, but not all carnivores are exclusively dependent on flesh. The Red Panda, for instance, belongs to the Order Carnivora but is mainly herbivorous while Palm Civets are largely frugivorous.

BIG AND SMALL PREY
*Lions mostly feed on ungulates weighing between 50 and 500 kg. Occasionally, they may eat rodents, hares, and even birds.*

ANOTHER'S PREY
*A Stripe-necked Mongoose feeds on a Black-naped Hare which may have been killed by it or abandoned by another predator.*

Most scavengers belong to the Order Carnivora but are omnivores with a variable diet, including prey that they may not have killed themselves. Almost all scavengers can kill their own prey if required, but given the opportunity, will eat the kill of other predators as an energy-saving mechanism that also enhances their chances of survival. Hyenas, jackals, bears, wild pigs, and mongooses epitomize scavenging; occasionally, predators such as leopards and wild dog are also known to scavenge. Scavengers are often thought to be lazy or dirty, both of which they are not. Scavenging and omnivory may not be associated with the magnificence of predation, but they are highly specialized skills.

BIG EATER
*This massive Gaur female weighing
close to 800 kg would need to feed
almost constantly to nourish itself
and provide milk for its calf.*

# HERBIVORES

Herbivores are adapted to a vegetarian diet, even if not solely confined to it. Proboscideans (elephants) and ungulates are the biggest and best-known herbivores. Ungulates include deer, antelope, goat, sheep, cattle, equids, pigs and rhinos. Some of them are browsers, plucking leaves and shoots off branches. Others are grazers, adapted to cropping grass. Many monkeys are primarily herbivorous, though they may eat fruits and insects as well. Some marine mammals such as Dugong, are also vegetarian. Most herbivores have few or no canine teeth; their incisors are modified to tear vegetation and their pre-molars and molars have large grinding surfaces.

## FRUGIVORES AND INSECTIVORES

Bats are an excellent example of a group of mammals adapted to a diet of fruits and insects. While the Megachiropterans such as the flying foxes are fruit-eating, a number of small bats, called Microchiropterans, catch insects on the wing. However, not all groups of animals are as clearly divided in their dietary preferences and fruit-eating and insect-eating habits vary from taxon to taxon. A specially interesting group of insect-eaters belongs to the Order Pholidota: the Pangolin or Scaly Anteater is devoid of all teeth and has a long snout with an equally long, sticky tongue used to suck insects out of termite mounds and ant-hills.

EXCLUSIVE FRUIT DIET
*The Flying Fox is one of India's most
common bat species and yet few people
know that it is strictly a fruit-eater.*

# Social Behaviour

ANIMALS SPEND most of their time foraging, eating or resting. Social and mating activities occupy less than 10 per cent of their time, but these are among the more interesting behaviour to watch. The basic social unit of most mammals is the family or larger aggregations of several families. These groupings are referred to in different terms, for example, herds in elephants, colonies in bats, pods in dolphins, and so on. Even in the case of solitary species, males and females come together during the breeding season and females stay with their young in temporary social units.

## Vocalization

Most mammals call in order to communicate with individuals of their own species – including to attract the opposite sex – and to threaten possible predators. Some animals such as monkeys and apes are very vocal while others such as hedgehogs are relatively quiet, yet each has a distinctive call that helps in identifying the species. Some animals have very different calls for different occasions, for example, wild dogs whistle to each other to reassemble, but may yap, yelp, or whimper at other times. Certain species such as cetaceans, elephants and bats have a range of vocalizations that are inaudible to the human ear.

AGGRESSION
*Primates may display their canines in an open-mouthed show of aggression or even fear. This can be accompanied at times by specific vocalizations.*

## Infanticide

While some behavioural traits such as vocalization, aggression, and territorial scent marking are well known, others such as infanticide are less known. Infanticide, as a mammalian strategy, has been recorded in over a hundred species, from hares, carnivores and rodents, to primates. In India, the Hanuman Langur is a classic example of males seeking out and killing children fathered by other males, to improve their breeding success. The reasons driving an animal to infanticide can be many, including the need to eliminate competitors, to secure food or other resources, and to manipulate the sex ratio of offspring.

## MARKING TERRITORY

Some animals use olfaction, or the sense of smell, along with sight and hearing, in order to communicate. Many mammals are equipped with specialized sweat glands that are used to stake territory. Urine and faeces are also used for this purpose. For example, lorises are known to urinate on their palms and leave scented prints as they clamber among branches, to let others know of their movements. Civets have anal sacs from which they spray foul-smelling liquid in defence, as well as to mark territory. Mongooses have stink glands that discharge nauseous and acrid fluids that repel predators effectively. Deer have glands on their legs, elephants near the eye, and the musk deer has it around the genitals and in the abdomen. Unlike vocalization, scent marks serve the purpose of messaging long after the sender has moved away.

## DOMINANCE HIERARCHIES

Many mammals live together in order to minimize the risk of predation, improve defence resources against rival groups and maximize foraging and reproductive success. Dominance hierarchies, with the biggest and strongest individual occupying the highest rank, are almost inevitable in such groupings. The pecking order changes constantly, with younger and healthier individuals taking over from the dominant members of the group. In many primate societies, the alpha male is the dominant animal, while in other species such as the elephant, an older female, or matriarch, leads the herd. Ritualistic combat is one of the ways in which dominance is asserted in several species. In some cases, these mock fights can lead to serious injury or death.

**SCENT MARKING**
*Otters urinate against familiar signposts, as do cats and dogs, to mark their territory.*

# VARIATIONS WITHIN SPECIES

While all the members of a species look more or less alike, they often differ from one another in significant ways, such as in fur colour and texture, body size, presence of appendages such as tusks and so on. In order to use an identification guide effectively, it is important to know why some animals look different even though they belong to the same species.

## SEXUAL DIMORPHISM

IN SOME ANIMALS males and females can be easily told apart in the field and in some it is virtually impossible to do so. Bats, for example, cannot be differentiated, while in most deer, the presence of an antler indicates a male. Some ungulates such as the Goral are monomorphic. Both sexes are horned and differentiating between them becomes difficult. Sexual dimorphism may also manifest itself in coat colour, size, length of canines, etc.

TUSKERS
In Asian elephants, tusks are an indication of being male, although some males are tuskless as well.

IMMATURE COAT
This Stump-tailed Macaque infant is golden yellow while the adult has brown fur and a red face.

## IMMATURE AND ADULT

AGE PLAYS AN IMPORTANT role in the way an animal looks. Infants may look completely different from adults and as they grow, may change coat colour several times before they reach adult colouration. In some species such as the langur, the difference in colour can be astonishing. In wild pigs, piglets are striped for the first few months, although the adults are uniformly brown, while the Gaur calf changes colour from golden yellow to fawn to light brown and then coffee-brown when it reaches a sub-adult state. At this stage, it closely resembles the adult female. In wild goats and antelopes (and many other species), younger males have shorter or less developed horns while other characteristics such as the saddle back of the Nilgiri Tahr or the beard of the Markhor are present only in the adult male.

# SEASONAL CHANGE

MAMMALS CHANGE COAT colour depending
on climatic conditions and this is striking in
sub-species that live in colder climates. In
winter, the coat of many animals becomes
thicker, while in summer it becomes more
sparse. In some cases this also results in a
change of colour, for example, the Himalayan
Stoat or Ermine goes from chestnut-brown in
summer to pure white in winter. Many males
turn more colourful and grow spectacular
appendages during the breeding season, none
more so than the males of the deer family. In
the non-breeding season, stags may be antler-
less or may have small velvet knobs, but in the
rutting season they sport the most impressive
headgear among mammals.

WINTER COAT
*Some sub-species of the Takin have a golden-yellow coat
in winter which changes to brown in summer.*

# RACE

DIFFERENT RACES OR sub-species can look
dramatically different, depending on the
geographical region they are found in. The
Indian Giant Squirrel, for example, has seven
different pelage colours. The sub-species of the
Red Fox are so distinct that they have three
different common names. There is considerable
scientific debate on whether the 16–17
different sub-species of the Common Langur
have enough variation to merit being called
different species. A host of other species such
as the Capped Langur and the Madras Tree
Shrew show marked sub-specific variations.

CANID VARIATIONS
*The Tibetan Wolf (**Canis lupus chanco**) is larger than the
peninsular sub-species. It has a longer crest of black hair on
its back, and in some cases is entirely black.*

# INDIVIDUAL APPEARANCE

ANIMALS SHOW INDIVIDUAL coat or pelage
differences, much like human beings, even
within the same race. This is particularly so in
the case of genetic aberrations such as albinism
and melanism which cause the famous white
tiger (see right) and black panther. Lesser
known and less common are the melanistic
tigers which are also called black tigers
(reported from Orissa). Individuals can also
differ in coat lustre and texture, depending on
their nutritional and health status. Similarly,
they can vary in size, sometimes being much
larger or smaller than is indicated in this book.

# HABITATS

FORESTS, GRASSLANDS, mountains, and deserts are some of the habitats inhabited by terrestrial mammals. The aquatic habitat, much larger in area, is populated by fish and invertebrates although a few specialized mammals exist in it as well. More adaptable mammals also inhabit urban areas.

## FOREST
Sixteen different forest types exist in India. These are the wet evergreen, semi-evergreen, dry evergreen, moist deciduous, dry deciduous, littoral and swamp, thorn scrub, broad-leaved, pine, dry montane sub-tropical evergreen, dry temperate montane, moist temperate montane, wet temperate montane, sub-alpine, dry alpine and moist alpine.

## DESERT
The Thar in western Rajasthan is the only true hot desert in India. Semi-arid habitats and saltflats exist in other parts of Rajasthan, Gujarat, and Madhya Pradesh. Cold deserts are found in the trans-Himalayan regions of Ladakh, Lahaul and Spiti valleys, and Sikkim.

## FRESHWATER AND MARINE
The aquatic ecosystem consists of rivers, wetlands, seas and oceans. Seas and oceans are by far the largest habitats for wildlife. While the Indian Ocean, the Arabian Sea, and the Bay of Bengal are vast stretches of marine habitats for cetaceans and the dugong, the Ganges River Dolphin and certain porpoises inhabit river systems and estuaries. The brackish water habitats of the Sunderbans and Bhittarkanika also harbour varied wildlife.

## MOUNTAINS
The montane habitats of India are divided amongst the Himalaya and the peninsular mountain chains. The highest mountain chain in the world, the Himalaya, comprises the Shivalik foothills, the lesser and the outer ranges. Peninsular mountains include the Aravallis, the Vindhyas, the Satpuras, and the Eastern and Western Ghats. Vast areas of these mountains are not wooded but still provide a habitat for mammals like wild goat and sheep.

## GRASSLAND
Ranging from the tall elephant grass habitats of the terai to the short montane grasslands of the Anamalai, grassland ecosystems interspersed with forests are some of the best areas for wildlife congregations. They are also home to several highly adapted grassland-dependent species.

# BIO-GEOGRAPHIC ZONES

INDIA IS DIVIDED INTO ten bio-geographic zones, for example, the Himalaya and the Deccan, based on a distinctive set of physical and historical conditions. These are further divided into 23 biotic provinces, such as the North-western Himalaya and Chhota Nagpur Plateau. The major ecosystem groupings that are found in each of the biotic provinces are called biomes, for example, coastal, alpine, and scrub.

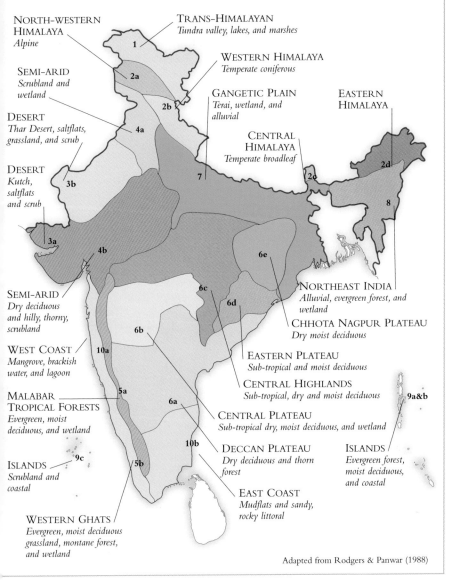

NORTH-WESTERN
HIMALAYA
*Alpine*

TRANS-HIMALAYAN
*Tundra valley, lakes, and marshes*

WESTERN HIMALAYA
*Temperate coniferous*

SEMI-ARID
*Scrubland and
wetland*

GANGETIC PLAIN
*Terai, wetland, and
alluvial*

EASTERN
HIMALAYA

DESERT
*Thar Desert, saltflats,
grassland, and scrub*

CENTRAL
HIMALAYA
*Temperate broadleaf*

DESERT
*Kutch,
saltflats
and scrub*

SEMI-ARID
*Dry deciduous
and hilly, thorny,
scrubland*

NORTHEAST INDIA
*Alluvial, evergreen forest, and
wetland*

CHHOTA NAGPUR PLATEAU
*Dry moist deciduous*

WEST COAST
*Mangrove, brackish
water, and lagoon*

EASTERN PLATEAU
*Sub-tropical and moist deciduous*

CENTRAL HIGHLANDS
*Sub-tropical, dry and moist deciduous*

MALABAR
TROPICAL FORESTS
*Evergreen, moist
deciduous, and wetland*

CENTRAL PLATEAU
*Sub-tropical dry, moist deciduous, and wetland*

DECCAN PLATEAU
*Dry deciduous and thorn
forest*

ISLANDS
*Evergreen forest,
moist deciduous,
and coastal*

ISLANDS
*Scrubland and
coastal*

EAST COAST
*Mudflats and sandy,
rocky littoral*

WESTERN GHATS
*Evergreen, moist deciduous
grassland, montane forest,
and wetland*

Adapted from Rodgers & Panwar (1988)

17

# USE OF STRATUM

SCIENTISTS DESCRIBE THE SPECIES that occupy different eco-niches in highly specialized terms such as canopy forager, littoral species, and mangrove dweller. As this book is intended primarily for the lay person, only broad strata have been indicated as a rough guide to the possible location of a species in a given habitat.

AERIAL
*In the air*

ARBOREAL
*Top of trees or high vegetation*

CAVE-DWELLING
*Inside caves*

FOSSORIAL
*Underground*

TERRESTRIAL
*Land surface, above ground*

AQUATIC
*Water, including rivers, ponds, lakes and oceans*

# STUDYING MAMMALS

AS SCIENTIFIC RESEARCH progresses, there is deeper and more complete understanding of the mammals around us. Yet, there are innumerable unexplained natural phenomena. Why does a stag decorate his antlers with tufts of grass during the rut? What are the infrasonic communications of an elephant? While ethologists grapple with such behavioural questions, taxonomists study mammals in order to understand the exact placement of a species in a scientific lineage. Evolutionary biologists study mammals or remains of mammals to deduce the evolutionary history of species, and parasitologists, virologists, and medical researchers try to understand the cause and cure of mammalian diseases.

While professional scientists focus on fundamental scientific issues, there are an ever increasing number of conservationists who have made studying mammals their mission in order to conserve species and ecosystems that are threatened. Amateur naturalists also study mammals, through brief incursions into the natural world where they may track an animal to its lair or watch it through binoculars, in order to observe its behaviour. Governments study mammals in order to estimate their population and to monitor the conservation projects that are run or funded by them.

Various methods are employed by specialists to study mammals, including long-distance observation and data collection, reading tracks and signs, radio-collaring and satellite-tracking, vegetation analysis and forest study, socio-economic analysis of humans living near wildlife, and disease investigations. It is only by putting together all the different streams of study that we can attempt to better understand the giant jigsaw that is nature.

KEEPING TRACK
*Radio-collaring has proven to be an expensive but reliable method of studying ranging patterns of animals. Here an elephant has been tranquilized by biologists, in order to attach a radio collar to its body.*

# VISIT TO A PROTECTED AREA

THERE ARE MORE THAN 500 national parks and sanctuaries in India, of which about half are accessible to the ordinary wildlife tourist. Visitors are expected to follow a prescribed code of conduct designed to have minimal impact on the fragile ecology and species of the region.

## TIPS FOR THE JUNGLE

■ Respect wildlife. Remember that all the animals you are watching are wild and many of them are dangerous. Many parks do not permit you to walk. Even if permitted, do not approach dangerous animals (indicated in this book by a red mark) on foot. Even if you are experienced in the field, treat wildlife with caution.

■ Give yourself time. Nature cannot be seen in a hurry and the more time you spend in the wild, the better are your chances of spotting elusive wildlife. Equally, the more time you spend watching animals, the more you will learn about them.

■ You can watch animals more unobtrusively by wearing clothes that merge with the background, such as muted shades of brown and green.

■ While a camera is desirable, a pair of binoculars is the most useful accessory in the forest. Carry essential food and water as well, in case of an emergency.

■ Leave the forest as you found it. Do not break branches, pluck wild flowers, or collect wildlife souvenirs from inside the park.

■ The quiet of the forest must be maintained. Take care to talk in hushed tones, attempt not to yell excitedly each time wildlife is sighted, and most definitely avoid radios and tape recorders. If driving a vehicle, remember that honking is not permitted.

■ The forest floor is not for plastic bags, cans, and other litter. Not only is it unaesthetic and unhygienic, it can prove fatal to wildlife if ingested.

KEEP YOUR DISTANCE
*Travel in small groups. Do not intrude on an animal's space.*

# BEST PLACE TO SEE

O N THE MAP BELOW are marked some of the best places to see wildlife in India. This is not an exhaustive list of protected areas; it is a compilation of the places at which different species are best seen, as mentioned in the species accounts within the book. NP stands for national park and WLS for wildlife sanctuary – the two categories of protected areas in India. Wildlife can also be seen outside the protected areas and these are indicated wherever appropriate.

# CONSERVATION

INDIA HAS A LONG HISTORY of conservation going back to a time when kings set aside areas as preserves for hunting. Communities like the Bishnois, concepts like the 'sacred groves' and in later years, schemes and projects of governments and non-government organizations (NGOs) have all contributed to conserving animals in the country. These measures are often built around large, charismatic fauna, but over two-thirds of India's mammal species is made up of shrews, rodents, bats, and small carnivores which are as threatened by habitat loss and alteration as the larger species.

## SUCCESS STORIES

TWO CLASSIC SUCCESS stories of mammalian conservation in India involve the Asiatic Lion and the One-horned Rhinoceros. Royal patronage, local zeal and national action plans have all helped the Lion to hold on to its last homeland, the Gir; over the past century, its numbers have gone up from a few dozen to a few hundred. The Rhino has fared even better and today numbers nearly 2000. While these may be better-known conservation stories, those involving less charismatic species are no less important. The Pygmy Hog (see above), for instance, is set to be the first low-key mammalian species in India to get a reprieve from extinction. A captive breeding facility in Guwahati has successfully completed the first phase of breeding the animal in captivity and is now on the brink of starting phase two – reintroduction of captive-bred animals into the wild. If this succeeds, the critically endangered Pygmy Hog might just become the unexpected hero in the story of India's conservation attempts.

## POACHING AND TRADE

POACHING AND TRADE in animal parts are among the major threats facing Indian wildlife. According to Interpol sources, international wildlife trade is the second largest illegal occupation in the world, totalling about US $ 25 billion. Mammals are under threat due to the lucrative trade in their parts and derivatives. Primates, cats, pandas, bears, and elephants are also threatened by the live animal trade that supplies the needs of zoos, circuses, and private owners both in India and abroad. Most of the demand is met from animals caught illegally in the wild. Traditional Oriental medicine utilizes tiger bones, rhino horn, pangolin scales, musk, bear bile, and other products. The soft underwool of the Tibetan Antelope is prized for being made into shawls; cat skins are used for display; and deer meat is widely eaten. Some of the most important conservation measures undertaken by the Indian government and NGOs, therefore, have been aimed at curtailing poaching and trade. Although awareness about this issue was not very high a few years ago, today non-wildlife agencies such as the customs and the police are also active in cracking down on the smuggling of wildlife products.

*Tiger skull and bones*

# HABITAT LOSS AND FRAGMENTATION

POACHING MAY BE the primary cause for sudden decline in species numbers, but habitat loss and fragmentation are the insidious, long-term problems that threaten Indian wildlife. Habitats are being lost largely because of the burgeoning needs of the human population. The enormous fuel and fodder requirements mean that more and more forests are being cut and pastures overgrazed. In addition, the timber needs of the country place a heavy burden on the forest reserves. Developmental projects such as mines and dams as well as industry not only take away vital habitats but also pollute and degrade forest fragments around them. Encroachment of forests by the landless and shifting cultivation in the Northeast have also led to fragmentation. The small number of wildlife left in these areas face acute extinction pressures. India protects approximately 4.5 per cent of its land surface through its protected area system, with about one per cent being highly protected as national parks. In some cases, villages, roads, and railway lines are found within the protected areas, making habitat conservation a challenging task. Mammals, especially large mammals, suffer the most as a result of such human-animal conflict; elephant corridors, tiger habitats, and the grassland that once nurtured the Cheetah and the Blackbuck are all equally threatened.

DEFORESTATION
*Northeast India and the Western Ghats are two global bio-diversity hotspots that are threatened by indiscriminate timber felling.*

POLLUTION
*Industrial effluents and toxic waters often find their way into river courses, seriously affecting the ecosystem through which the river flows and the species that utilize the water.*

# HOW THIS BOOK WORKS

T HIS BOOK COVERS the different Mammalian Orders that are found in India. The sample species profile shown below is a typical entry, with information presented in a combination of written text, bands, symbols, and abbreviations.

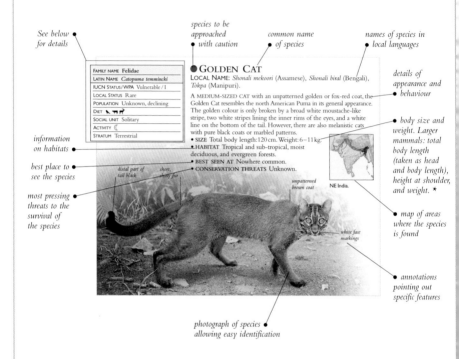

See below for details

species to be approached with caution

common name of species

names of species in local languages

### ● GOLDEN CAT

LOCAL NAME: *Shonali mekoori* (Assamese), *Shonali biral* (Bengali), *Tokpa* (Manipuri).

A MEDIUM-SIZED CAT with an unpatterned golden or fox-red coat, the Golden Cat resembles the north American Puma in its general appearance. The golden colour is only broken by a broad white moustache-like stripe, two white stripes lining the inner rims of the eyes, and a white line on the bottom of the tail. However, there are also melanistic cats with pure black coats or marbled patterns.
• SIZE Total body length:120 cm. Weight: 6–11 kg.
• HABITAT Tropical and sub-tropical, moist deciduous, and evergreen forests.
• BEST SEEN AT Nowhere common.
• CONSERVATION THREATS Unknown.

details of appearance and behaviour

body size and weight. Larger mammals: total body length (taken as head and body length), height at shoulder, and weight. ★

NE India.

map of areas where the species is found

| FAMILY NAME | Felidae |
|---|---|
| LATIN NAME | *Catopuma temmincki* |
| IUCN STATUS/WPA | Vulnerable / I |
| LOCAL STATUS | Rare |
| POPULATION | Unknown, declining |
| DIET | 🐾 🐗 🦅 |
| SOCIAL UNIT | Solitary |
| ACTIVITY | ☾ |
| STRATUM | Terrestrial |

information on habitats

best place to see the species

most pressing threats to the survival of the species

distal part of tail black

short, shiny fur

unpatterned brown coat

white face markings

annotations pointing out specific features

photograph of species allowing easy identification

scientific name of family

scientific name of genus

scientific name of species

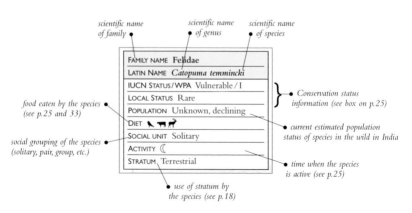

| FAMILY NAME | Felidae |
|---|---|
| LATIN NAME | *Catopuma temmincki* |
| IUCN STATUS/WPA | Vulnerable / I |
| LOCAL STATUS | Rare |
| POPULATION | Unknown, declining |
| DIET | 🐾 🐗 🦅 |
| SOCIAL UNIT | Solitary |
| ACTIVITY | ☾ |
| STRATUM | Terrestrial |

food eaten by the species (see p.25 and 33)

social grouping of the species (solitary, pair, group, etc.)

Conservation status information (see box on p.25)

current estimated population status of species in the wild in India

time when the species is active (see p.25)

use of stratum by the species (see p.18)

★ *Abbreviations: In the Insectivores, Rodents, and Bats sections certain abbreviations have been used to indicate size. These are:* **HBL**: *Head and body length;* **FA**: *Forearm length;* **Tail**: *Tail length.*

# SYMBOLS

## DIET SYMBOLS

The variety of foods consumed by the different mammals is represented by symbols that are explained below. Wherever relevant, more details are given in the text for individual species entries.

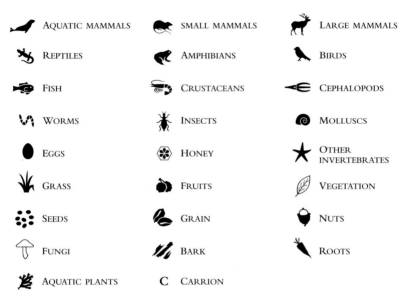

## ACTIVITY SYMBOLS

Species activities are listed by day (diurnal), night (nocturnal), and at dawn or dusk (crepuscular).

# PRIMATES

PRIMATE CHARACTERISTICS

PRIMATE CHARACTERISTICS
- Five digits on hands and feet
- Can grasp with fingers and thumb
- Forward-facing eyes
- Can walk on two limbs
- Simple dentition
- Developed cerebral hemispheres

| INDIAN PRIMATES AT A GLANCE | | | |
|---|---|---|---|
| | PRIMATES | MACAQUES | LANGURS |
| NUMBER OF SPECIES | 15 (16) | 7 (8) | 5 |
| LARGEST | Hanuman Langur | Stump-tailed | Nilgiri |
| SMALLEST | Slender Loris | Bonnet | Phayre's Leaf |
| MOST COMMON | Rhesus Macaque | Rhesus | Hanuman |
| MOST ENDANGERED | Golden Langur | Lion-tailed | Golden |

PROSIMIANS, NEW AND OLD WORLD MONKEYS, apes and man are closely related and belong to an Order known as Primates, comprising over 200 species worldwide. While macaques are found throughout Asia and Northern Africa, langurs, gibbons, and lorises are restricted to Asia. Current evolutionary theories propose that primates evolved for a life on trees. They developed forward-facing eyes to be able to judge distances between trees, and the ability to grasp with thumb and forefinger to hold on to branches. Somewhere along the evolutionary tree, a few primates such as macaques and chimpanzees became semi-arboreal while gorillas and man took to life on the ground. However, an arboreal life is a factor that links most members of this Order.

## SOCIAL BONDING

An exceptional degree of social bonding is a behavioural trait that links all primates except the prosimians. It is well known that elephants and monkeys suffer more than any other creature if kept alone in captivity, since they have a complex social organization in the wild. Apart from prosimians, all monkeys have a distinct social unit, though the way it is structured may differ. For example, in a macaque group a multi-male organization means that there is much more competition to become alpha male, while in a langur troop, a single adult male with a harem ensures more peaceable routine interactions. Being mainly fruit and leaf eaters, it makes sense evolutionarily for most primates to forage together in the forest and behaviour such as grooming helps in bonding and keeping the group together.

WELL-GROOMED
*Primates groom each other as a part of everyday life (like the **Bonnet Macaque** mother and baby shown here), as well as to display hierarchy.*

# PRIMATE FORMS

Indian primates can be divided into four groups: the small, round-eyed lorises; the stocky, comparitively short-tailed macaques; the long-tailed langurs and the tailless Hoolock Gibbon. Other than the gibbon, all Indian primates have males and females that look alike except in terms of size.

### LORIS
*India has two small nocturnal prosimians: the* Slow Loris *and* Slender Loris *(shown here). Belonging to the sub-order* Strepsirhini, *these furry primates are characterized by large, round eyes, insectivorous diets, and a solitary lifestyle.*

### MACAQUE
*This sub-family comprises fruit, insect, and seed eaters with stocky bodies and tails of varying size. The most commonly seen monkeys in Indian cities are the* **Rhesus Macaque** *(see p. 30) and the Bonnet Macaque (see p. 31), although there are five other forest macaques in the country. Macaques live in groups with males, females, and young.*

### GIBBON
*The only ape in India, the* **Hoolock Gibbon** *(see p. 29) is found in forests of Northeast India and is extremely endangered. Gibbons have very long arms and no tail. They move by brachiation – hanging by the arms and swinging hand over hand from branch to branch – and are the most dependent on trees. Both sexes are of the same size.*

### LANGUR
*Langurs are predominantly leaf eating monkeys that have long tails and limbs as an adaptation for an arboreal lifestyle. They normally live in uni-male bi-sexual troops although all-male troops are also common. The* **Common Langur** *(see p. 37) is worshipped as Hanuman or the Monkey God, while several rarer langur species lead a precarious existence in small pockets of forest.*

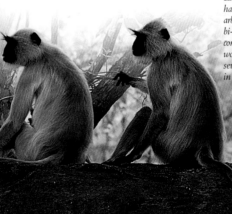

| | |
|---|---|
| FAMILY NAME | **Loridae** |
| LATIN NAME | *Nycticebus bengalensis* |
| IUCN STATUS/WPA | Data deficient/I |
| LOCAL STATUS | Uncommon |
| POPULATION | app. 10,000 |
| DIET | 🐛 🪱 🌱 ● 🌿 |
| SOCIAL UNIT | Solitary/Pairs |
| ACTIVITY | ☾ |
| STRATUM | Arboreal |

# SLOW LORIS

**LOCAL NAME:** *Lajuki bandor* (Assamese), *Nilaji makhra* (Bodo), *Galwee* (Garo), *Samrok gamkok* (Manipuri), *Sahuai* (Mizo).

A SMALL PRIMATE, the Slow Loris has large glistening eyes that dominate its round face. Its velvety fur is buff yellow, with the head and shoulders a lighter shade. Very little is known about this secretive animal. However, once spotted, it is very distinctive and cannot be confused with any other animal except the Slender Loris, from which it is geographically separated. Like most prosimians it has a claw on its second toe which it uses to dig out grubs from tree trunks.

*dark dorsal stripe*

*small ears*

• **BEHAVIOUR** The Slow Loris can hang upside down while feeding on fruit and stalks its prey in slow motion, springing erect and grabbing it with both hands. It signposts trees by spraying urine on its palms and leaving scented handprints on the branches.

• **SIZE** Total body length: 30– 40 cm. Weight: 1.2 – 1.3 kg.

• **HABITAT** Dense, moist deciduous, semi-evergreen and evergreen forests.

*brown eye-patches*

• **BEST SEEN AT** Panbari and Kanchanjuri, Kaziranga NP (Assam).

*soft velvet fur*

• **CONSERVATION THREATS** Poaching and habitat loss.

Throughout NE India, more commonly S of R Brahmaputra.

| | |
|---|---|
| FAMILY NAME | **Loridae** |
| LATIN NAME | *Loris lyddekerianus* |
| LOCAL STATUS | Uncommon |
| IUCN STATUS/WPA | Vulnerable/I |
| POPULATION | Unknown, declining |
| DIET | 🐛 🪱 🌿 🌱 🐝 |
| SOCIAL UNIT | Solitary / Pairs |
| ACTIVITY | ☾ |
| STRATUM | Arboreal, terrestrial |

# SLENDER LORIS

**LOCAL NAME:** *Chinge koollie* (Kodava), *Kaadu pappa* (Kannada), *Thevangu* (Tamil, Malayalam), *Devanga pilli* (Telegu).

THIS IS THE SOUTHERN grey-brown cousin of the Slow Loris. Lankier, with less fur, it has an indistinct spinal stripe. Both lorises have very sharp teeth and bite savagely. During the day this loris lives in leaf cover or in tree hollows, coming out at night to feed. In both lorises sexes are alike, though males are slightly larger. Of the two Indian sub-species, *L.l. malabaricus* is considerably smaller than *L.l. lyddekerianus.*

*large ears*

• **BEHAVIOUR** Lorises have to hang upside down to mate. The Slender Loris stands erect on branches, peering for its prey.

• **SIZE** Total body length: 20–25 cm. Weight: 125 – 340 gm.

• **HABITAT** Open scrub jungle, dry deciduous and evergreen forests.

*lanky legs*

• **BEST SEEN AT** Dindugal RF (Tamil Nadu).

• **CONSERVATION THREATS** Poaching.

*white muzzle*

Throughout S India, S of R Tapti and Godavari (up to 800 m).

| | |
|---|---|
| FAMILY NAME | Hylobatidae |
| LATIN NAME | *Bunopithecus hoolock* |
| LOCAL STATUS | Uncommon |
| IUCN STATUS/WPA | Endangered/I |
| POPULATION | app. 2,500, declining |
| DIET | 🐵 ✿ 🌿 |
| SOCIAL UNIT | Groups of 2–3 |
| ACTIVITY | ☼ |
| STRATUM | Arboreal |

# HOOLOCK GIBBON

LOCAL NAME: *Holou bandor* (Assamese), *Ulluck* (Hindi/Bengali), *Uluman* (Bengali), *Hulu makhra* (Bodo), *Heru* (Garo), *Hulu* (Khasi), *Yommu* (Manipuri), *Hahuk* (Mizo).

THE ONLY INDIAN APE, this tailless primate is a jungle gymnast that is known more by its distinctive haunting songs, than by sight. The male is fully black with silvery white brows and young females are of a similar appearance. Adult females, however, turn a golden blonde colour. Newborns are greyish-yellow, but turn dark in a couple of weeks. Very visible white brows give this ape the alternative name of White-browed Gibbon. Long arms, almost double the length of its legs, help in locomotion on trees. However, on the ground they become an impediment to walking and are thus held above the head. When standing upright, the Hoolock Gibbon measures up to 1 m, the height of a small human child. Adult gibbons are reportedly monogamous and pair for life.

• BEHAVIOUR Gibbons swing from tree to tree using brachiation – a specialized, swing-arm type of locomotion. They hang by the arms and swing at high speed, hand over hand, from branch to branch. Since the fingers are hooked on to branches, the thumbs are irrelevant and set well into the palms. Gibbons can also stand up and run along branches. Gibbon songs are the loudest sound of the northeastern forest and resound at dawn. Vocalized as a loud "hookoo-hookoo-hookoo", gibbon songs are sung by one group at a time, with other groups taking over in turns, the chorus continuing till the sun is high up in the sky.

• SIZE Total body length: 90 cm. Weight: 6–8 kg.
• HABITAT Evergreen, semi-evergreen and moist deciduous forests.
• BEST SEEN AT Borajan and Gibbon WLS (Assam).
• CONSERVATION THREATS Habitat loss, fragmentation, and poaching.

DIFFERENT FEMALE
*The only Indian primate species in which the male and female are differently coloured, the adult male Hoolock Gibbon is uniformly black whereas the adult female is a golden blonde.*

Throughout NE India, S of R Brahmaputra.

long arms

white brows

no tail

| | |
|---|---|
| FAMILY NAME | Cercopithecidae |
| LATIN NAME | *Macaca mulatta* |
| IUCN STATUS/WPA | Lower risk/II |
| LOCAL STATUS | Abundant |
| POPULATION | Unknown |
| DIET | 🐚 🍖 🌿 🍃 🐛 🌱 |
| SOCIAL UNIT | Groups of 5–50 |
| ACTIVITY | ☼ |
| STRATUM | Terrestrial, arboreal |

# ●RHESUS MACAQUE

LOCAL NAME: *Molua bandar* (Assamese), *Bandor, Markat* (Bengali), *Bandar* (Hindi), *Makhre* (Garo), *Ponz* (♂), *Punz* (♀) (Kashmiri), *Chree* (Khasi), *Yong* (Manipuri), *Lak makad* (Marathi), *Makda* (Gujarati), *Zawng* (Mizo), *Pati makada* (Oriya).

THE MOST WIDESPREAD monkey of northern India, living in close association with humans (commensal), the Rhesus is an aggressive primate that is found in multi-male groups dominated by a single male (alpha male). It has a range of vocalizations: a short bark, a food call ("ooo-ooo") and grunt being most common; the young can screech disconcertingly. Although the Hanuman Langur is considered to be the holy monkey of India, the Rhesus is also fed by humans at temples. Being intelligent, they gather at such spots for food and demand it with impunity. In urban and rural areas they often raid homes for eatables.

• BEHAVIOUR Male monkeys maintain their ranking by threat displays, such as shaking branches. In cities this translates into shaking electric lines (causing blackouts) or even wrenching car mirrors.
• SIZE Total body length: 47–63 cm. Weight: 5–11 kg.
• HABITAT Urban areas, deciduous and evergreen forests, and scrub.
• BEST SEEN AT Northern Indian towns.
• CONSERVATION THREATS Habitat loss, urban migration, and capture as pests.

All over N and NE India, except deserts and high Himalaya, N of R Tapti and Godavari (up to 2,400 m).

MOTHER AND CHILD
*Rhesus have olive brown coats and pink faces.*

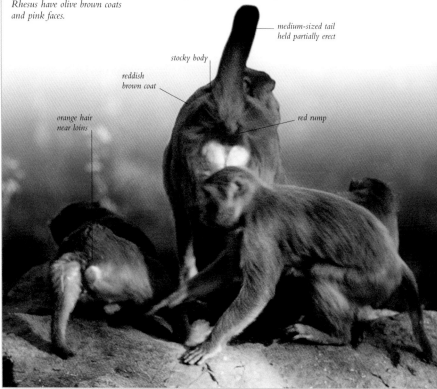

medium-sized tail held partially erect

stocky body

reddish brown coat

orange hair near loins

red rump

| | |
|---|---|
| FAMILY NAME | Cercopithecidae |
| LATIN NAME | *Macaca radiata* |
| IUCN STATUS/WPA | Lower risk/II |
| LOCAL STATUS | Abundant |
| POPULATION | Unknown |
| DIET | 🐾 🦎 🌿 🐛 ❀ |
| SOCIAL UNIT | Groups of 20–30 |
| ACTIVITY | ☼ |
| STRATUM | Arboreal, terrestrial |

# ● BONNET MACAQUE

LOCAL NAME: *Korangan* (Malayalam), *Makad* (Marathi), *Kapi, Manga* (Kannada), *Pati makada* (Oriya), *Vella korangu* (Tamil), *Kothi* (Telegu).

A PECULIAR CAP OF long hair, arranged in a whorl, gives the Bonnet Macaque its name. It is a medium-sized species with a tail that is longer than its body. Its colour changes from a lustrous brown in winter to scraggy buff-grey in summer. This is the common commensal monkey of South India and can be seen around temples.

*pale puffy face*

*bonnet of long dark hair*

● BEHAVIOUR Like the Rhesus, it loses its fear of man easily. Males have to continually show dominance to prevent losing rank and thus can be aggressive at times. It spends a lot of time in trees, or high perches in urban areas, but also comes down to the ground frequently.
● SIZE Total body length: 35–65 cm. Weight: 4–9 kg.
● HABITAT Urban and rural areas, deciduous forest, and scrub.
● BEST SEEN AT Periyar NP (Kerala), southern Indian towns.
● CONSERVATION THREATS Habitat loss, urban migration, and capture as pests.

*whitish under-parts*

S India, Mumbai in the W to R Godavari in the E.

| | |
|---|---|
| FAMILY NAME | Cercopithecidae |
| LATIN NAME | *Macaca fascicularis* |
| IUCN STATUS/WPA | Lower risk/I |
| LOCAL STATUS | Locally common |
| POPULATION | 360, declining |
| DIET | 🦀 🐾 🐟 |
| SOCIAL UNIT | Groups of 5–30 |
| ACTIVITY | ☼ |
| STRATUM | Terrestrial, arboreal |

Great Nicobar Island.

# ● CRAB-EATING MACAQUE

LOCAL NAME: *Makphoum* (Nicobarese).

Restricted to the Nicobar Islands in India, the Crab-eating or Long-tailed Macaque is a medium-sized monkey that eats fruits and nuts but is also adapted to a diet of crustaceans. Like the Bonnet Macaque, it also feeds on coconuts, ripping them open with its teeth. Grizzled olive brown in colour, it has a long tail and short stout legs. Males have a prominent blotched scrotum. It is mainly found in Southeast Asia, and India is at the tip of its range.
● BEHAVIOUR The Crab-eating Macaque is an adept swimmer and lives near streams or rivers whenever found inland.
● SIZE Total body length: 35–45 cm. Weight: 2.5–8.3 kg.
● HABITAT Coastal forests, mangroves, and coconut plantations.
● BEST SEEN AT Great Nicobar Island.
● CONSERVATION THREATS Habitat loss and human interference.

*short, stout legs*

*long tail*

# ASSAMESE MACAQUE

| | |
|---|---|
| FAMILY NAME | Cercopithecidae |
| LATIN NAME | *Macaca assamensis* |
| IUCN STATUS/WPA | Vulnerable/II |
| LOCAL STATUS | Uncommon |
| POPULATION | app. 25,000 |
| DIET | 🐚🍃🌾🐌🦎🌱 |
| SOCIAL UNIT | Groups of 15-20 |
| ACTIVITY | ☀ |
| STRATUM | Terrestrial, arboreal |

Throughout NE India except Tripura, and North Bengal and Sikkim (up to 3,000 m).

**LOCAL NAME:** *Bandor* (Assamese), *Pio* (Bhutia), *Makre dow* (Garo), *Asamia bandar* (Hindi), *Sahu* (Lepcha), *Zawng* (Mizo), *Tepfi* (Naga).

THE ASSAMESE MACAQUE is a heavy, thickset forest macaque with a brownish-grey coat. It superficially resembles the Rhesus Macaque, but does not have the orange fur near the loins that characterizes its commensal cousin. It carries its tail parallel to the ground rather than erect. The adult male has a pronounced beard of long facial hair. The Assamese Macaque's call is a loud "pio" note, rendered musically.

• BEHAVIOUR Like all macaques, it drops from trees to the ground when alarmed, and scampers into the bushes. It frequents crop fields in north Bengal and Sikkim where it is often hunted by irate villagers.
• SIZE Total body length: 44 – 68 cm. Weight: 4.6 – 12 kg.
• HABITAT Dense deciduous and semi-evergreen forests of the Northeast.
• BEST SEEN AT Bherjan-Borajan WLS (Assam).
• CONSERVATION THREATS Habitat loss and poaching.

*bearded, thickset face*

*brownish-grey fur*

## EXTRALIMITAL MACAQUE
*There have been reports of a macaque being sighted in Northeast India which is most likely* **Macaca thibetana** *or the* **Tibetan Macaque.** *However, there is considerable debate on whether this monkey recorded in West Kamang, Arunachal Pradesh is the Tibetan Macaque or a sub-species of the Assamese Macaque. The Tibetan Macaque is a large, dark brown monkey with a long, thick pelage. Its face is pale brown, tending towards pink in females, partially hidden by long cheek whiskers and a prominent pale buff beard. There is a whitish patch around its eyes and a distinctive whorl of hair on its head.*

| | |
|---|---|
| FAMILY NAME | Cercopithecidae |
| LATIN NAME | *Macaca leonina* |
| IUCN STATUS / WPA | Vulnerable / II |
| LOCAL STATUS | Rare |
| POPULATION | Unknown |
| DIET | 🍎 🌿 ✳ 🐛 🗡 |
| SOCIAL UNIT | Small groups |
| ACTIVITY | ☀ |
| STRATUM | Terrestrial, arboreal |

# PIG-TAILED MACAQUE

LOCAL NAME: *Gahori nejiya bandor* (Assamese), *Bara haleji bandar* (Bengali), *Peko* (Garo/Karbi), *Suar poonch bandar* (Hindi), *Zawng muat* (Mizo), *Kangh* (Naga).

A LARGE FOREST MONKEY, the Pig-tailed Macaque might at first sight resemble the Assamese and Rhesus Macaques. It can be distinguished from them by its dark cap of short, neatly parted hair and short erect tail, slightly curled at the tip. It also differs from the Stump-tailed Macaque in its pink and not red face.

dark cap of parted hair

short erect tail

white eyebrows

• BEHAVIOUR Like most members of the macaque family, it grunts, whimpers and murmurs.
• SIZE Total body length: 43−60 cm. Weight: 4−16 kg.
• HABITAT Lowland and montane deciduous, and evergreen forests.
• BEST SEEN AT Garampani WLS (Assam).
• CONSERVATION THREATS Habitat loss and poaching.

Throughout NE India, S of Brahmaputra (up to 2,000 m).

| | |
|---|---|
| FAMILY NAME | Cercopithecidae |
| LATIN NAME | *Macaca arctoides* |
| IUCN STATUS / WPA | Vulnerable / II |
| LOCAL STATUS | Rare |
| POPULATION | Unknown, declining |
| DIET | 🍎 🌿 🐛 🗡 |
| SOCIAL UNIT | Groups of 12 − 65 |
| ACTIVITY | ☀ |
| STRATUM | Terrestrial |

# STUMP-TAILED MACAQUE

LOCAL NAME: *Senduri bandor* (Assamese), *Makre khimidonza* (Garo), *Sinduri bandar* (Hindi), *Zawng hmalsen* (Mizo), *Chantee* (Naga).

ALSO KNOWN AS the Bear Macaque, this stocky monkey is the largest and heaviest macaque species in India. It is also one of the country's most endangered primates. The Stump-tailed Macaque has a unique crown of hair that radiates from a central whorl and falls sleekly to the back of the head. It has long cheek hair that covers the ears and extends to its throat to form a ruff-like beard. It has the shortest tail among macaques and is very terrestrial by nature.

blotched, reddish face

short tail

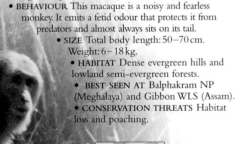

• BEHAVIOUR This macaque is a noisy and fearless monkey. It emits a fetid odour that protects it from predators and almost always sits on its tail.
• SIZE Total body length: 50−70 cm. Weight: 6−18 kg.
• HABITAT Dense evergreen hills and lowland semi-evergreen forests.
• BEST SEEN AT Balphakram NP (Meghalaya) and Gibbon WLS (Assam).
• CONSERVATION THREATS Habitat loss and poaching.

Throughout NE India, S of R Brahmaputra (up to 2,400 m).

| | |
|---|---|
| FAMILY NAME | Cercopithecidae |
| LATIN NAME | *Macaca silenus* |
| IUCN STATUS/WPA | Endangered/I |
| LOCAL STATUS | Rare |
| POPULATION | app. 3,000 –4,000, declining |
| DIET | 🍃 ❀ 🌸 🌰 ● |
| SOCIAL UNIT | Groups of 7 – 40 |
| ACTIVITY | ☀ |
| STRATUM | Arboreal |

Western Ghats and associated hills of Karnataka, Kerala, and Tamil Nadu.

# LION-TAILED MACAQUE

LOCAL NAME: *Singalika* (Kannada), *Nella manthi, Singhawalan, Neelan* (Malayalam), *Arakkan, Singhaval manthi* (Tamil).

THIS ENDANGERED MONKEY of evergreen forests may be distinguished from the other black monkey of southern India, the Nilgiri Langur, by its grey facial mane and much shorter, tufted tail that looks like a lion's tail. The Lion-tailed Macaque is a medium- to large-sized macaque, which is very arboreal in its natural undisturbed habitat. It moves in a characteristic slow motion style on tree tops.
• BEHAVIOUR The call of this monkey sounds like a "coyeh" or "coo".
• SIZE Total body length: 46 – 60 cm. Weight: 6 – 8 kg.
• HABITAT Dense evergreen and semi-evergreen forests.
• BEST SEEN AT Silent Valley NP (Kerala), Kalakkad and Anamalai WLS (Tamil Nadu).
• CONSERVATION THREATS Habitat loss and poaching.

*ashy grey mane around face*

*all-black coat*

# NILGIRI LANGUR

**LOCAL NAME:** *Kari Manthi* (Tamil), *Karin korangan* (Malayalam), *Kurri korunga* (Badaga, Kurumba), *Turuni kodan* (Toda).

| | |
|---|---|
| FAMILY NAME | Cercopithecidae |
| LATIN NAME | *Trachypithecus johnii* |
| IUCN STATUS/WPA | Vulnerable/I |
| LOCAL STATUS | Locally common |
| POPULATION | app. 10,000 |
| DIET | 🌿🐌🌱 |
| SOCIAL UNIT | Troops of 8–15 |
| ACTIVITY | ☀ |
| STRATUM | Terrestrial, arboreal |

Western Ghats S of Kodagu, and Palni and Anamalai Hills.

yellowish hair

black body

long tail

SLIM AND BLACK, this langur is the common rainforest monkey of the southern Western Ghats. It has yellow-tinted hair on its head and is often confused with the stockier Lion-tailed Macaque which has an ashy grey mane. Also, the Nilgiri Langur's tail is longer. Females have a white patch on the inside of their thighs. Newborns are pink with reddish hair. It is hunted extensively for alleged medicinal properties.
• **BEHAVIOUR** The characteristic "hoo-hoo" call of the adult male langur can be heard mostly at dawn and sometimes at dusk.
• **SIZE** Total body length: 60–80 cm. Weight: 11–14 kg.
• **HABITAT** Primarily rainforests, also deciduous patches, plantations, and edges of estates.
• **BEST SEEN AT** Anamalai WLS (Tamil Nadu), Periyar NP (Kerala).
• **CONSERVATION THREATS** Habitat loss and poaching.

# PHAYRE'S LEAF MONKEY

**LOCAL NAME:** *Chasma chakwa bandor* (Assamese), *Chasma, Dodhi bandor* (Bengali), *Dawr* (Mizo), *Dodhi, kaala bandor* (Tripuri).

| | |
|---|---|
| FAMILY NAME | Cercopithecidae |
| LATIN NAME | *Trachypithecus phayrei* |
| IUCN STATUS/WPA | Endangered/I |
| LOCAL STATUS | Uncommon |
| POPULATION | app. 1,000, declining |
| DIET | 🌿🐌🔲 |
| SOCIAL UNIT | Troops of 8–30 |
| ACTIVITY | ☀ |
| STRATUM | Arboreal, terrestrial |

pale patches around lips and eyes

A SMALL, LITTLE-KNOWN leaf-eater found only in the lower northeastern states bordering Bangladesh, the Phayre's Leaf Monkey mainly has a Southeast Asian distribution. It is also called the Spectacled Monkey because of its white eye-patches that stand out in its black face. Its body is slate-grey, tending to black in the limbs, with a lighter underside. It is hunted by the Mizos and Lushais for its gallstones which are supposed to have medicinal qualities.
• **BEHAVIOUR** A less noisy langur, it leaps on to tree branches in a spread-eagled fashion rather than jumping on to a single chosen branch.
• **SIZE** Total body length: 45–59 cm. Weight: 6–8 kg.
• **HABITAT** Mixed moist deciduous, semi-evergreen and secondary forests, bamboo patches, and forest fringes.
• **BEST SEEN AT** Sepahijala WLS (Tripura).
• **CONSERVATION THREATS** Habitat loss and poaching.

Tripura, Mizoram, and Cachar, Hailakandi and Karimganj districts of Assam.

| | |
|---|---|
| FAMILY NAME | Cercopithecidae |
| LATIN NAME | *Trachypithecus geei* |
| LOCAL STATUS | Uncommon |
| IUCN STATUS/WPA | Endangered/I |
| POPULATION | < 1000, declining |
| DIET | 🌿🐛🌰 |
| SOCIAL UNIT | Troops of 5–10 (22 max.) |
| ACTIVITY | ☼ |
| STRATUM | Arboreal |

# GOLDEN LANGUR

LOCAL NAME: *Sonali bandar* (Assamese), *Makre gophur* (Bodo), *Sugrib* (Bhotia).

black face

ARGUABLY THE MOST beautifully coloured langur, the Golden Langur has deep cream to golden fur with tinges of red on the flanks. It has a black face with long cheek whiskers and a cap of hair on its head. This langur also has a distinctive long, tasselled tail. Males appear more golden, while females verge on cream. Discovered in 1956, it has been the flagbearer of langurs ever since.
• BEHAVIOUR A very silent langur, it comes down rarely to drink water.
• SIZE Total body length: 50 – 60 cm. Weight: 9.5 –11 kg.
• HABITAT Evergreen and moist deciduous forests.
• BEST SEEN AT Manas and Chakrashila WLS (Assam).
• CONSERVATION THREATS Poaching.

long tasselled tail

Between R Manas and R Sankosh, in Kokrajhar, Bongaigaon and Dhubri districts of Assam (up to 2,400 m in Bhutan).

| | |
|---|---|
| FAMILY NAME | Cercopithecidae |
| LATIN NAME | *Trachypithecus pileatus* |
| LOCAL STATUS | Locally common |
| IUCN STATUS/WPA | Endangered/I |
| POPULATION | Unknown, stable |
| DIET | 🌿🐛🌰 |
| SOCIAL UNIT | Troops of 5–16 |
| ACTIVITY | ☼ |
| STRATUM | Arboreal |

# CAPPED LANGUR

LOCAL NAME: *Tupimuria* (Assamese), *Golija makhre* (Bodo), *Rangol* (Garo), *Tongo* (Khasi), *Bilaspuri* (Manipuri), *Ngau* (Mizo).

THE COMMON FOREST LANGUR of Northeast India, the Capped Langur has a number of sub-species with varying colouration. A few sub-species are more golden than the Golden Langur, while the males of some sub-species have tinges of red on their bodies and cobalt blue on the inner thighs. A conspicuous cap of different coloured hair is a good identification for different sub-species. All of them, however, vary from golden-cream to grey in the upper body with a fulvous (brownish yellow) under body and have tails that are blackish on the lower half and tipped black. The cheeks have large tufts of pale hair.

cap of dark erect hair

pale cheek hair

• BEHAVIOUR It lives exclusively on trees and seldom comes down to the ground. It draws most of its water needs from the dew on foliage.
• SIZE Total body length: 50– 70 cm. Weight: 10 – 12 kg.
• HABITAT Dense deciduous and evergreen forests.
• BEST SEEN AT Kaziranga NP and Gibbon WLS (Assam).
• CONSERVATION THREATS Habitat loss and poaching.

Throughout NE India (up to 2,000 m).

| FAMILY NAME | Cercopithecidae |
|---|---|
| LATIN NAME | *Semnopithecus entellus* |
| LOCAL STATUS | Abundant |
| IUCN STATUS / WPA | Lower risk / II |
| POPULATION | app. 250,000, stable |
| DIET | 🌿 🐾 🌱 |
| SOCIAL UNIT | Troops of 10 – 100 |
| ACTIVITY | ☀ |
| STRATUM | Terrestrial, arboreal |

# HANUMAN LANGUR

LOCAL NAME: *Koda* (Kodava), *Hanuman langur* (Hindi/Marathi), *Wandra* (Gujarati), *Dodda manga* (Kannada), *Vella manthi* (Tamil), *Kondamucchu* (Telegu), *Wandur* (Kashmiri), *Hanuman* (Bengali/Assamese), *Hanuman makada* (Oriya).

THE MOST WIDESPREAD langur in India, the Common or Hanuman Langur is silver-grey with a black face. Venerated by Hindus as a god, it is commonly recognized by most Indians. There are several races of Hanuman Langur, differing in colour and size. Scientists are currently debating whether this langur is a single species with several sub-species, or whether these are different species.

- BEHAVIOUR In certain sub-species, male langurs possess a harem and do not tolerate sub-adult or even very young males in the troop. The rate of infanticide by adult males in these sub-species is very high and females shelter newborn babies with much care. Usually, surviving males leave the troop and form all-male bands till they can lead their own troop. The Hanuman Langur is known for its unique association in the forest with the Cheetal or Spotted Deer, each warning the other of the approach of predators, and the Cheetal eating leaves and fruit dropped by langurs from trees.
- SIZE Total body length: 60 –75 cm. Weight: 16 – 21 kg (Western Himalaya), 9 – 16 kg (Peninsular India).
- HABITAT All habitats except high mountains and desert, also found in human settlements.
- BEST SEEN AT Sariska NP (Rajasthan) and Corbett NP (Uttaranchal). Also seen around temples.
- CONSERVATION THREATS Habitat loss and urban migration.

## VARYING COLOURS

*Coat and crest colours vary dramatically. The back ranges from chocolate brown to pale silver and some sub-species have darker limbs.*

Throughout India, except upper Himalaya (up to 3000 m), NE India, and arid/desert areas of Gujarat and Rajasthan.

black face

face fringed by hair

silver-grey coat

long tail

# DEER, MUSK DEER AND CHEVROTAINS

| INDIAN DEER, MUSK DEER & CHEVROTAINS AT A GLANCE | |
|---|---|
| NUMBER OF SPECIES | 9 (12) |
| LARGEST | Sambar |
| SMALLEST | Mouse Deer |
| MOST COMMON | Spotted Deer |
| MOST ENDANGERED | Brow-antlered Deer |

### DEER CHARACTERISTICS
• Ungulate or hoofed mammal
• Ruminant
• No incisors in the upper jaw,
although canines are normally present
• Prominent facial glands
• Moist, naked nose
• No gall bladder, except in one
species – the Musk Deer

THE CERVIDAE or deer family occurs
throughout the two Americas, Europe and
Asia, and is absent from Australia, Antarctica and
most of Africa. Deer are the most common
herbivores found throughout India and form the
principal prey for the Tiger and the Leopard. Musk
Deer are primitive ruminants that do not have
antlers or the facial glands that true deer possess.
Chevrotains are small ruminants that are
intermediates between pigs and deer. This section
looks at various species of Cervidae or true deer,
including muntjacs (which some taxonomists feel
are not deer), as well as the dimunitive chevrotains
and the alpine musk deer.

*A male* **Himalayan Musk Deer** *does not have
antlers but displays prominent canines – these are
rudimentary in females.*

*The pointed antlers of the* **Swamp
Deer** *are among the most developed
headgear in Indian deer.*

# ANTLERS

Most male deer can be distinguished by their antlers which differ from the horns of goats, sheep, antelope, and cattle in three unique ways. They are solid; they are usually branched (perhaps to allow non-lethal combat among males); and they are deciduous or shed annually. Antlers are among the most rapidly growing tissues in the animal world and within a month or two of the deer shedding its full-grown bony antlers, new ones spring up in "velvet". This is a finely furred skin that covers the antler and has a network of capillaries. Gradually, a hard burr or ring develops at the base of the antler, choking off the blood supply, and the velvet "dries up". Deer then rub this skin off on branches and on the ground to expose their new, solid headgear. Evolutionary biologists theorize that this device is used for sexual display and male-male fights. The months when deer can be seen in hard antlers and velvet vary considerably according to locale and the season. At times one can see two deer in the same herd with hard and velvet antlers (see opposite).

# SOCIAL ORGANIZATION & RUT

A characteristic behaviour of the deer family, rutting denotes the period when male deer display and battle each other for breeding access to females. The males of large forest and grassland species especially, have spectacular ruts as stags fight one another for mates. Loud vocalizations and sparring at each other with branched antlers are typical of the rut. Other behavioural traits such as decorating the headgear with vegetation are also part of the display. The birth of the fawn follows a 5-8 month gestation period. This is the only time that the female deer turns carnivorous, when she consumes the afterbirth. The social organization of deer and deer-like ruminants varies greatly with the Mouse Deer, Barking Deer, and Musk Deer being solitary, while true deer are found in groups of up to 100 individuals at times. Barking Deer are monogamous while many large cervids have harems.

| | |
|---|---|
| FAMILY NAME | Moschidae |
| LATIN NAME | *Moschus chrysogaster* |
| IUCN STATUS/WPA | Lower risk/I |
| LOCAL STATUS | Uncommon |
| POPULATION | >5,000, declining |
| DIET | 🌿 🍂 🌱 🍄 |
| SOCIAL UNIT | Solitary/pairs |
| ACTIVITY | ◑ ☾ |
| STRATUM | Terrestrial |

# HIMALAYAN MUSK DEER

LOCAL NAME: *Kastura* (Hindi), *Roos* (♂), *Roos-kutt* (♀) (Kashmiri).

A SHY DOG-SIZED mountain ruminant, the Himalayan or Alpine Musk Deer has a thick, bristly coat speckled with white on the flanks, white-stockinged legs, and a naked tail that lies buried in the thick rump hair. The speckles are more visible in summer and are more prominent in the young. The only deer with a gall bladder, a musk gland and no facial glands, the Musk Deer is considered to be evolutionarily primitive. A loud hiss or peep is the normal call in both the sexes, with a shorter chirp indicating alarm. Some experts believe that the Musk Deer that is found in Sikkim, Assam and Arunachal Pradesh is *Moschus fuscus* or the Black Musk Deer. The adult male has a gland or pod under the abdominal skin that secretes musk, a substance valued highly in the making of Oriental medicines and to a limited extent, perfumes.

• BEHAVIOUR Male Musk Deer fight each other during the winter rutting season, cutting deep slashes on rivals with their long canines. Communication is chiefly by olfaction. The deer scent mark by defecation and secretions of the caudal, musk and inter-digital glands.
• SIZE Height at shoulder: 50 cm. Weight: 13 −15 kg.
• HABITAT Sub-alpine oak and rhododendron forests, alpine scrub and meadows and upper temperate oak forests.
• BEST SEEN AT Kedarnath WLS (Uttaranchal).
• CONSERVATION THREATS Poaching and habitat disturbance.

FEMALE WITH YOUNG ONE
*The female Musk Deer does not have visible canines. Both male and female can be identified by their unique bounding gait.*

long hare-like ears, fringed white inside

no antlers in either sex

brown-grey coat

long canines in male

J&K, excluding Ladakh, to Arunachal Pradesh (2,500 m to treeline).

| FAMILY NAME | Cervidae |
| --- | --- |
| LATIN NAME | *Cervus unicolor* |
| IUCN STATUS/WPA | Lower risk/III |
| LOCAL STATUS | Common |
| POPULATION | app. 50,000–100,000, declining |
| DIET | 🌿 ✿ 🐾 |
| SOCIAL UNIT | Herds of 2–12, solitary ♂ |
| ACTIVITY | ☀ ☾ (feeding) |
| STRATUM | Terrestrial |

# SAMBAR

LOCAL NAME: *Tekha* (Naga), *Sambar* (Hindi/Marathi/Bengali), *Kaduve* (Kannada), *Kadama* (Kodava), *Kadaa maan* (Tamil), *Kezha maan, Mlave* (Malayalam), *Khar pohu* (Assamese), *Sabar* (Gujarati), *Sazuk* (Mizo), *Kadathi* (Telegu).

A TYPICAL FOREST DEER with a shaggy, dark brown coat, and large spreading antlers, the Sambar is India's largest deer. Females are lighter and less shaggy. The adult males are largest in Central India and on account of their size, they form the preferred prey base of tigers. This is the only widespread large forest deer – the other three species (see p. 42-43) are endangered and restricted in their range.

• **BEHAVIOUR** The Sambar alarm call is a loud "dhonk". Mostly browsers, Sambar are rarely seen grazing. They often feed in shallow water and when chased by predators such as dholes, they take to water, splashing loudly with their hooves to confuse their attacker. Stags fight each other during rutting season for access to females. During the rut stags wallow like cattle and pigs.

• **SIZE** Height at shoulder: 150 cm. Weight: 225–320 kg.

• **HABITAT** Mixed deciduous forest and grassland scrub.

• **BEST SEEN AT** Sariska and Ranthambhor NPs (Rajasthan).

• **CONSERVATION THREATS** Poaching, habitat loss, and disease.

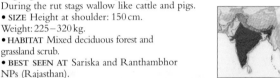

Throughout India, except deserts, mangroves, and high mountains.

**SORE SPOT**
*Some Sambar sub-species develop a raw red throat patch seasonally, surrounded by naked skin, as in the female above.*

large antler with three tines in stag

large size

coarse dark brown coat

| | |
|---|---|
| FAMILY NAME | **Cervidae** |
| LATIN NAME | *Cervus elaphus* |
| IUCN STATUS/WPA | Crit. endangered/I |
| LOCAL STATUS | Rare |
| POPULATION | app. 200-400, declining |
| DIET | ❦ ✿ |
| SOCIAL UNIT | Herds of 2-8 (summer), 20-30 (winter) |
| ACTIVITY | ☼ ☾ (feeding) |
| STRATUM | Terrestrial |

N of Kashmir Valley (Dachigam) and Himachal Pradesh (Gamagul).

# KASHMIR RED DEER
**LOCAL NAME:** *Hangul* (♂), *Minemer* (♀) (Kashmiri).

THE KASHMIR RED DEER or Hangul is a sub-species of the Eurasian Red Deer restricted to a portion of the North-west Himalaya. A large, dingy brown animal with an orange-white rump patch, the Hangul may be identified by its white lips and chin and large, spreading antlers. Further east of the Hangul's range is found the Sikkim Red Deer, locally called Shou. The Shou (*C. e. wallichi*) is thought to be extinct in Bhutan and is found in small numbers in Tibet. There are unconfirmed reports of the animal straying into India. It is larger than the Hangul, with bigger antlers and a larger rump patch.

• BEHAVIOUR Stags migrate above the snow line, to heights of 2,700m−3,600m in summer, and come down to join the hinds (which migrate up to lower heights in October). Stags are known to roar during rutting.
• SIZE Height at withers: 120−125 cm.
Weight: Up to 180 kg.
• HABITAT Broad-leaved and coniferous forests, and meadows between 1,500−3,600 m.
• BEST SEEN AT Dachigam NP (J&K).
• CONSERVATION THREATS Habitat loss and poaching.

large antler with 4-5 tines in stag

orangish-cream rump

dull brown coat

HANGUL HIND
*All female deer in India are without antlers, and identification is best done by viewing the males in a herd.*

## BROW-ANTLERED DEER

LOCAL NAME: *Thamin* (Burmese), *Sangai* (Manipuri).

| | |
|---|---|
| FAMILY NAME | Cervidae |
| LATIN NAME | *Cervus eldii* |
| IUCN STATUS/WPA | Vulnerable/I |
| LOCAL STATUS | Rare |
| POPULATION | app. 100, declining |
| DIET | 🌾 🥬 🐌 |
| SOCIAL UNIT | Small herds |
| ACTIVITY | ☾ |
| STRATUM | Terrestrial |

THE MALE DEER has a dark brown winter coat which turns to fawn in summer; the female is fawn all year round. The young are spotted. The Brow-antlered Deer has splayed hooves and long dewclaws. Keen eyesight and speed allow it to be an open ground deer. A sharp grunt indicates alarm, while rutting calls are longer and louder.

• BEHAVIOUR This deer walks on the hind surface of its pasterns, which are thus horny and not hairy. It moves with mincing hops over floating foliage and is also called Dancing Deer. It is known to raid crops at night.

circular antler with 6 or more tines in stag

male's dark brown winter coat

• SIZE Height at shoulder: 105–120 cm. Weight: 170 kg.

• HABITAT Open flat grasslands and phumdis or floating vegetation in marshes; avoids forests.

• BEST SEEN AT Keibul Lamjao NP (Manipur).

• CONSERVATION THREATS Habitat loss, cattle grazing, and inbreeding.

Northern shores of Lake Loktak, Manipur.

## SWAMP DEER

LOCAL NAME: *Dal horina* (Assamese), *Baradali horin* (Bengali), *Barasingha* (Hindi), *Goinjak, Gaoni, Salsamar, Newari* (C India).

| | |
|---|---|
| FAMILY NAME | Cervidae |
| LATIN NAME | *Cervus duvaucelii* |
| IUCN STATUS/WPA | Vulnerable/I |
| LOCAL STATUS | Locally common |
| POPULATION | >2,000, declining |
| DIET | 🌾 🥬 |
| SOCIAL UNIT | Herds of 50–100 or more |
| ACTIVITY | ☀ ☾ |
| STRATUM | Terrestrial |

THE TWELVE-TINED antlers of stags give this deer the name Barasingha. Adult males have a dark brown coat in winter and a light brown coat in summer, like females. The hard-ground sub-species of Central India has different ecology from the swamp deer of the North and Northeast.

• BEHAVIOUR The stags bray loudly during the rut. Deer in swamps wallow in mud and have splayed hooves.

large antler with 6 tines in stag

swollen neck and ruff in stag

• SIZE Height at shoulder: 115–135 cm. Weight: 170–180 kg.

• HABITAT Grasslands, swamps (N and NE India), and sal forests (C India).

• BEST SEEN AT Kanha NP (Madhya Pradesh) and Kaziranga NP (Assam).

• CONSERVATION THREATS Habitat loss, poaching, and cattle grazing.

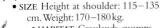

W Terai, Assam and C India.

| | |
|---|---|
| FAMILY NAME | **Tragulidae** |
| LATIN NAME | *Moschiola meminna* |
| IUCN STATUS/WPA | Lower risk/I |
| LOCAL STATUS | Locally Common |
| POPULATION | Unknown |
| DIET | 🌿 🍂 |
| SOCIAL UNIT | Solitary/pairs |
| ACTIVITY | ◑ ☾ |
| STRATUM | Terrestrial |

# MOUSE DEER

LOCAL NAME: *Pisura* (Hindi), *Pisori haran* (Marathi), *Koora* (Kannada), *Kooran panni* (Malayalam), *Saruhu maan* (Tamil).

INDIA'S SMALLEST DEER, the Mouse Deer or the Asian Chevrotain, is a unique species with a three-chambered stomach instead of the four-chambered one in all other ruminants. It also has large hooves and a wedge-shaped body that allows it to scurry through bushes. Its coat is speckled olive brown. Neither sex has antlers but both have long canines. This primitive deer has relatives in Southeast Asia and West Africa.

• BEHAVIOUR The Mouse Deer usually makes its den in a tree hollow. As it is shy, small, well-camouflaged and has no vocalizations, it is usually overlooked. In hot weather it pants with its mouth open.

• SIZE Height at shoulder: 25 – 30 cm. Weight: 2 – 4 kg.
• HABITAT Deciduous and evergreen forests.
• BEST SEEN AT Mudumalai (Tamil Nadu) and Bandipur NP (Karnataka).
• CONSERVATION THREATS Poaching and habitat disturbance.

white spots merging into bands on flank

small size

three white stripes on throat

Throughout S India (up to 24° N).

| | |
|---|---|
| FAMILY NAME | **Cervidae** |
| LATIN NAME | *Muntiacus muntjak* |
| IUCN STATUS/WPA | Lower risk/III |
| LOCAL STATUS | Locally common |
| POPULATION | Unknown |
| DIET | 🌿 🍂 |
| SOCIAL UNIT | Solitary/ pairs |
| ACTIVITY | ☀ ◑ ☾ (feeding) |
| STRATUM | Terrestrial |

# INDIAN MUNTJAC

LOCAL NAME: *Kutra* (Bengali), *Kakar* (Hindi), *Kadu koorie* (Kannada), *Bhekar* (Marathi), *Kelaiyadu* (Tamil/Malayalam), *Shaji* (Manipuri), *Sagoli pohu* (Assamese), *Chize* (Naga), *Sakhi* (Mizo).

THE MORE COMMON OF THE two small Indian forest ruminants, the Barking Deer or Indian Muntjac has a glossy brown coat with no underfur. Its forelimbs are longer than the hind limbs. Males have long upper canines that are not always visible. Two other small Southeast Asian species, the Burmese Leaf Deer *(M. putaoensis)* and the Black Muntjac *(M. crinifrons),* have been reported from Arunachal Pradesh.

• BEHAVIOUR This muntjac is more likely to be heard in the late mornings and evenings. A sharp bark indicates alarm while a slightly longer, shriller version is its normal call.
• SIZE Height at shoulder: 50 –75 cm. Weight: 14 – 28 kg.
• HABITAT Prefers hilly and moist areas in thick deciduous and evergreen forests.
• BEST SEEN AT Corbett NP (Uttaranchal).
• CONSERVATION THREATS Poaching and habitat loss.

short antlers

dark chestnut-brown coat

V-shaped bony ridge

Throughout India, except J&K, high Himalaya (up to 2,500 m), and arid/desert areas of Gujarat and Rajasthan.

# HOG DEER

**LOCAL NAME:** *Horina pohu, Hugori pohu* (Assamese), *Kaala khatia* (Bengali), *Para* (Hindi/Punjabi), *Kharsa* (Manipuri).

THE CLOSEST RELATIVE of the Spotted Deer, the Hog Deer is stouter, with shorter legs. Its stout rump and lowered stance give it a pig-like appearance. The young are sandy and spotted indistinctly on the flanks while the adults have a speckled appearance due to the white-tipped hairs on their olive brown coat. The underside of the body and tail is white and the large rounded ears fringed white. Stags have very short antlers with three tines.

- **BEHAVIOUR** When alarmed, it erects its tail, calls in a low bark like the Cheetal and scurries into the grass with its neck lowered and stretched out.
- **SIZE** Height at shoulder: 61–71 cm. Weight: 36–50 kg.
- **HABITAT** Tall grasslands and forest swamp interspersed with grassland.
- **BEST SEEN AT** Kaziranga NP (Assam) and Dudhwa NP (Uttaranchal).
- **CONSERVATION THREATS** Habitat loss and poaching.

| FAMILY NAME | Cervidae |
|---|---|
| LATIN NAME | *Axis porcinus* |
| IUCN STATUS/WPA | Lower risk/III |
| LOCAL STATUS | Locally common |
| POPULATION | Unknown, declining |
| DIET | |
| SOCIAL UNIT | Solitary/herds (feeding) |
| ACTIVITY | (feeding) |
| STRATUM | Terrestrial |

*three-tined antler in stag*

*large round ears, fringed white*

*olive-brown speckled coat*

Terai and duars, from Uttaranchal to Assam, Mizoram, and Manipur.

# SPOTTED DEER

**LOCAL NAME:** *Cheetal* (Hindi/Bengali/Marathi), *Saraga jinke* (Kannada), *Pulli maan* (Tamil/Malayalam), *Chukala jinka* (Telegu).

THIS IS INDIA'S MOST COMMON and visible deer. It is also the only predominantly spotted deer in the country. Its coat varies geographically, becoming redder in southern India. The sexes are almost identical except for size and antlers in the male.

- **BEHAVIOUR** Acts as a look-out for langurs, as well as feeds on leaves and fruit dropped by them from trees. Has a sharp "ack ack" call and a loud "wow" alarm call.
- **SIZE** Height at shoulder: 90 cm. Weight: 85 kg.
- **HABITAT** Deciduous forest, especially around fringes.
- **BEST SEEN AT** Corbett NP (Uttaranchal), Bandipur NP (Karnataka), and Kanha NP (Madhya Pradesh).
- **CONSERVATION THREATS** Poaching and cattle grazing.

| FAMILY NAME | Cervidae |
|---|---|
| LATIN NAME | *Axis axis* |
| IUCN STATUS/WPA | Lower risk/III |
| LOCAL STATUS | Abundant |
| POPULATION | Unknown, stable |
| DIET | |
| SOCIAL UNIT | Herds of 10–30, 100+ winter |
| ACTIVITY | |
| STRATUM | Terrestrial |

*large antler with 3 tines in stag*

*dark dorsal stripe*

*white throat*

*white spots on rufous coat*

Throughout India, except J&K, high Himalaya and deserts, E to Assam.

# ANTELOPES

| INDIAN ANTELOPES AT A GLANCE | |
|---|---|
| NUMBER OF SPECIES | 6 |
| LARGEST | Nilgai |
| SMALLEST | Four-horned Antelope |
| MOST COMMON | Nilgai |
| MOST ENDANGERED | Tibetan Antelope |

ANTELOPE CHARACTERISTICS

*In common with all bovids:* Four-chambered stomach
• Permanent horns with bony cores • No incisors in upper jaws and no canines • Fused or absent outer toes

*Unlike other bovids:* Slender legs and graceful build
• Muzzle hairy up to the nostrils • Glands on face and between digits • Hair tufts on the knees in most species

HOOFED MAMMALS that have an even number of toes are called Artiodactyls and they include pigs, deer, musk deer, chevrotains, camels and bovids. The family Bovidae includes antelopes, goats, sheep, and cattle. The six species of antelope that exist in India belong to three sub-families. The Nilgai and Chowsingha belong to the Boselaphini tribe of sub-family Bovinae which is restricted to peninsular India and is believed to be the primitive stock from which wild cattle evolved. Females do not have horns in the sub-family. The two gazelles and the Blackbuck belong to the Antilopinae sub-family and are slender-bodied, long-limbed creatures with annulated horns. If females have horns, they are thinner and shorter. The Tibetan Antelope belongs to a separate monotypic sub-family, Pantholopinae.

## RUT

As in deer, rutting in antelopes can be spectacular. Male **Blackbuck,** for instance, prance around with a mincing gait, their corkscrew horns laid flat against their backs, as they impress females. As in other antelopes, they spar with each other, clashing horns, but normally avoid direct injury to the body. They use posture and positioning of horns to indicate moods and threats. Most antelopes are completely oblivious of their surrounding when they compete for sexual favours. In Pakistan a shepherd is recorded to have crept up close to a pair of sparring Chinkara and caught them by their hind legs, without their even noticing his presence. During rut, almost all antelopes indulge in scent marking and pile up their faeces at spots marked as toilets.

| ANTELOPE SPECIES | RUT (PEAK) | GESTATION PERIOD | BIRTH MONTHS |
|---|---|---|---|
| BLACKBUCK | Feb–Mar | 6 months | Aug–Sep |
| CHINKARA | Variable. Mar–Apr and Sep–Oct | 5.5 months | Variable. Mar–Apr and Sep–Oct |
| CHIRU | Dec | 6 months | June–July |
| CHOWSINGHA | No rut | 8 months | Oct–Feb |
| TIBETAN GAZELLE | Jan–Feb | 6 months | July–Aug |
| NILGAI | Sep–Feb | 8–9 months | May–Sep |

## DROPPINGS

Even when an antelope (or any other animal) is not sighted in the forest, its droppings point to its presence. Normally in pellet-form, they can be found scattered, or heaped together in clumps. Many antelope species such as the Nilgai and Blackbuck are known to mark their territory by using constant open-air toilets or even communal latrines where a single animal or a whole herd accumulates dung. However, solitary species such as the Chowsingha do not have this communal habit. Pellets may be round, slightly tapered, spindle shaped, or flat.

| FAMILY NAME | Bovidae |
| --- | --- |
| LATIN NAME | *Boselaphus tragocamelus* |
| IUCN STATUS/WPA | Lower risk/III |
| LOCAL STATUS | Abundant |
| POPULATION | Unknown, increasing |
| DIET | 🌾 🍃 🍎 🌿 🍂 |
| SOCIAL UNIT | Herds of 4–10, solitary ♂ |
| ACTIVITY | ☼ ☾ |
| STRATUM | Terrestrial |

Throughout India, S of Himalaya up to Karnataka (except deserts, West Bengal, and NE).

# NILGAI

LOCAL NAME: *Nilgai, Nil* (Hindi), *Roz* (Punjabi/Haryanvi), *Rohu* (Marathi), *Roj* (Gujarati).

INDIA'S LARGEST ANTELOPE, the Blue Bull, or Nilgai, is said to resemble a horse more than a bull. In appearance it is quite similiar to the African Eland. The shoulder, which is the same height as that of a horse in full-grown males, slopes downwards to a low rump. Adult males are iron-blue, while females and calves are sandy brown. Normally silent, the Nilgai grunts loudly when alarmed. It is one of the major raiders of crops and crop yields can be drastically low in areas where it is found in large numbers. Despite the extensive damage done by this animal, it is tolerated almost everywhere in India as its name suggests "cow", an animal venerated by Hindus.

• BEHAVIOUR Defecates at regular "toilets", forming large clumps of saucer-shaped droppings. The male stalks the female during the mating season with its tail up in a characteristic "cobra-like" stance.

• SIZE Height at shoulder: 130–150 cm. Weight: 170 kg – 240 kg.

• HABITAT Dry deciduous savanna country, open scrub, and agricultural land.

• BEST SEEN AT Ranthambhor and Sariska NPs (Rajasthan).

• CONSERVATION THREATS Poaching and severe cattle grazing.

conical horns in males

TAWNY FEMALE
*Female Nilgais are sandy brown—a typical antelope colour, while males are iron-blue.*

white throat and lips

large iron-blue body

sloping shoulder

| FAMILY NAME | Bovidae |
| --- | --- |
| LATIN NAME | *Antilope cervicapra* |
| IUCN STATUS / WPA | Vulnerable / I |
| LOCAL STATUS | Common |
| POPULATION | app. 50,000, increasing |
| DIET | 🌿 🍂 🌱 🌾 |
| SOCIAL UNIT | Herds of 10–50 or more |
| ACTIVITY | ☼ |
| STRATUM | Terrestrial |

Throughout India, S of terai (except deserts, W coast, and NE).

# BLACKBUCK

LOCAL NAME: *Mrig, Harna* (Hindi), *Hulla karu* (Kannada), *Kalweet* (Marathi), *Veli maan* (Tamil), *Krishna jinka* (Telegu), *Kaliyar* (Gujarati).

AN ANTELOPE FOUND exclusively in the Indian subcontinent, the Blackbuck is glorified in many religious and mythological texts. Adult males are dark brown to velvet black with white undersides. The colour varies with the season and region – it appears darkest after the rains, while males found in southern India are dark brown. Females and young are fawn above and white below. By the end of the third year, males attain beautifully spiralled horns.

• BEHAVIOUR Dominant males remain with the herd through the year, while other males form separate herds outside of rut. During rut the male walks in a mincing gait, with his tail curled upward and horns held parallel to his back (see below). When alarmed the Blackbuck leaps up as if on a spring (a movement known as "pronking").

• SIZE Height at shoulder: 73–83 cm.
Weight: 32–42 kg.
• HABITAT Arid grassland, open scrub, and semi-desert areas.
• BEST SEEN AT Velavadar NP (Gujarat).
• CONSERVATION THREATS Poaching and habitat loss.

BUCK AND YEARLING
*An adult male and a reddish yearling drink at the same pool. The females do not have horns (see below, forefront).*

*white patch around eye*

*white muzzle*

*spiralled horns in stag (45–60 cm)*

*pied colour in stag*

| | |
|---|---|
| FAMILY NAME | **Bovidae** |
| LATIN NAME | *Tetracerus quadricornis* |
| IUCN STATUS/WPA | Vulnerable/I |
| LOCAL STATUS | Uncommon |
| POPULATION | app. 10,000 |
| DIET | ↓ ⊘ |
| SOCIAL UNIT | Solitary/groups of 2–6 |
| ACTIVITY | ☾ |
| STRATUM | Terrestrial |

# FOUR-HORNED ANTELOPE

LOCAL NAME: *Chowsingha* (Hindi/Marathi), *Koondu koori poki* (Kannada), *Naal kombu maan* (Tamil).

A SMALL, LIGHT BROWN antelope, the Chowsingha is reddish when young, turning yellower with age. It is slightly darker than the Indian Gazelle (see below), which it resembles superficially. Males have two pairs of horns, the front pair being very short. Its horns are keeled and not ringed as in most antelopes. Dark stripes run along each of its legs. The Chowsingha's call is a low whistle, or a bark similar to the Barking Deer's.

*four-keeled horns*

*chestnut coat*

- **BEHAVIOUR** It often lives near water, on which it is very dependent. Unlike other antelopes, it is found singly, in pairs, or small groups.
- **SIZE** Height at shoulder: 55–65 cm. Weight: 20 kg.
- **HABITAT** Dry deciduous forest and scrub, prefers undulating terrain.
- **BEST SEEN AT** Mudumalai NP (Tamil Nadu) and Bandipur NP (Karnataka).
- **CONSERVATION THREATS** Poaching, grazing, and habitat loss.

Throughout India S of Himalaya, till northern slopes of Nilgiri, excluding NE.

| | |
|---|---|
| FAMILY NAME | **Bovidae** |
| LATIN NAME | *Gazella bennettii* |
| IUCN STATUS/WPA | Lower risk/I |
| LOCAL STATUS | Common |
| POPULATION | app. 100,000, stable |
| DIET | ↓ ⊘ ♣ ⚬ |
| SOCIAL UNIT | Herds of 3–30 |
| ACTIVITY | ☼ |
| STRATUM | Terrestrial |

# INDIAN GAZELLE

LOCAL NAME: *Chinkara* (Hindi/Marathi), *Burra jinka* (Telegu).

AN INHABITANT OF ARID regions, the Indian Gazelle is light chestnut or biscuit-coloured, with very glossy fur to minimise heat absorption. Its horns are S-shaped in profile but appear straight from the front and are sometimes present in females. The gazelle's call resembles a sneeze. It has been traditionally protected by ethnic communities in western India.

- **BEHAVIOUR** Chinkara can survive without water for many days. It obtains water from vegetation and dew and is physiologically adapted to conserve it.
- **SIZE** Height at shoulder: 65 cm. Weight: 23 kg.
- **HABITAT** Desert and arid regions.
- **BEST SEEN AT** Desert NP (Rajasthan).
- **CONSERVATION THREATS** Poaching.

*closely ringed horns (25 cm) in males*

*furred tail*

*white underparts*

*white streaks around nose*

Throughout NW and C India, especially Rajasthan and Gujarat (up to 1,500 m).

# TIBETAN GAZELLE
LOCAL NAME: *Gowa* (Ladakhi).

| | |
|---|---|
| FAMILY NAME | **Bovidae** |
| LATIN NAME | *Procapra picticaudata* |
| IUCN STATUS/WPA | Lower risk/I |
| LOCAL STATUS | Uncommon |
| POPULATION | <100 |
| DIET | 🌱 |
| SOCIAL UNIT | Solitary/herds of 5–15 |
| ACTIVITY | ☼ |
| STRATUM | Terrestrial |

Eastern Ladakh and Sikkim (3,250 –5,500 m).

THE TIBETAN GAZELLE is a small antelope with horns that rise up straight and then take a sudden sharp curve backwards. Its fur is short and greyish fawn in summer and turns luxuriant and pale fawn in winter. This antelope associates with other mountain species such as the Kiang, Yak, Chiru, and Argali. Found in the cold desert plateau of Tibet, it comes into Ladakh and Sikkim in very small numbers and is now close to extinction in India.
• BEHAVIOUR The Tibetan Gazelle ruts during winter and is territorial during this period.
• SIZE Height at shoulder: 60 cm. Weight: 26–40 kg.
• HABITAT Alpine meadows and steppes.
• BEST SEEN AT Chang Chen Mo Valley, Ladakh (J&K).
• CONSERVATION THREATS Poaching.

backward-curving horns (10–12 cm)

white rump patch

# TIBETAN ANTELOPE
LOCAL NAME: *Chiru, Chuku, Tsus* (♂), *Chus* (♀) (Tibetan).

| | |
|---|---|
| FAMILY NAME | **Bovidae** |
| LATIN NAME | *Pantholops hodgsonii* |
| IUCN STATUS/WPA | Endangered/I |
| LOCAL STATUS | Uncommon |
| POPULATION | app. 200–500, declining |
| DIET | 🌱 |
| SOCIAL UNIT | Herds of 5–25 |
| ACTIVITY | ☼ ☾ |
| STRATUM | Terrestrial |

THE TIBETAN ANTELOPE or Chiru has a luxuriant coat to help it survive temperatures of up to -40°C. A woolly tan and grey winter coat (with a white undercoat) replaces the reddish fawn summer coat. Its soft down hair is known as *shahtoosh* or the "king of wools" and the antelope is hunted relentlessly for this. Migratory by nature, it comes into Ladakh through the Lanak La Pass from Tibet.
• BEHAVIOUR The Chiru scoops out shallow depressions with its hooves to lie in. When alarmed, it runs with its head held low.
• SIZE Height at shoulder: 74–83 cm. Weight: 26–40 kg.
• HABITAT Trans–Himalayan deserts (3,250 –5,500 m). Prefers steppe grassland.
• BEST SEEN AT Chang Chen Mo Valley, Ladakh (J&K).
• CONSERVATION THREATS Poaching and habitat loss.

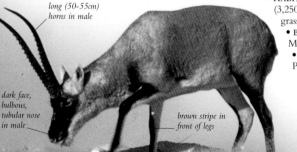

long (50-55cm) horns in male

dark face, bulbous, tubular nose in male

brown stripe in front of legs

Chang Chen Mo Valley, Ladakh.

# WILD GOAT, SHEEP, AND GOAT-ANTELOPES

**GOAT CHARACTERISTICS**
- Anal glands
- Pedal glands only on forefeet
- Body odour
- Beards
- Flat tails, naked underneath
- Knee callouses

**SHEEP CHARACTERISTICS**
- Facial and groin glands
- Pedal glands (on all legs)
- Round and hairy tails

| WILD GOAT, SHEEP, AND GOAT-ANTELOPES AT A GLANCE | |
|---|---|
| NUMBER OF SPECIES | 10 |
| LARGEST | Takin |
| SMALLEST | Goral |
| MOST COMMON | Goral |
| MOST ENDANGERED | Nilgiri Tahr/Argali |

MORE THAN 30 SPECIES of wild goat, sheep, and goat-antelopes evolved into a diverse group around four million years ago. Goat-antelopes are the more primitive of this lot with stockier bodies and shorter, sharper horns. True goats and sheep have longer horns and different behaviour patterns. However, all of them are creatures of rugged mountains or hills. Wild sheep are found in North America, throughout Asia, and in Europe, whereas wild goats are found in North America, Asia, North Africa (Sudan), and Europe (Spain and the Alps). In India, they can be found from the low rolling tropical hills of the Northeast to the high Himalaya and the Western Ghats. Some scientists list the Red Goral (*Naemorhedus bailey*) and the Wild Goat (*Capra sibrica*) as occuring within Indian territory, but this book limits itself to the 10 species that have been conclusively proven to exist in India.

HIGH ON THE HILLS
*The* **Nilgiri Tahr** *is an endangered goat that is endemic to the Western Ghats.*

# RUT

GOATS LIVE ON CRAGS and cliffs, and during breeding season, males compete by rearing up on their hind legs and battering their opponents with their horns. Male goats associate with herds and mate with the females in the herd.

Wild sheep prefer flat plateaux or plains. Unlike goats, rams wander from herd to herd looking for ewes to mate with. When challenged, rival males run at each other and spar with a loud thud of the horns. Sheep huddle in flocks and subordinates often appease dominant males by rubbing against them cheek to cheek.

Goat-antelopes have sharp horns and do not contest by ramming them. Instead they wrestle-spar with horn butting in the abdomen and flanks of their rivals.

FRIENDLY RIVALS
*Nilgiri Tahr sub-adults spar playfully with their horns.*

IMPOSING PRESENCE
**Ibex** *males are among the most spectacular goats of the Himalaya with their sweeping horns and beards.*

| | |
|---|---|
| FAMILY NAME | Bovidae |
| LATIN NAME | *Budorcas taxicolor* |
| IUCN STATUS/WPA | Vulnerable/I |
| LOCAL STATUS | Rare |
| POPULATION | Unknown |
| DIET | 🌾 🍂 |
| SOCIAL UNIT | Groups of 10–20 or more |
| ACTIVITY | ☀ |
| STRATUM | Terrestrial |

# TAKIN

LOCAL NAME: *Takin* (Adi).

THE NATIONAL ANIMAL of Bhutan, the Takin has a hairy muzzle and resembles a Gnu. Calves are fully black with juveniles turning reddish-brown in the front half. In adult males, this colouration changes to golden yellow in front and dark brown or black in the rear. Males also have a dark dorsal stripe, a black face, and a short beard on the chin. Females are greyish in colour with a black nose.

• BEHAVIOUR The Takin is attracted to hot sulphur springs where it gathers in large numbers. Its body is covered by an oily substance with a characteristic odour.

• SIZE Height at shoulder:110 –130 cm. Weight: 200– 300 kg.

• HABITAT Dense bamboo and rhododendron thickets, especially on steep slopes.

• BEST SEEN AT Jorging Valley, Siang (Arunachal Pradesh).

• CONSERVATION THREATS Poaching.

Musk Ox-like horns

dark face

sloping back

dorsal stripe in males

Mishmi hills, Arunachal Pradesh (2,100–3,000m).

| | |
|---|---|
| FAMILY NAME | Bovidae |
| LATIN NAME | *Naemorhedus sumatraensis* |
| IUCN STATUS/WPA | Vulnerable/I |
| LOCAL STATUS | Rare |
| POPULATION | Unknown |
| DIET | 🌾 🍂 |
| SOCIAL UNIT | Solitary/ groups of 2–5 |
| ACTIVITY | ☾ |
| STRATUM | Terrestrial |

# MAINLAND SEROW

LOCAL NAME: *Deo sagoli* (Assamese), *Jongli chagol* (Bengali), *Sarao* (Hindi), *Halj* (Kashmiri), *Gya* (Bhotia), *Tellu* (Naga), *Saza* (Mizo).

A GOAT-LIKE BODY with long donkey-like ears, and a habit of standing with forelegs astraddle, make the Serow an ungainly goat-antelope. Its coarse coat varies from red to black with some white on the chest and lower parts. The conical, wrinkled horns are thicker in the male. There are two sub-species of Serow in India: the Himalayan race (*N. s. thar*) is greyish-black, while the Burmese (*N. s. rubidus*) is chestnut-brown. The difference between them is most evident in Assam where north of the Brahmaputra the Serow is grey and south of the river it is brown. These animals are agile on rocky terrain.

• BEHAVIOUR When alarmed, the Serow bounds away with a hissing snort or a whistling scream.

• SIZE Height at shoulder:90 –110 cm. Weight: 60 –140 kg.

• HABITAT Thickly forested gorges, valleys, and sub-alpine scrub.

• BEST SEEN AT Kalatop WLS (Himachal Pradesh) and Kedarnath WLS (Uttaranchal).

• CONSERVATION THREATS Poaching and habitat disturbance.

grey-black stiff mane

short beard

Himalaya, from J&K to Arunachal Pradesh, Manipur, Mizoram, Nagaland, and Meghalaya (1,000 – 2,000 m, and up to 3,000 m in the NE).

| FAMILY NAME | Bovidae |
|---|---|
| LATIN NAME | *Naemorhedus goral* |
| IUCN STATUS/WPA | Lower risk/III |
| LOCAL STATUS | Locally common |
| POPULATION | Unknown |
| DIET | 🌿 🍂 🍒 |
| SOCIAL UNIT | Groups of 5-10, solitary ♂ |
| ACTIVITY | ☾ ☼ |
| STRATUM | Terrestrial |

W Himalaya to Arunachal Pradesh, Nagaland, Manipur, and Mizoram.

# GORAL

LOCAL NAME: *Goral* (Hindi), *Pij, Pijur, Rai* (Kashmiri), *Ra giyu* (Bhotia), *Deo sagoli* (Assamese), *Ram chagol* (Bengali), *Sathar* (Mizo).

This goat-antelope differs from true goats in four distinct ways: it has small facial glands (like antelopes), both sexes are approximately the same size (as with the Serow), the male does not have a beard, and the female has four mammae. In India there are two distinct sub-species of Goral – the Grey Goral and the Brown Goral. The former inhabits the western Himalaya and the latter is found east of Nepal and in Northeast India. While both have banded fur, giving them a salt-and-pepper look, the Grey Goral has a black spinal band till its withers, while the Brown Goral has the band till its tail. The horns of the male are thicker and more divergent than in females.

• BEHAVIOUR The Goral seems to prefer steep slopes. If alarmed it stands its ground, sneezing and hissing, and then bounds away in a zig-zag course into scrub cover.
• SIZE Height at shoulder: 65–70 cm. Weight: 25–35 kg.
• HABITAT Steep slopes with low tree cover, moderate shrubs and open grassy banks interspersed with cliffs.
• BEST SEEN AT Rajaji NP (Uttaranchal) and Majhatal WLS (Himachal Pradesh).
• CONSERVATION THREATS Poaching.

small ringed horns (10–15 cm)

bell-shaped ears, fringed white

white lips

greyish-brown fur

white throat patch

| FAMILY NAME | Bovidae |
|---|---|
| LATIN NAME | *Hemitragus jemlahicus* |
| IUCN STATUS/WPA | Vulnerable/I |
| LOCAL STATUS | Uncommon |
| POPULATION | Unknown, declining |
| DIET | 🌿 🍃 |
| SOCIAL UNIT | Herds of 10–15 |
| ACTIVITY | ☼ |
| STRATUM | Terrestrial |

# HIMALAYAN TAHR

LOCAL NAME: *Kras, Jegla* (Kashmiri), *Jharal* (Nepalese), *Tehr, Jehr* (W Himalayas).

THE HIMALAYAN TAHR is a deep copper-brown mountain goat that lives in extremely inaccessible terrain. Ewes and younger males are light brown while adult males are darker. The male Tahr has a coarse, tangled mane (straw coloured in summer) over its neck, chest, and shoulders. The rump, abdomen, and back of lower legs are rusty. Its long, robust limbs end in soft hoof pads with horny rims.

• BEHAVIOUR Adult males live alone during late summer and rejoin herds in autumn.
• SIZE Height at shoulder: 80 – 100 cm. Weight: 60 – 100 kg.
• HABITAT Forested precipitous terrain, prefers oak and bamboo forests.
• BEST SEEN AT Kedarnath WLS (Uttaranchal).
• CONSERVATION THREATS Poaching and habitat loss.

*short, heavily keeled horns*

*black face*

*long mane in males*

*copper-red body*

Himalaya, from J&K to Sikkim (2,500–4,400 m).

| FAMILY NAME | Bovidae |
|---|---|
| LATIN NAME | *Hemitragus hylocrius* |
| IUCN STATUS/WPA | Endangered/I |
| LOCAL STATUS | Locally common |
| POPULATION | app. 2,500, gen. decline |
| DIET | 🌿 🍃 |
| SOCIAL UNIT | Herds of 10–15, occ. up to 100 |
| ACTIVITY | ☼ |
| STRATUM | Terrestrial |

# NILGIRI TAHR

LOCAL NAME: *Vara aadu* (Malayalam), *Varai aadu* (Tamil).

A HANDSOME GOAT, the male Nilgiri Tahr looks like a shorn version of its close cousin, the male Himalayan Tahr, without the flowing mane and hair of its northern relative. The short, greyish-brown coat of the females and young bucks is dark brown tending to blue-black in adult males, with a whitish saddle-shaped patch across the shoulders and back. The throat and abdomen are white. The horns of both male and female are parallel and curve backwards.

• BEHAVIOUR While the herd rests in the hot afternoon hours, a very conspicuous sentinel stands guard.
• SIZE Height at shoulder: 100–110 cm.
• HABITAT Montane grassland and rocky crags, interspersed with shola forests.
• BEST SEEN AT Eravikulam NP (Kerala).
• CONSERVATION THREATS Poaching and habitat disturbance.

*close-set, wrinkled horns*

*short, coarse coat*

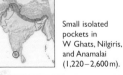

Small isolated pockets in W Ghats, Nilgiris, and Anamalai (1,220–2,600 m).

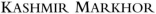

| | |
|---|---|
| FAMILY NAME | **Bovidae** |
| LATIN NAME | *Capra falconeri* |
| IUCN STATUS/WPA | Endangered/I |
| LOCAL STATUS | Rare |
| POPULATION | <250, declining |
| DIET | ⌇ ✿ |
| SOCIAL UNIT | Herds of 5–10 |
| ACTIVITY | ☼ ☽ |
| STRATUM | Terrestrial |

# KASHMIR MARKHOR

LOCAL NAME: *Markhor* (Punjabi/Kashmiri), *Rapoche* (♂), *Rawache* (♀) (Ladakhi).

THE LARGEST MOUNTAIN GOAT in the world, the Markhor has long fur like the Himalayan Tahr, a flowing beard, and corkscrew horns. Males vary from iron-grey to off-white in winter with hints of red-brown in summer. Females are fawn and much smaller. Both sexes have dark brown muzzles, brown upper legs, and a brown flank stripe. The belly and upper legs are creamy white. The name "Markhor" is probably a corruption of the Persian "mar-akhur" or "snake-horned", referring to the shape of the horns. However, it is often mistakenly believed to mean "snake-eater".

- BEHAVIOUR Can climb trees like goats do.
- SIZE Height at shoulder: 80–100 cm. Weight: 90–100 kg.
- HABITAT Dense pine and birch forests, or open barren slopes (adapts to both with equal ease).
- BEST SEEN AT Kishtwar WLS (J&K).
- CONSERVATION THREATS Poaching, insurgency, and disease.

*corkscrew horns*

*long beard*

*white legs*

*small horns of female*

J&K.

| | |
|---|---|
| FAMILY NAME | **Bovidae** |
| LATIN NAME | *Capra ibex* |
| IUCN STATUS/WPA | Vulnerable/I |
| LOCAL STATUS | Uncommon |
| POPULATION | app. 15–20,000 |
| DIET | ⌇ ✿ |
| SOCIAL UNIT | Herds of 12–50 |
| ACTIVITY | ☼ |
| STRATUM | Terrestrial |

# ASIATIC IBEX

LOCAL NAME: *Sakin* (♂), *Dabmo* (♀) (Ladakhi), *Kail* (Kashmiri).

THE IBEX IS CLOSEST in appearance to the Wild Goat (*Capra hircus*), which is found in Pakistan. The dense coat of the male is brownish in summer. From autumn to spring males are dark brown or black with dull white saddle patch. There is a dorsal stripe from neck to tail in both sexes. The male Ibex has distinctive thick, scimitar-shaped horns; this shape is used to identify various sub-species. Females have thin parallel horns.

- BEHAVIOUR The Ibex does not always migrate to lower heights in winter and prefers steep slopes where snow does not gather. Sentries are usually female; the alarm call is a shrill exhalation of breath.
- SIZE Height at shoulder: 80–100 cm. Weight: 90 kg.
- HABITAT Steep crags above the tree line.
- BEST SEEN AT Pin Valley NP (Himachal Pradesh), Kanji WLS (J&K).
- CONSERVATION THREATS Poaching, cattle grazing, and habitat loss.

*scimitar horns*

*white rump patch*

*pointed beard in male*

West of Sutlej gorge in Himachal Pradesh and Western Ladakh (3,650 – 6,700 m) .

# LADAKH URIAL

**LOCAL NAME:** *Shapu* (♂), *Shamo* (♀) (Ladakhi), *Urial* (Punjabi).

| | |
|---|---|
| FAMILY NAME | **Bovidae** |
| LATIN NAME | *Ovis vignei* |
| IUCN STATUS/WPA | Vulnerable/I |
| LOCAL STATUS | Uncommon |
| POPULATION | app. 1,500+ |
| DIET | ↓ ∅ |
| SOCIAL UNIT | Herds of 10-30, 2-3 ♂ |
| ACTIVITY | ☼ |
| STRATUM | Terrestrial |

ALSO KNOWN AS THE Red Sheep, the Urial resembles the Argali (see below), but is smaller with shorter horns. The Urial has three sub-species: Afghan, Punjab, and Ladakh Urial. Adult males are copper-red with a black-and-white saddle patch and a long black throat ruff that is lost in the spring. The face bib, undersides and lower legs are white. Ewes do not have the saddle patch or bib and are lighter while the young are grayer and smaller. Ewes have short horns and the lateral stripe is restricted to a black spot under forelegs. The Ladakh Urial's horn tips point forward, while those of the Punjab Urial point down towards the neck.

copper-red coat / arched horns / black ruff in male / whitish legs

- **BEHAVIOUR** Rams in rut visit several herds, unlike wild goats that keep to a single herd.
- **SIZE** Height at shoulder: 70–90 cm. Weight: 35–90 kg.
- **HABITAT** Alpine grassland above the tree line; usually avoids steep slopes.
- **BEST SEEN AT** Nimdum WLS and Rong Nallah, Ladakh (J&K).
- **CONSERVATION THREATS** Poaching and cattle grazing.

Ladakh (Indus Valley), Karakoram, and Gilgit and Skardu (POK) (2,750–4,000 m).

# ARGALI

**LOCAL NAME:** *Nayan* (♂), *Nayanmo* (♀) (Ladakhi), *Kuchan* (♂), *Mesh* (♀) (Wakhan).

| | |
|---|---|
| FAMILY NAME | **Bovidae** |
| LATIN NAME | *Ovis ammon* |
| IUCN STATUS/WPA | Vulnerable/I |
| LOCAL STATUS | Rare |
| POPULATION | app. 250, declining |
| DIET | ↓ ∅ |
| SOCIAL UNIT | Herds of 12-100, 2-5 ♂ |
| ACTIVITY | ☼ |
| STRATUM | Terrestrial |

THE ARGALI IS India's largest wild sheep and has eight sub-species, of which two could occur in India: the Great Tibetan Sheep or Nayan, and the Marco Polo Sheep or Kuchan. Both are red-brown or greyish in colour. In winter the Kuchan turns creamy white, while Nayan males develop creamy ruffs on their necks. Argali young are dark grey. Females are much bigger than all other sheep and have characteristic horns.

- **BEHAVIOUR** In spring males wander in bachelor herds close to the snow-line. In autumn they move lower down to join the herds of female and young. It is common for females to give birth to twins.

large, wrinkled horns / long antelope-like legs / grey coat / white chest

- **SIZE** Height at shoulder: 110–120 cm. Weight: 100–140 kg.
- **HABITAT** Desolate habitat – sand hills and plains (Nayan); boulder-strewn nullahs further north (Kuchan).
- **BEST SEEN AT** Khymer Valley and Tsokar basin, Ladakh (J&K).
- **CONSERVATION THREATS** Poaching and cattle grazing.

Nayan: Tibet (core range) to Ladakh and Sikkim. Kuchan: Hunza (Pakistan) to Tagdumbash Pass, Ladakh.

# BLUE SHEEP

**LOCAL NAME:** *Bharal, Bharar, Bharut* (Hindi), *Na, Sna* (Ladakhi), *Nao* (Bhutia), *Nervati* (Nepali).

| | |
|---|---|
| FAMILY NAME | Bovidae |
| LATIN NAME | *Pseudois nayaur* |
| IUCN STATUS/WPA | Lower risk/I |
| LOCAL STATUS | Locally common |
| POPULATION | app. 10,000, stable |
| DIET | ☘ 🌿 🌱 |
| SOCIAL UNIT | Herds of 10–50 or more, –5 ♂ |
| ACTIVITY | ☼ |
| STRATUM | Terrestrial |

Ladakh, through higher altitudes of Kumaon, to Arunachal Pradesh (3,500–5,500 m).

THE BLUE SHEEP or Bharal lives in slate-blue shale country and has a coat to match. In winter this colouration becomes more pronounced (see inset), while in summer the coat becomes red-brown (see below) for better camouflage. Adult rams are dark brown to black on the chest and front of the legs. This species displays both goat- and sheep-like characteristics. The ram lacks a beard and has feet glands, like others in the sheep family. However, it also shares goat-like traits such as smooth horns and the absence of facial glands. The Bharal has a squirrel-like "chirrt" alarm call. Males are usually solitary or found in small groups of 4–5, while females and young are found in herds of 10–50, even going up to 200. The Bharal lives in areas with crags and cliffs but uses them largely as retreats from danger. When foraging they are found in alpine meadows and along with Argalis are the only representatives of the family that prefer open ground.

• **BEHAVIOUR** During rut, males rear up and strike each other like goats. However, they court females by raising their forelegs and stretching out their head in sheep-like fashion. They may mouth their own red penis as a threat display (like goats), but they may rub their face on the rival's backside in appeasement (like sheep).

• **SIZE** Height at shoulder: 80 – 90 cm. Weight: 40–70 kg.

• **HABITAT** Mountainous regions above the tree line, open grassy or boulder-strewn ground and high cliffs.

• **BEST SEEN AT** Nanda Devi NP (Uttaranchal).

• **CONSERVATION THREATS** Poaching and cattle grazing.

CROWNING GLORY
*The Blue Sheep has smooth, rounded olive-black horns (60 cm).*

white rump patch

white legs and belly

thin divergent horns in female

# WILD CATTLE

| WILD CATTLE AT A GLANCE | |
|---|---|
| NUMBER OF SPECIES | 3 (4) |
| TALLEST | Gaur |
| HEAVIEST | Wild Buffalo |
| MOST COMMON | Gaur |
| MOST ENDANGERED | Wild Yak |

## CATTLE CHARACTERISTICS
- Well-developed sense of smell
- Massive size • Low, wide skull
- Pad in upper jaw instead of incisors or canines
- Fused incisors and canines in lower jaw
- Four-chambered, complex stomach
- Big horns that are not shed, in both sexes

CATTLE ARE AMONG the mammals most familiar to man, because of the large number of domestic varieties in existence. Their wild progenitors, however, are relatively unknown. Some of these are the largest herbivores found in the wild. In India, the Gaur, Yak, and Wild Buffalo are wild species that have related domestic varieties. Wild cattle normally achieve maturity at two years and females can bear a calf every year all through their lives, which in captivity can be for as long as 15–20 years. In the wild, however, their life span may be considerably shorter. In Wild Buffaloes and Yaks, the males and females look superficially alike and can be told apart only by the males being slightly larger and by their genitalia. The Gaur (see below), however, is sexually dichromatic.

**THE BANTENG**
*This is a handsome Southeast Asian cattle, with the bulls a dark chestnut in colour and the females ruddy brown. It is about the size of a large domestic cow and has a white muzzle, a white patch over the eyelids, and white rump and stockings. Males have a dewlap and dorsal ridge. The Banteng is mainly found in Southeast Asia. However, occasional sightings have been reported from Manipur and a few other parts of the Northeast.*

| FAMILY NAME | Bovidae |
|---|---|
| LATIN NAME | *Bubalus arnee* |
| IUCN STATUS/WPA | Endangered / I |
| LOCAL STATUS | Locally common |
| POPULATION | >1,200, declining |
| DIET | 🌾 |
| SOCIAL UNIT | Solitary/groups of up to 20 |
| ACTIVITY | ☼ ☾ |
| STRATUM | Terrestrial |

Assam and C India.

# ● ASIATIC WILD BUFFALO

LOCAL NAME: *Arna* (Hindi), *Bonoria moh* (Assamese), *Jongli monsh* (Bengali).

LARGE, BLACK, AND ROBUST, with flat sweeping horns, the Wild Buffalo is considered to be one of the most dangerous animals to encounter. It is a sleeker, heavier version of the domestic buffalo and has the largest horns on any animal in the world. There are two horn types – in one, the horns curve upwards in a semicircle and almost meet at the tips; in the other, they grow in a parallel fashion upwards and then inwards. The Wild Buffalo has dirty white stockings that are telltale markings as well. Its propensity to breed with domestic buffaloes has posed a serious problem to the population in Assam and it is believed that the highly endangered population found in Central India is of a purer strain. It is now found in small isolated pockets in Northeast India (Kaziranga, Dibru-Saikhowa, Laokhawa-Burrha Sapori, and Manas National Park), Central India (Indravati, Bhairamgarh, Udanti and Pamer sanctuaries in Bastar district of Chattisgarh), and Orissa (Koraput district).

• BEHAVIOUR The Buffalo snorts, stomps its feet, and shakes its head as it prepares to charge. It forms a tight herd around the young calves when threatened by predators.
• SIZE Height at shoulder: 155–180 cm. Weight: 800 – 1200 kg.
• HABITAT Grassland and marshes.
• BEST SEEN AT Kaziranga NP (Assam).
• CONSERVATION THREATS Habitat loss, cattle grazing, and hybridization.

DOMESTIC BUFFALO
*Different breeds of domestic buffalo closely resemble the wild one, but they do not have the magnificent sweep of horns.*

large flat horns

shiny black, hairless body

| FAMILY NAME | **Bovidae** |
|---|---|
| LATIN NAME | *Bos gaurus* |
| IUCN STATUS/WPA | Vulnerable/I |
| LOCAL STATUS | Common |
| POPULATION | app. 20,000+, declining in pockets |
| DIET | 🌿 ⌀ ⫽ |
| SOCIAL UNIT | Solitary/herds of 5–30 |
| ACTIVITY | ☀ ☾ |
| STRATUM | Terrestrial |

Western Ghats,
C and SE peninsula,
West Bengal,
and NE.

# ● GAUR

LOCAL NAME: *Gaur* (Hindi), *Gawa* (Marathi), *Kadu kona* (♂), *Kadu emmai* (♀) (Kannada), *Kattu pothu, Kattee* (Malayalam), *Methun* (Assamese), *Kattu madu* (Tamil).

THE LARGEST BOVINE in the world, the Gaur is often mistakenly called the Indian bison although it is not related to the North American Bison. It has a massive head, deep chest, and muscular shoulder ridge. Adult males are glossy black, while the young and females are coffee-brown. The newborn calf changes colour from golden yellow to fawn, light brown, and then red-brown.

• **BEHAVIOUR** Very shy and calm for a creature of its size, the Gaur rarely attacks unless tormented, and in most parts of South India will allow humans to approach very close. It has an acute sense of smell. If a herd is taken by surprise, it might start a stampede with calves getting run over in the process.

• **SIZE** Height at shoulder: 165–195 cm. Weight: 800–1200 kg.

• **HABITAT** Mixed deciduous, scrub and evergreen hill forests, and grassland.

• **BEST SEEN AT** Mudumalai NP (Tamil Nadu) and Bandipur NP (Karnataka).

• **CONSERVATION THREATS** Poaching, habitat loss, cattle grazing, and disease.

## MITHUN

*Believed to be a hybrid of Gaur and domestic cattle, the* **Mithun** *(Bos frontalis) is the state animal of Arunachal Pradesh. It is characterized by pinkish patches on its dark body. The number of Mithun a man owns signifies his wealth.*

ashy forehead — pointed horns

dorsal ridge

black hairless body

two dewlaps

white stockings

| AMILY NAME | Bovidae |
|---|---|
| ATIN NAME | *Bos grunniens* |
| JCN STATUS/WPA | Vulnerable/I |
| OCAL STATUS | Uncommon |
| OPULATION | >100, declining |
| )IET | 🌾 |
| OCIAL UNIT | Groups of 10–20 |
| CTIVITY | ☼ |
| TRATUM | Terrestrial |

# YAK

LOCAL NAME: *Brong dong* (Tibetan), *Ban chour* (Hindi).

THICKSET, SHAGGY CATTLE of the mountains, Yaks have been domesticated across most of their range. In comparison to its domestic cousins, the Wild Yak has shaggy blackish-brown fur and has larger horns (76 cm over the curves), that are more sweeping (the tips are apart by nearly 90 cm).
• BEHAVIOUR Although a type of cattle, the Wild Yak is behaviourally akin to the Wild Bison of America. During rut, the male Yak behaves differently from its close relatives, the Gaur and Banteng. It often wallows in mud during the rut – a bison or buffalo characteristic. It also grunts hoarsely and grinds its teeth – a habit unique to the Yak.
• SIZE Height at shoulder: 160–180 cm. Weight: 500–550 kg.
• HABITAT Mountain pastures in cold deserts.
• BEST SEEN AT Chang Chen Mo Valley, Ladakh (J&K).
• CONSERVATION THREATS Hybridization.

Ladakh, Sikkim, and
Arunachal Pradesh
(4,000–6,000 m).

DOMESTIC YAK
*Pure-bred domestic Yaks are as large as their wild cousins. Male Yaks are also interbred with domestic cows to produce the Zo (see above), used as a beast of burden at lower heights.*

humped shoulder

handlebar horns

long, shaggy knotted hair

grey muzzle

# WILD PIGS

T HE WILD PIG and the Pygmy Hog are found in India along with several breeds of domestic pigs that evolved from the wild ones around 9,000 years ago. Pigs are social animals that live in groups called sounders, comprising the female or sow and the piglets. While most hoofed mammals give birth to one or two offspring, pigs bear a litter of up to a dozen. Adult boars join the sounders only during the breeding season when they fight for sows by slashing laterally at the flanks and shoulders of rivals. This fighting style is peculiar to some species as other pigs head-butt or snout-nudge their way to dominance. Once it gains access to a sounder, the boar may froth at the mouth or produce lip pheromones to attract the sow to mate. The female gestates for 100 days in the case of the Pygmy Hog and 115 days in case of the Wild Pig. The pig's fondness for mud wallows, that protect it against parasites, and its omnivorous diet that includes scavenging garbage, have earned it the reputation of being filthy and gluttonous. Pigs rely on their sense of smell although other senses are also well developed.

## WILD PIG CHARACTERISTICS
- Even-toed ungulates with well-developed outer toe
- Non-ruminant
- Capped molars
- Barrel-shaped body with small neck, large head, and spindly legs
- Snout ends in a cartilaginous disc that helps in rooting for tubers

## SIGNS OF PIGS AT WORK

Wild pigs leave behind obvious signs that make them easy to detect.
- They leave behind tracks of very clear, cloven hoof-marks.
- They scrape and dig up the forest floor in a very characteristic manner. Shallow scrapes indicate a resting place, while deeper ones indicate signs of feeding.
- They lay down piles of grass and shrubby vegetation and burrow beneath them to make rough nests.

WILD PIGS

# ● WILD PIG

**LOCAL NAME:** *Jungli suar* (Hindi/Bengali), *Ran dukkar* (Marathi), *Kadu handi* (Kannada), *Kattu panni* (Malayalam/Tamil), *Vawk* (Mizo).

| | |
|---|---|
| FAMILY NAME | Suidae |
| LATIN NAME | *Sus scrofa* |
| IUCN STATUS/WPA | Lower risk/III |
| LOCAL STATUS | Common |
| POPULATION | Unknown |
| DIET | 🍃 ⚘ ✳ 🐛 C |
| SOCIAL UNIT | Sounders of 5–30 |
| ACTIVITY | ☼ ☾ |
| STRATUM | Terrestrial |

A LARGE FOREST PIG, this ancestor of the common pig is dark greyish-brown with a black mane. This is the same species of boar that is found in Europe except that its coat is thinner. The coat is lightest in the northwest and more deeply coloured in the south and east. Southern Indian boars are also slightly larger in size. Wild boars litter through the year and the piglets are light brown with pale stripes. This camouflage colouration lasts for 6–7 months, when they become independent of their mothers.
• BEHAVIOUR Extremely pugnacious, an angry wild boar can cause more damage than larger beasts, as it rarely abandons a charge. The dorsal crest is erected during fierce fights.
• SIZE Total body length: 90–180 cm. Weight: 90–100 kg.
• HABITAT Scrub, grassland, mixed deciduous and evergreen forests.
• BEST SEEN AT Almost all Indian sanctuaries.
• CONSERVATION THREATS Poaching.

black mane from nape to loin

long snout

curved tushes

visibly naked tail

thin legs

Throughout India, except J&K, high Himalaya, and deserts.

# PYGMY HOG

**LOCAL NAME:** *Nal gahori* (Assamese).

| | |
|---|---|
| FAMILY NAME | Suidae |
| LATIN NAME | *Sus salvanius* |
| IUCN STATUS/WPA | Crit. endangered/I |
| LOCAL STATUS | Rare |
| POPULATION | 250–500 |
| DIET | 🍃 ⚘ ✳ 🐛 C |
| SOCIAL UNIT | Sounders of 5–10 |
| ACTIVITY | ☾ |
| STRATUM | Terrestrial |

RESTRICTED TO THE "DUARS" of the Northeast and Nepal, the Pygmy Hog was feared to be extinct until it was re-discovered in 1971. Rounded in shape, it has a very short tail. Adults are grey-brown to black in colour. The male has small tusks that can inflict gashes as deep as those of the Wild Pig. The young, born in the dry months of April and May, are lighter with reddish stripes.
• BEHAVIOUR Pygmy Hogs are known to groom each other often and make soft grunting sounds as they forage, both of which help them form and keep sounders together. They are unique in building nests for sleeping at night.
• SIZE Total body length: 50–70 cm. Height at shoulder: 25 cm. Weight: 6–9 kg.
• HABITAT Wet, tall terai grassland and riverine forest.
• BEST SEEN AT Barnadi WLS and Manas NP (Assam).
• CONSERVATION THREATS Habitat loss and poaching.

no visible tail

miniature size

no mane

Duars of lower Assam near the Bhutan border.

65

# ELEPHANT

THE ELEPHANT IS ONE of the largest, best-known and most charismatic animals on earth. Although several species flourished in different parts of the world in the 50 million years of its evolution, currently the elephant persists only in Africa and Asia. Asian elephants range across 13 countries in South and Southeast Asia and number a tenth of the African elephant population. Recently, taxonomists separated the African elephant into two species: the Savanna Elephant (*Loxodonta africana*) and the Forest Elephant (*Loxodonta cyclotis*).

**ELEPHANT CHARACTERISTICS**
- Large size • Naked, wrinkled grey skin
  - Enlarged incisors to form tusks
  - Elongated snout to form a trunk
- Extra-large ears to aid cooling of body
  - Columnar legs with four or five toes
  - Medium-sized tail with stiff bristles forming a tuft at the end

AFRICAN ELEPHANT
*The female African elephant, unlike the Asian elephant, bears tusks.*

Elephants are social animals that live in closely-knit family groups led by a matriarch. These form larger herds that can have young males, while adult males are solitary and associate with herds only for mating. Occasionally, all-male groups are also seen.

African elephants of both sexes and most male Asian elephants have tusks—a pair of enlarged incisors growing outward and upward – that are used to establish hierarchy, as feeding aids, and for defense. These are prized for ivory, which is used to make curios and seals and are the primary reason for poaching which is driving many populations to extinction. Elephants use a range of vocalizations to communicate, from tummy rumbles to low growls, infrasonic calls, and loud trumpetings. They have a long life span averaging 60 years.

| | |
|---|---|
| FAMILY NAME | Elephantidae |
| LATIN NAME | *Elephas maximus* |
| IUCN STATUS/WPA | Endangered/I |
| LOCAL STATUS | Common |
| POPULATION | app. 25,000–27,000 |
| DIET | 🌿 🍃 🐾 🌾 |
| SOCIAL UNIT | Family/solitary ♂ |
| ACTIVITY | ☀ |
| STRATUM | Terrestrial |

NE India, West Bengal, N Indian terai, Orissa, Jharkhand, and S India.

# ● ASIAN ELEPHANT

LOCAL NAME: *Hathi* (Hindi/Bengali/Assamese), *Yanai* (Tamil), *Aana* (Malayalam), *Aane* (Kannada), *Yenugu* (Telegu).

THE LARGEST LAND MAMMAL in India, the Asian Elephant's grey wrinkled skin, long trunk and sail-like ears make it one of the most easily recognized animals. It is revered by Hindus due to its association with the god Ganesha. The Asian Elephant is slightly smaller than the African Savanna Elephant and differs from it anatomically in many ways. The Asian Elephant has a rounded or humped back as opposed to the saddle-shaped one of the African elephant. Its trunk ends in one tip or "finger" as opposed to two, it has a two-domed forehead, and its ears are smaller in size. Only male Asian Elephants have large tusks, while females have very small dental protuberances called "tushes". Some males, called "makhnas", are tuskless and can be distinguished from adult females by the penis bulge below the tail.

• BEHAVIOUR Elephants migrate over long distances in search of food and water, or for security, and use the same forest corridors for many hundreds of years. If these corridors are blocked, they enter human settlements. Elephants are also attracted to human settlements by crop or by domestic alcohol distilleries that they can smell from miles away. The resulting human-elephant conflict is a major threat to the survival of the species.

• SIZE Height at shoulder: 245–275 cm. Weight: 3,000 kg.

• HABITAT Mixed deciduous and evergreen forests, scrub, and grassland.

• BEST SEEN AT Nagarahole NP (Karnataka) and Corbett NP (Uttaranchal).

• CONSERVATION THREATS Poaching, habitat loss, and human-animal conflict.

two-domed forehead

humped back

large circular ears with front fold

tusks in male

columnar legs

# WILD EQUIDS

HOOFED ANIMALS WITH an odd number of toes are known as Perissodactyls. They include horses, zebras, asses, rhinos, and tapirs, most of which are endangered in the wild. Only 18 species of Perissodactyls are in existence globally. Of these, eight species, known as equids, are specialized grazers, including horses, zebras, and asses. All equids are social animals that live in large herds, and gallop over open stretches with a grace and power that is unique to the family. The habit of putting their entire weight on the central toe gives them a springy gait and therefore speed in flight. Specialized molars allow them to eat a broad range of high fibre diet in large quantities – critical for survival in an arid countryside. Equids originated in North America 55 million years ago and colonized Europe and Asia around 1.8 million years ago. Today, however, they are not found in their continent of origin.

India has two species of wild equids: the Khur of the hot deserts of Gujarat and the Kiang (below) of the plateaux of Ladakh. These are closely related to the domestic horse *(Equus caballus)* and the domestic donkey *(E. asinus)*, though they are all marginally different from one another. Wild asses are larger than the domestic donkey but smaller than horses. Their ears are longer than those of donkeys, but shorter than those of horses. Both wild and domestic asses have an erect mane of short hair and a paintbrush tip to the tail, while horses have a flowing silky mane and tail. Horses have a horny pad on each hind leg known as a "chestnut" that asses do not have. Wild asses are plain coloured while domestic asses have horizontal stripes on the shoulder and sometimes on the legs.

## WILD EQUID CHARACTERISTICS
- Odd-toed ungulate, with a single toe enclosed in a hoof
- Non-ruminant
- Long incisors for clipping and large cheek teeth for grinding grass
- Long head and neck with a long mane
- Slender limbs

**Feral horses**
*The Przewalski's Horse of Mongolia is the only true wild horse in the world. However, feral horses do exist in Assam (Dibru-Saikhowa) and Tamil Nadu (Point Calimere). These horses are descendants of domestic breeds that escaped into the forest many years ago. They are wild in behaviour and habit although they contain very few wild genes (right).*

## ASIATIC WILD ASS

LOCAL NAME: *Khur* (Hindi), *Ghudkhar* (Gujarati).

THE KHUR or the Asiatic Wild Ass is a large fawn or pale chestnut donkey with a dark chocolate fringe of hair on its neck. This fringe thins down to a stripe on the spine, and extends till the tail. Stallions are slightly larger and darker than mares, though the difference is not easily distinguishable. The group stays together except in the foaling season when the mares and the foals stay separate from the stallions.

• BEHAVIOUR A swift animal, this wild ass gallops at an average speed of 30–35 km per hour, touching 50 km at top speed. Its sense of smell is extremely well developed. It is known to raid wheat, millet, and cotton fields at night.

• SIZE Height at shoulder: 110–120 cm. Weight: 250–290 kg.

• HABITAT Open salt mudflats.

• BEST SEEN AT Dhrangadhara WLS (Gujarat).

• CONSERVATION THREATS Habitat disturbance and competition from livestock.

| FAMILY NAME | Equidae |
|---|---|
| LATIN NAME | *Equus onager* |
| IUCN STATUS/WPA | Vulnerable/I |
| LOCAL STATUS | Locally common |
| POPULATION | app. 3,000 |
| DIET | ✹ 🐾 |
| SOCIAL UNIT | Small groups, occasionally > 100 |
| ACTIVITY | ☼ ☾ (feeding) |
| STRATUM | Terrestrial |

pale chestnut coat

dark stripe from mane to tail

white underparts

Rann of Kutch, Gujarat.

## TIBETAN WILD ASS

LOCAL NAME: *Kiang/Kyang* (Ladakhi).

THE KIANG IS AN animal of the trans-Himalayan cold deserts. It is bigger and more ruddy than the Khur (see above). The Kiang congregates in groups wherever grass and sedge are abundant.

• BEHAVIOUR This adaptable grazer co-exists with Gazelles, Yaks, and Tibetan Antelopes. The vast open areas that it lives in encourage the Kiang to share the same space with other animals. Its tolerance to predators such as wolves has been documented, but it flees rapidly when predators such as the Snow Leopard come into view.

• SIZE Height at shoulder: 135–140 cm. Weight 250–300 kg.

• HABITAT High open plateau, hill, and valley.

• BEST SEEN AT Changthang WLS, Ladakh (J&K).

• CONSERVATION THREATS Competition from livestock and disease.

| FAMILY NAME | Equidae |
|---|---|
| LATIN NAME | *Equus kiang* |
| IUCN STATUS/WPA | Vulnerable/I |
| LOCAL STATUS | Locally common |
| POPULATION | 3,000–4,000 |
| DIET | ✹ |
| SOCIAL UNIT | Small groups, occasionally 100 |
| ACTIVITY | ☼ |
| STRATUM | Terrestrial |

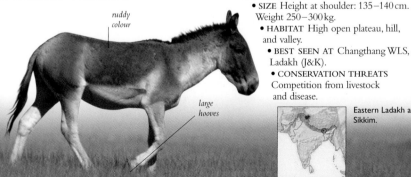

ruddy colour

large hooves

Eastern Ladakh and Sikkim.

# RHINOCEROS

- Heavy thickset body weighing over 1,000 kg
- Thick, almost hairless skin with folds
- One or two horns on tip of nose
- Short stumpy legs with three toes
- Tiny eyes and tubular ears

THERE ARE FIVE SPECIES of rhinoceros in the world, of which two are African and three Asian. The latter are so endangered that the numbers of all three of them put together do not match the population of any one species found in Africa. Rhinoceroses are mega-herbivores with one or two sharp conical horns at the tip of the nose. The Indian and the Javan Rhinoceros have only one horn, while both the African species and the Sumatran have two horns. The rhinoceros family evolved nearly 50 million years ago and they are truly pre-historic creatures that have survived in an increasingly hostile world. India had all three Asian rhinoceroses till the 19th century but today it is a refuge for only the Greater One-horned Rhinoceros, the largest of the Asian rhinoceroses.

The other two Asian rhinoceroses are today restricted to Java and Vietnam (Javan Rhinoceros), Malaysia, Sumatra, and Myanmar (Sumatran Rhinoceros). The Javan Rhinoceros is a miniature version of the Indian rhinoceros and is also called the Lesser One-horned Rhinoceros. The Sumatran Rhinoceros is sometimes called the Woolly or Two-horned Rhinoceros due to the fuzzy hair on its body and its two horns.

RHINO HORN
*The rhinoceros's horn grows throughout its life and can be regrown if broken. It is the sole reason for poaching of this animal, since it is believed to have medicinal properties.*

large grey body

single horn (20 cm)

| | |
|---|---|
| FAMILY NAME | Rhinocerotidae |
| LATIN NAME | *Rhinoceros unicornis* |
| IUCN STATUS / WPA | Endangered / I |
| LOCAL STATUS | Locally common |
| POPULATION | app. 1,750 |
| DIET | ↯ |
| SOCIAL UNIT | Solitary/pairs/groups |
| ACTIVITY | ☼ ☾ |
| STRATUM | Terrestrial |

SUMATRAN RHINOCEROS
*There are unconfirmed reports of the Sumatran Rhinoceros straying into India from Myanmar.*

# ● GREATER ONE-HORNED RHINOCEROS

LOCAL NAME: *Gainda* (Hindi), *Gaur* (Assamese), *Gondar* (Bengali).

This animal is a relic of five million years of evolution. The large folds of skin across its flanks and tubercles, that look like rivets on the skin, give it an armour-plated look. The actual colour of its skin is a deep slate-grey, but it looks ashy when encrusted with alluvial mud, or ink-black when wet. Males are larger and have thicker neck folds as compared to females. The male genitalia are also easily visible.

● BEHAVIOUR A creature of habit, the rhinoceros regularly follows the same walking paths or "dandis" when foraging. It also uses the same spot to defecate, forming large "toilets". This behaviour makes it vulnerable to poachers who wait for it at pre-determined locations. The rhinoceros is best seen from a safe distance. If an intruder unwittingly separates mother and calf in the tall grass, the female charges without fail. Although many charges are bluffs, some may be actually carried out, harming the intruder seriously. Indian rhinoceroses do not use their horn to gore victims, but use their sharp teeth to bite off chunks of flesh instead. The teeth are also used while fighting among themselves.

● SIZE Height at shoulder: 170–185 cm. Weight: 1,500–2,100 kg.
● HABITAT Alluvial grassland.
● BEST SEEN AT Kaziranga NP (Assam).
● CONSERVATION THREATS Poaching and habitat loss.

N West Bengal (Jaldapara and Gorumara), and Assam (Kaziranga, Manas, Orang, Laokhawa and Pabitora).

*armour plating on flanks*

# PANDA

The Red Panda is a taxonomic conundrum. It was once classified with a group of primitive carnivores called procyonids. The Red Panda, however, shows close similarities to bears and also to the unrelated Giant Panda of China. Many taxonomists place it in a separate family while others place it in the sub-family Ailurinae of family Ursidae.

The Red Panda is mainly vegetarian although it may occasionally eat small prey. It bears one or two young after a gestation period of 112–158 days. The Red Panda is confined to South and East Asia.

| | |
|---|---|
| FAMILY NAME | Ursidae |
| LATIN NAME | *Ailurus fulgens* |
| IUCN STATUS / WPA | Endangered / I |
| LOCAL STATUS | Rare |
| POPULATION | Unknown, declining |
| DIET | |
| SOCIAL UNIT | Pairs/groups |
| ACTIVITY | |
| STRATUM | Terrestrial |

## RED PANDA

**LOCAL NAME:** *Oakdonga* (Bhotia), *Wah, Ye, Nigalva, Ponva* (Nepalese), *Sankam* (Lepcha).

THE RED PANDA is one of the most striking creatures of the northeastern forests. The chestnut colour of its body is offset by the white snout, inner ears and cheek patches. The tip of the nose is glossy black. This panda has a wiry white moustache, chestnut "teardrop stains" on its white cheek mask and large liquid brown eyes that lend it a peculiar appeal. Its tail is ringed with light and dark chestnut bands. The young are buff in colour. Red Pandas are unique among sub-tropical creatures in having white furred soles.

• **BEHAVIOUR** The Red Panda scent marks its territory with urine, droppings, and powerful secretions from its anal glands. Other pandas detect these by taste and not smell. Communication is through a wide repertoire of squeaks, snorts, and whistles. Red Pandas feed only on fresh bamboo leaves at the base of the stalk and do not eat the stalk itself like the Giant Panda of China.

• **SIZE** Total body length: 50–60 cm. Weight: 3–6 kg.

• **HABITAT** Mixed forest with dense bamboo undergrowth.

• **BEST SEEN AT** Singhalila NP, Sikkim.

• **CONSERVATION THREATS** Habitat loss and poaching.

short pointed ears

masked face

chestnut body

long banded tail

Sikkim, West Bengal, and Arunachal Pradesh.

# BEARS

| INDIAN BEARS AT A GLANCE | |
|---|---|
| NUMBER OF SPECIES | 4 |
| LARGEST | BROWN BEAR |
| SMALLEST | SUN BEAR |
| MOST COMMON | SLOTH BEAR |
| MOST ENDANGERED | SUN BEAR |

### BEAR CHARACTERISTICS
- Broad head with small eyes
- Stump tail
- Strong and heavily built
- Long, non-retractable claws
- Protrusible lips that separate from gum
- Good sense of smell, poor eyesight and hearing
- Omnivorous diet

MEMBERS OF THE Ursinae or bear sub-family number eight in all and have a common appearance and form. Though classified as carnivores, their diet is omnivorous and they have grinding molars that are usual in herbivores, as well as sharp canines that are present in carnivores. Except for the Polar Bear, all other bears are dark coloured and predominantly vegetarian. They spend long hours foraging for berries, fruits and nuts, supplementing their diet with insects. Globally, only two species of bear are not endangered; the rest are persecuted for their meat and gall bladders (used to make traditional medicines) and face the constant pressure of a shrinking habitat. Bears are adept at bipedal walking. When faced with intruders they stand up, peer shortsightedly and sniff the air for unfamiliar scents, before deciding whether to run or charge. The strong white or yellow chest markings present on three of the Indian bear species probably serve as threat symbols when they rear up on their hind limbs. Bears are found in the Americas, Europe, and Asia.

**BEARS TOGETHER**
*The Sloth Bear often carries its young piggy-back while it forages for food.*

| | |
|---|---|
| FAMILY NAME | Ursidae |
| LATIN NAME | *Ursus arctos* |
| IUCN STATUS/WPA | Vulnerable/I |
| LOCAL STATUS | Rare |
| POPULATION | app. 300, declining |
| DIET | 🌿🐟🪲🌾🐄🐀C |
| SOCIAL UNIT | Solitary |
| ACTIVITY | ☾ |
| STRATUM | Terrestrial |

Himalaya, J&K and Sikkim (3,000-6,000 m).

# ●HIMALAYAN BROWN BEAR

LOCAL NAME: *Barf ka reech, Lal bhalu, Siala reech* (Hindi), *Kane haput* (♂), *Kane hapich* (♀) (Kashmiri), *Denmo* (Ladakhi), *Dub* (Nepali).

THE BROWN BEAR IS the world's largest terrestrial carnivore. The Himalayan Brown Bear *(Ursus a. isabellinus)* is a sub-species of the Brown Bear and is considerably smaller than its more famed relatives–the Grizzly and the Kodiak bears. However, it is still a very large bear with a thick, reddish-brown coat and no clear chest markings (that are present in most other bears).

• BEHAVIOUR This is the least arboreal bear and is largely terrestrial as an adaptation to life in the rolling uplands, above the tree line. It hibernates in winter.
• SIZE Total body length: 245 cm.
• HABITAT Alpine scrub and meadows, occasionally sub-alpine forests.
• BEST SEEN AT Great Himalayan NP (Himachal Pradesh).
• CONSERVATION THREATS Habitat disturbance and poaching.

*coarse reddish-brown fur*

*yellow or ivory-coloured claws*

| | |
|---|---|
| FAMILY NAME | Ursidae |
| LATIN NAME | *Ursus thibetanus* |
| IUCN STATUS/WPA | Vulnerable/I |
| LOCAL STATUS | Uncommon |
| POPULATION | 3,000, declining |
| DIET | 🐀🍯🌸🪲🌾🐀🐄C |
| SOCIAL UNIT | Solitary |
| ACTIVITY | ☀ ☾ |
| STRATUM | Terrestrial |

Himalaya, from J&K to Arunachal Pradesh and hills of NE (1,200 – 3,000 m).

# ●ASIATIC BLACK BEAR

LOCAL NAME: *Reech* (Hindi), *Haput* (♂), *Hapich* (♀) (Kashmiri), *Sanar* (Nepali), *Dom* (Bhutia).

A LARGE FOREST-DWELLING bear of the Himalaya, the Asiatic Black Bear is also called the Moon Bear due to the crescent-shaped white mark on its glossy black chest. Its fur is much shorter than that of the other black bear of India, the Sloth Bear. Longer hairs are present in the neck region, probably an evolutionary adaptation to escape the bites of predators such as tigers.
• BEHAVIOUR This bear hibernates in the upper Himalaya. It is fairly arboreal though it does not sleep on trees like the Sun Bear.
• SIZE Total body length:140–170 cm. Weight: 90–115 kg.
• HABITAT Heavily forested broad-leaved and coniferous forests. In the Northeast, also mixed deciduous and semi-evergreen forests.
• BEST SEEN AT Dachigam NP (J&K).
• CONSERVATION THREATS Poaching and human interference.

*white crescent chest patch*

*short, glossy black fur*

*black claws*

| FAMILY NAME | Ursidae |
|---|---|
| LATIN NAME | *Helarctos malayanus* |
| IUCN STATUS/WPA | Data deficient/I |
| LOCAL STATUS | Rare |
| POPULATION | Unknown |
| DIET | ✳ ◑ ➘ ✿ ❋ |
| SOCIAL UNIT | Solitary |
| ACTIVITY | ☼ ☾ |
| STRATUM | Terrestrial, arboreal |

# ● SUN BEAR

LOCAL NAME: *Gos bhaluk* (Assamese).

A SMALL FOREST BEAR with a Southeast Asian distribution, the Sun Bear is present only in a few pockets in Northeast India. Its short black coat has an attractive golden-yellow V- or U-shaped mark on the chest. With its small stocky frame it looks almost like a large dog and is called Dog Bear in parts of its range in Southeast Asia. The Sun Bear has a very long tongue (25 cm) that it uses to lick out grubs from tree holes and honey from hives. It also thrusts its arms into termite mounds and licks the insects off its paws.

• BEHAVIOUR The most arboreal bear, it makes rough nests of bent branches in trees to sleep in. It uses its teeth to haul itself up trees, and its long claws for digging and tearing up bark.

*pale muzzle*

• SIZE Total body length: 104–140 cm. Weight: 27–65 kg.

*golden yellow or off-white V mark*

• HABITAT Subtropical hardwood forests.
• BEST SEEN AT Nowhere common.
• CONSERVATION THREATS Habitat loss and poaching.

*long dark brown claws*

*short, black coat*

Assam, Arunachal Pradesh (S of R Brahmaputra), Mizoram, and Manipur.

| FAMILY NAME | Ursidae |
|---|---|
| LATIN NAME | *Melursus ursinus* |
| IUCN STATUS/WPA | Vulnerable/I |
| LOCAL STATUS | Locally common |
| POPULATION | app. 10,000, declining |
| DIET | ✳ ◑ ➘ ❋ ⦿ ➚ C |
| SOCIAL UNIT | Solitary |
| ACTIVITY | ☼ ☾ |
| STRATUM | Terrestrial |

Throughout India, except J&K, high Himalaya, and arid/desert areas of Gujarat and Rajasthan.

# ● SLOTH BEAR

LOCAL NAME: *Bhalu* (Hindi), *Reech* (Gujarati), *Asval* (Marathi), *Karadi* (Tamil/Kannada/Malayalam), *Elugu banti* (Telegu), *Bhalluk* (Bengali).

THIS WIDESPREAD INDIAN BEAR is familiar as a performing bear in the streets. A shaggy black animal with a long snout and lumbering gait, it can be lethal if confronted. The Sloth Bear is dim-sighted and rears up on its hind legs and bites or claws when alarmed.

• BEHAVIOUR This bear sucks up termites and ants through the gap caused by its missing front incisors. Its long claws are used to tear up termite mounds.
• SIZE Total body length: 140–170 cm. Weight: 65–145 kg.
• HABITAT Deciduous forest, scrub, and grassland.
• BEST SEEN AT Mudumalai WLS (Tamil Nadu) and Melghat NP (Maharashtra).
• CONSERVATION THREATS Habitat loss and poaching.

*protruding snout*

*creamish "V" on chest*

*shaggy black coat*

*ivory-white claws*

# CANIDS AND HYENAS

## CANID CHARACTERISTICS

- Cursorial predatory lifestyle
- Five digits on forefeet (one vestigial) and four on hind feet
- Non-retractile claws
- Long, sharp, upstanding ears
- Long, bushy tail
- Long limbs
- Long, pointed muzzle
- Deep chest

| CANIDS AT A GLANCE | |
|---|---|
| NUMBER OF SPECIES | 7 |
| LARGEST | WOLF |
| SMALLEST | DESERT FOX |
| MOST COMMON | JACKAL |
| MOST ENDANGERED | DHOLE |

The 34 species of canids in the world represent a successful family of predators, many of which hunt on the run (although some like the South American Maned Wolf are chiefly vegetarian). This lifestyle has endowed them with slender elongated bodies and limbs, and digitigrade feet with non-retractile claws. The tail is normally long and bushy and the ears are long and pointed. Jackals, wolves, foxes, and wild dogs are found in India in the wild; domestic dogs also belong to the same family. The Dhole or the Indian Wild Dog and wolves live in packs. Jackals and foxes are usually seen alone or in pairs. In India, canids are not dense forest species; they prefer open or lightly wooded country.

Hyenas are dog-like carnivores with large heads, strong jaws and muscular forequarters. Like canids, they are efficient scavengers and hunters with complex social lives that include meeting and mating ceremonies and ritualized dominance and appeasement behaviour. Hyenas differ from canids in their dentition, which resembles that of felids, and in having an anal gland like mustelids.

Both canids and Hyenas share a reputation bordering on the negative, with successive governments in the past ordering their extermination and giving rewards for their ears and tails as proof of their having been killed. However, they are now fully protected under law.

## CORNERED STAG
*The Dhole or Wild Dog is a pack hunter that surrounds its prey after a collaborative chase.*

| | |
|---|---|
| AMILY NAME | Canidae |
| ATIN NAME | Canis aureus |
| UCN STATUS/WPA | Lower risk/II |
| OCAL STATUS | Common |
| OPULATION | Unknown |
| IET | 🦴 🐾 🦎 🐦 🐍 C |
| OCIAL UNIT | Solitary/pairs/packs |
| CTIVITY | ☼ ☾ |
| TRATUM | Terrestrial |

# JACKAL

**LOCAL NAME:** *Gidar* (Hindi), *Kolha* (Marathi), *Shiyal* (Bengali/Gujarati), *Naree* (Tamil), *Gulle naree* (Kannada), *Kurukkan* (Malayalam), *Nakka* (Telegu), *Shaal* (Kashmiri), *Bilua* (Oriya).

A MEDIUM-SIZED CANID, the Jackal's scraggy, buff-grey coat is not as smooth as the fox's, nor as dense as the wolf's. The buff coat is interspersed with black hair while the underside, throat and the area around the eyes and lips are white. Jackals found in North India are larger and heavier than their peninsular counterparts.

- **BEHAVIOUR** A successful hunter, the Jackal has an undeserved reputation as a scavenger. Its eerie howls are characteristic of the Indian countryside and jungle. It also yelps, barks, and uses shorter calls.
- **SIZE** Body length: 60–75 cm. Weight: 7–15 kg.
- **HABITAT** Urban and semi-urban areas, and forests.
- **BEST SEEN AT** Sariska and Ranthambhor NPs (Rajasthan).
- **CONSERVATION THREATS** Poaching.

Throughout India (up to 3,000 m).

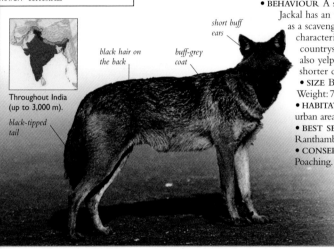

*short buff ears*
*black hair on the back*
*buff-grey coat*
*black-tipped tail*

| | |
|---|---|
| MILY NAME | Hyaenidae |
| TIN NAME | Hyaena hyaena |
| CN STATUS/WPA | Lower risk/III |
| OCAL STATUS | Uncommon |
| OPULATION | Unknown |
| ET | 🦴 🐾 C |
| OCIAL UNIT | Solitary/family groups |
| CTIVITY | ☾ |
| TRATUM | Terrestrial |

# STRIPED HYENA

**LOCAL NAME:** *Lakkad bagga* (Hindi), *Taras* (Marathi), *Domulagundu* (Telegu), *Kadu keeruba* (Kannada), *Jharak* (Gujarati), *Heta bagha* (Oriya), *Kazhutha puli* (Tamil/Malayalam).

THIS UNGAINLY skulking scavenger has a sloping back, spindly legs, a buff body with black stripes on the flanks and legs, and coarse, long fur. The back has a dark crest and the throat and breast are black.

- **BEHAVIOUR** Laughing call that ends in a cackle.
- **SIZE** Total body length: 150–160 cm. Weight: 26–41 kg.
- **HABITAT** Scrub forests, and near human habitation.
- **BEST SEEN AT** Gir NP (Gujarat).
- **CONSERVATION THREATS** Poaching and road kills.

*striped body*

Throughout India except J&K and NE (up to 1,500 m).

| | |
|---|---|
| FAMILY NAME | Canidae |
| LATIN NAME | *Canis lupus* |
| IUCN STATUS/WPA | Data deficient/I |
| LOCAL STATUS | Uncommon |
| POPULATION | 2000–3000, declining |
| DIET | 🐾 🐄 🐃 ↖ |
| SOCIAL UNIT | Packs |
| ACTIVITY | ☼ ☾ |
| STRATUM | Terrestrial |

# ● WOLF

**LOCAL NAME:** *Bheriya, Nekra, Hundar* (Hindi), *Landga* (Marathi), *Tholla* (Kannada), *Thodelu* (Telegu), *Onai* (Tamil), *Changu* (Tibetan), *Rame Hoon* (Kashmiri), *Hendol* (Bengali), *Nar* (Gujarati), *Bhagad* ( Kutchhi).

A LARGE CANID THAT LOOKS like a slim Alsatian with a big head, the Wolf has grey fur intermingled with black, especially on the dorsal crest, forehead, and tip of the tail. The undersides are buff in colour. Despite being one of the largest canids of the Indian subcontinent, the Indian Wolf is smaller than the sub-species found in Europe and America. The Wolf readily adapts to a variety of food including domestic livestock, bringing it into direct conflict with villagers. Occasional incidents of children being lifted have given it a notoriety that it finds difficult to shrug off. The Tibetan sub-species, *Canis lupus chanco,* is larger than the peninsular sub-species. It has a longer crest of black hair on its back, and in certain cases is completely black in colour.

• BEHAVIOUR Wolf packs communicate by howling and using gestures involving the ears, tail, and facial muscles. These indicate hierarchical disputes and play.
• SIZE Total body length:100–130 cm. Weight:15–20 kg.
• HABITAT Dry open country, desert, and barren uplands.
• BEST SEEN AT Velavadar NP (Gujarat) and Nanaj WLS (Maharashtra).
• CONSERVATION THREATS Hybridization, poaching, habitat loss, and human-animal conflict.

WOLF IN PROFILE
*The Wolf's face is rufous with white around the eyes and ears. The nose pad, lips and gum are moist black.*

Western and Peninsular India, and Trans-Himalaya, Ladakh to Sikkim.

grey coat interspersed with black

large, pointed ears

bushy tail with black tip

long, slender muzzle

long, slim legs

| | |
|---|---|
| ΛMILY NAME | **Canidae** |
| ΛTIN NAME | *Cuon alpinus* |
| JCN STATUS/WPA | Vulnerable/II |
| ƆCAL STATUS | Locally common |
| ƆPULATION | 5000–8000 |
| ƎT | 🐾 🦌 🐄 🐗 |
| ƆCIAL UNIT | Packs |
| ƆTIVITY | ☼ ☾ (hunting) |
| ⁻RATUM | Terrestrial |

Peninsular, central and NE India. Trans-Himalaya, Ladakh to Sikkim.

# WILD DOG

**LOCAL NAME:** *Dhole* (Hindi), *Ramkum* (Kashmiri), *Kolsun* (Marathi), *Kutra* (Gujarati), *Kadu nai* (Kannada), *Resu kukka* (Telegu), *Chen nai* (Malayalam/ Tamil), *Ram kutta* (Bengali), *Rang kukur* (Assamese), *Balia kukura* (Oriya), *Farra* (Ladakhi), *Huithou* (Manipuri).

A UNIQUELY ASIAN reddish-brown forest dog, the Dhole has shorter legs, a more bushy tail, and a thicker muzzle than both the Wolf and the domestic dog. Also known as the Asiatic Wild Dog, it varies from light sandstone to rust-red, the pelt turning deeper further south. Pups are sooty brown when born, turning russet in about three months. Dhole packs fluctuate in size, according to the season.

• BEHAVIOUR Dholes hunt in packs of six or seven and start eating their prey before it is dead, cleaning it to the bones within a few hours. They whistle as they hunt, and also yelp and whine.

• SIZE Total body length: 90 cm. Weight: 12–18 kg.

• HABITAT Open woodland interspersed with grassy meadows.

• BEST SEEN AT Bandipur and Nagerahole NPs (Karnataka).

• CONSERVATION THREATS Habitat loss, decline in prey species, and human-animal conflict.

ORIGINAL STOCK
*The Dhole is considered to be a primitive dog as it has six molars in its lower jaw as opposed to the seven of other canids.*

bushy, black-tipped tail

rust-red coat

short ears

thick muzzle

short legs

# FOXES

| | |
|---|---|
| FAMILY NAME **Canidae** | |
| IUCN STATUS/WPA Lower risk/II | |
| LOCAL STATUS Locally common (Indian Fox)/uncommon (Red Fox) | |
| POPULATION Unknown | |
| DIET 🐾 ✳ 🦎 🍖 C | |
| SOCIAL UNIT Solitary/pairs | |
| ACTIVITY ☾ | |
| STRATUM Terrestrial | |
| CONSERVATION THREATS Poaching, habitat disturbance | |

THREE SPECIES OF FOX inhabit India, two of which are widespread while the third is known from only a single record. Compared to the Jackal, Wolf, and Wild Dog, foxes are smaller, have shorter legs, a bushier tail, and longer ears. They also have a flatter head with a more slender muzzle. The two common foxes are the Indian Fox and the Red Fox, which has three sub-species (see opposite page). The Blanford's Fox *(Vulpes cana)*, which has been reported once from the Rann of Kutch, can be distinguished from the other two foxes by its smaller size, bushy black tail (sometimes with a small white tip), extensive black masking on the muzzle and flowing white hair in the chest area.

All foxes are opportunistic hunters and foragers, equally at ease catching small prey and scavenging. They den in burrows and females are known to move the den site once in a while if danger threatens, or as a precautionary measure.

## INDIAN FOX (*Vulpes bengalensis*)

**LOCAL NAME:** *Lomri* (Hindi), *Lokeria* (Central India), *Kokri* (Marathi), *Sanna nari* (Kannada), *Kulla naree* (Tamil), *Kuru naree* (Malayalam), *Gunta nakka* (Telegu), *Khek-shiyal* (Bengali), *Hiyal* (Assamese), *Kodisilai* (Oriya), *Lamhui* (Manipuri).

THE COMMON PENINSULAR Indian or Bengal Fox is more daintily built than the Red Fox and can be easily distinguished by its black-tipped tail and greyish appearance (more like a small Jackal). Its legs always look slightly browner than the body. The ears are brown with a black fringe and there are small black patches of hair on the muzzle in front of the eyes.

- **SIZE** Total body length: 45-60 cm. Weight: 1.8-3.2 kg.
- **HABITAT AND OCCURRENCE** Open rocky country, desert, and near human habitation (up to 1,350 m) throughout India; avoids dense forest.
- **BEST SEEN AT** Velavadar NP (Gujarat) and Rollapadu WLS (Andhra Pradesh).

black-tipped tail

black patch on muzzle

ears fringed
with white
hair

reddish
fur

white
tail-tip

## ED FOX (*Vulpes Vulpes*)

**CAL NAME:** *Lomri* (Hindi), *Loh* (Kashmiri), *Lokadi* (Gujarati).

IE COMMON FOX of the hills, deserts, and parts of northern Indian plains, the Red Fox is extremely
iable in body colour and size. The three sub-species of the fox found in India can be readily
inguished from the Indian Fox and Jackal by their characteristic white-tipped tail and black patches
ind the ears. The Tibetan Fox (*V. v. montana*) is the common fox of Ladakh and the Himalaya. It is foxy-
in colour, with thick luxuriant underfur during the winters. The ears are large and fringed with white
r. The chest, belly, muzzle and cheeks have white fur mixed with the red. The Kashmir Fox (*V. v. griffithi*)
lightly smaller than the Tibetan Fox and has a rust-orange coat, dark grey throat, chest, and outer part of
legs. The Desert Fox (*V. v. pusilla*) is the smallest and lightest of the three, with short, greyish fur mixed
h rust-brown hairs. The feet often have white patches on them and the back of each ear is dark brown.
tail is less bushy than in the other two sub-species.

**IZE** Total body length: 46 – 70 cm. Weight: 2-4 kg.
**IABITAT AND OCCURRENCE** The Himalaya, from J&K to Sikkim, and desert and arid areas
Rajasthan and Kutch, Gujarat.
**EST SEEN AT** Himalayan hill-stations and Desert NP (Rajasthan).

*Desert Fox (left) is smaller and greyer than the Tibetan Fox (right).*

# FELIDS

| INDIAN FELIDS AT A GLANCE | |
|---|---|
| NUMBER OF SPECIES | 15 |
| LARGEST | TIGER |
| SMALLEST | RUSTY SPOTTED CAT |
| MOST COMMON | JUNGLE CAT |
| MOST ENDANGERED | ASIATIC LION |

### FELID CHARACTERISTICS
• Rounded head and short muzzle
• Digitigrade feet with retractile claws
• Reduced number of pre-molars and molars
• Four toes on hind feet
• No anal scent gland
• Hunting by ambush

CATS EVOLVED SOME 40 million years ago. The 36 species found around the world vary considerably in size and colour but all have slender, graceful bodies with round head, shortened muzzle and erect ears. Unlike canids, many of which hunt by running flat out at their prey, most cats hunt by stealth, aided by pads on the soles of their feet. They bring down prey by swiping at them with their forepaws and have thus developed powerful forearms and sharp claws, which unlike in canids are retractable into sheaths. While traditionally the Tiger, Lion, Leopard, Snow Leopard, and Clouded Leopard are referred to as Big Cats, there are ten other species of wild felids, which are called smaller cats. The Cheetah is the only big cat to have become extinct in India in the twentieth century (see box).

**Cheetah**
*Once the fastest predator of the Indian plains, the Cheetah became extinct here in the twentieth century. Today, it is found only in Africa and parts of Iran. The Cheetah is taller than a Leopard but has a smaller head and shorter ears. Its yellow body is stippled with black spots, and a black "scar" line running from the eye to the upper lip gives it a menacing look. This big cat resorts to a short, fast burst of speed to capture prey and not stealth like other cats.*

#### TIGER IN WATER
*Tiger distribution is influenced by availability of water and prey, and lack of disturbance. In summer, cool, shaded areas are the best places to sight a Tiger.*

LION PRIDE
*Male cubs live with
the pride until they
are sub-adults, when
they disperse. Females
may stay on to become
members of the natal
pride.*

## DIFFERING LIFESTYLES

Wild cats range from the solitary to the social.
Lions are among the most social of felids, living in
prides and hunting cooperatively. This togetherness
is marked in the way they defend their territory by
roaring, scent-marking, and joint patrolling. In
comparison, the Tiger, the Leopard, and many
smaller cats epitomize the life of a loner, coming
together only to mate.

There are, however, certain common characteristics
that link the cat family, including excellent
binocular and colour vision, sharp hearing and a
peculiar ability to always land on their feet. All wild
cats are essentially nocturnal, but they can be seen
during day time, largely resting.

NOCTURNAL HUNTER
*Leopards prey on medium- to
small-sized wild animals. When
facing a shortage of prey, they can
take dogs, livestock, poultry, and
rarely small children.*

| | |
|---|---|
| FAMILY NAME | **Felidae** |
| LATIN NAME | *Panthera tigris* |
| IUCN STATUS/WPA | Endangered/I |
| LOCAL STATUS | Uncommon |
| POPULATION | 3,750–4,000, declining |
| DIET |  |
| SOCIAL UNIT | Solitary |
| ACTIVITY | ☾ ◑ |
| STRATUM | Terrestrial |

Isolated pockets
throughout India
(up to 3,600 m).

# ● TIGER

**LOCAL NAME:** *Bagh, Sher* (Hindi), *Bagh* (Bengali/Assamese), *Pedda pu*
(Telegu), *Patery Wagh* (Marathi), *Vengai Puli* (Tamil), *Kaduwa, Naree*
(Malayalam), *Hoolee* (Kannada), *Bagha* (Oriya).

UNDOUBTEDLY THE MOST CHARISMATIC animal of India, the majestic
Tiger has an orange coat patterned with broad black stripes. It has black
ears, each with a winking white spot on the back, powerful forepaws, and
a long banded tail. The Indian Tiger is one of five races or sub-species
distributed through Asia. Today, shrinking Tiger numbers and habitat are
major conservation issues. It is estimated that there are only 3,750-4,000
tigers left in India, comprising about 65% of the world's population. This
makes the national animal of India a very endangered species.

• BEHAVIOUR The Tiger prefers to hunt large deer, especially Sambar,
where available. Quite adaptable, it can survive on smaller prey, or even
fish in mangroves. It may attack humans if prey is unavailable or if it is
old or injured. This behaviour has earned it the fearsome title of man-
eater, although other mammals such as the leopard or the elephant take
far more human lives.

• SIZE Total body length: 2.6–3 m. Weight: 135–230 kg.

• HABITAT Deciduous, thorn, and evergreen forests, mangroves,
and grassland.

• BEST SEEN AT Ranthambhor NP (Rajasthan) and Bandhavgarh NP
(Madhya Pradesh).

• CONSERVATION
THREATS Poaching, habitat
loss, fragmentation and
decline in prey.

*large, powerful
body*

## CONSERVING THE TIGER

Project Tiger, started in 1973, is one of India's best-known conservation ventures. The government-sponsored scheme has been responsible for keeping tiger numbers at over 3,500, up by almost three times since its inception. The network of 27 reserves today protects nearly 40,000 sq km of tiger habitat.

black stripes on
orange coat

white patch on
back of ear

| | |
|---|---|
| FAMILY NAME | **Felidae** |
| LATIN NAME | *Panthera leo* |
| IUCN STATUS/WPA | Crit. endangered/I |
| LOCAL STATUS | Locally common |
| POPULATION | 250–350, increasing |
| DIET | 🐾 🐄 |
| SOCIAL UNIT | Prides of 2–15 |
| ACTIVITY | ☾ |
| STRATUM | Terrestrial |

# ● ASIATIC LION

LOCAL NAME: *Sher, Babbar sher, Singh* (Hindi), *Sinh* (Gujarati), *Sawach* (Kathiawari).

A LARGE TAWNY CAT WITH an unpatterned body and a long naked tail with a tuft at the tip, the male Asiatic Lion is known by its distinctive mane which varies in colour from pale blonde to jet black. The mane is sparser than in the African Lion (the ears are more clearly visible, therefore). Lionesses do not have a mane while cubs have a faint spotted pattern that fades as they mature. Both sexes have a distinct fold of skin along the belly. The Asiatic Lion separated as a sub-species as recently as 100,000 years ago and had a close brush with extinction as numbers plummeted to approximately 20 about 100 years ago. Like the Indian rhinoceros, the Lion has staged an amazing recovery. Today, there are more than 250 Lions found only in a single, tiny pocket in Gujarat and their number is increasing.

• BEHAVIOUR The Asiatic Lion is less social than the African Lion. It lives in small prides comprising 2-5 females with their young. Males join in only to eat and mate. Cattle contribute significantly to the Lion's diet, which changed from being mostly livestock in the early 1970s to mostly wild ungulates in the late 1980s.

• SIZE Total Body Length: 2.75 m. Weight: 110-190 kg.

• HABITAT Dry deciduous teak, scrub jungle, and dry savanna forests.

• ONLY SEEN AT Gir NP (Gujarat).

• CONSERVATION THREATS Habitat loss, disease, and inbreeding.

**STALKING PREY**
*As in the African sub-species, female Asiatic Lions hunt more often than males.*

Gir Forest, Gujarat.

mane in male

tawny brown,
unpatterned coat

| | |
|---|---|
| FAMILY NAME | Felidae |
| LATIN NAME | *Panthera pardus* |
| IUCN STATUS / WPA | Lower risk / I |
| LOCAL STATUS | Uncommon |
| POPULATION | app. 20,000, declining |
| DIET | 🐾 🐿 🐗 🐄 |
| SOCIAL UNIT | Solitary |
| ACTIVITY | ☾ |
| STRATUM | Terrestrial |

# ● COMMON LEOPARD

LOCAL NAME: *Tendua, Chita, Guldar* (Hindi), *Diblya Wagh* (Marathi), *Chirathe* (Kannada), *Chirutai puli* (Telegu / Tamil), *Pulli puli* (Malayalam), *Cheeta bagh* (Bengali), *Kelral* (Mizo), *Teku* (Naga), *Khare-suh* (Kashmiri), *Dipdo* (Gujarati), *Pendra* (Oriya).

THE MOST ADAPTABLE BIG CAT of the Indian subcontinent, the Leopard has a clear yellow coat marked with black rosettes. It has a small spotted head with powerful jaws, and a long tail, and its underside is white. The colour of the coat varies considerably in intensity from gold to tawny in commoner forms. The rasping call of the Leopard (called "sawing" because it resembles the sound of wood being sawed) is a familiar nocturnal call in the Indian jungle.

• BEHAVIOUR Leopards manage to co-exist with Tigers by hunting smaller prey and hauling the carcasses up trees. They prey upon cattle, dogs and even children, thus earning notoriety as man-eaters. As they are often sighted near habitation in rural India, the Leopard is mistakenly considered to be a common species.

• SIZE Total Body Length: 1.85-2.15 m. Weight: 39-68 kg.

• HABITAT Deciduous and evergreen forests, scrub jungle, open country, and fringes of human habitation.

**"BLACK PANTHER"**
*The Leopard's coat may vary in colour and the jet black melanistic form is also sometimes called the "Black Panther".*

• BEST SEEN AT Sanjay Gandhi NP, Borivili NP (Maharashtra) and Gir NP (Gujarat).

• CONSERVATION THREATS Poaching, habitat loss, human-animal conflict, and decline in prey species.

Throughout India
(up to 3,000 m).

long, spotted and partially ringed tail

black rosettes all over body

tawny yellow or gold coat

| | |
|---|---|
| FAMILY NAME | **Felidae** |
| LATIN NAME | *Uncia uncia* |
| IUCN STATUS/WPA | Endangered/I |
| LOCAL STATUS | Rare |
| POPULATION | 400–600, declining |
| DIET |  |
| SOCIAL UNIT | Solitary |
| ACTIVITY | ☾ ◑ |
| STRATUM | Terrestrial |

**MOUNTAIN MONARCH**
*There are 4,500–7,500 Snow Leopards in the world today.*

# ● SNOW LEOPARD

**LOCAL NAME:** *Barhal he* (Pahari), *Barfani cheetah* (Urdu), *Shan* (Ladakhi), *Burhel haye* (Bhotia), *Sheen-e-suh* (Kashmiri).

ONE OF THE MOST aptly named animals, the Snow Leopard is adapted completely to live in snow-covered areas. It is marginally smaller than the Common Leopard, with a more luxuriant coat. It has black spots on its limbs and face, and its pale smoky-grey coat, with ghostly, dark grey rosettes, allows for excellent camouflage. The Snow Leopard's paws are massive in comparison to its body, and help to fell the larger prey that it often needs to hunt. An enlarged nasal cavity which warms the air that it breathes, and dense, long fur enable this cat to live in places where the temperatures can dip to -40° C.

• **BEHAVIOUR** Despite being a large carnivore, the harsh terrain and climate that it lives in forces the Snow Leopard to have a wide dietary range, including rodents, birds, and wild goats. During the lean season, small alpine mammals such as pikas and hare comprise a fair share of its diet. In February and March, during its peak breeding months, it is known to feed on a shrub, *Myricaria germanica*.

• **SIZE** Total body length: 100–130 cm. Weight: 35–55 kg.

• **HABITAT** Alpine steppe, grassland, and scrub above the tree line.

• **BEST SEEN AT** Hemis NP, Ladakh (J&K).

• **CONSERVATION THREATS** Poaching, human-animal conflict, and decline in prey.

Himalaya, Trans-Himalaya, Ladakh to Arunachal Pradesh (3,000–5,500 m).

grey rosettes all over body

dirty snow-coloured coat

thick tail

| | |
|---|---|
| FAMILY NAME | Felidae |
| LATIN NAME | *Lynx lynx* |
| IUCN STATUS/WPA | Lower risk/I |
| LOCAL STATUS | Rare |
| POPULATION | Unknown |
| DIET | 🐾 🦌 🐦 |
| SOCIAL UNIT | Solitary |
| ACTIVITY | ◑ |
| STRATUM | Terrestrial |

## ● EURASIAN LYNX

LOCAL NAME: *Patsalam* (Kashmiri), *Eeh* (Ladakhi).

THE EURASIAN LYNX IS FOUND throughout Eurasia, with India forming the southern edge of its range. It has a buff or sandy-grey coat that is spotted profusely. Unpatterned and striped forms are also known, although they are not common in India. The lynx can be distinguished from other mountain cats by its long ear tufts. It is often poached for its fur.

• BEHAVIOUR It breeds once a year for two or three years and then skips a year.
• SIZE Total body length: 85–90 cm. Weight: 18–21 kg.
• HABITAT Cold desert, scrub woodland, and barren outcrops of rock above the tree line. Rarely found on southern slopes.
• BEST SEEN AT Nubra River Valley, Ladakh (J&K).
• CONSERVATION THREATS Habitat loss and poaching.

long, black
ear tufts

white moustache
and face ruff

buff-grey
patterned
coat

large
furry feet

Ladakh (J&K) and
Lahaul and Spiti
(Himachal
Pradesh)
(2,500–3,000 m).

| | |
|---|---|
| FAMILY NAME | Felidae |
| LATIN NAME | *Otocolobus manul* |
| IUCN STATUS/WPA | Lower risk/I |
| LOCAL STATUS | Rare |
| POPULATION | Unknown |
| DIET | 🐾 🐦 |
| SOCIAL UNIT | Solitary |
| ACTIVITY | ◑ |
| STRATUM | Terrestrial |

## PALLAS'S CAT

LOCAL NAME: *Ribilik* (Ladakhi)

EURASIAN IN ITS RANGE, the Pallas's Cat is found only in Ladakh in India, and is popularly known by its German and Russian name – Manul. A greyish cat, the white tips of its hair give it a frosted appearance. Like the Snow Leopard, it has very long fur on its undersides and tail to keep it warm in its frozen habitat. The Pallas's Cat's flat head with small rounded ears gives it a low profile that helps it hunt stealthily in open mountainous regions. Pallas's Cats are rare in snow-bound areas inhabited by lynxes.

• BEHAVIOUR Known to occupy dens of foxes or marmots, it also uses rock crevices or caves for shelter.
• SIZE Total body length: 50–55 cm. Weight: 2–5 kg.
• HABITAT Open rock-strewn mountain steppe; prefers south-facing mountain slopes.
• CONSERVATION THREATS Habitat loss and poaching.

flat face

white-tipped
grey fur

short, black-
tipped tail

Ladakh (2,500–
4,800 m).

| | |
|---|---|
| FAMILY NAME | **Felidae** |
| LATIN NAME | *Neofelis nebulosa* |
| IUCN STATUS/WPA | Vulnerable/I |
| LOCAL STATUS | Rare |
| POPULATION | Unknown, declining |
| DIET |  |
| SOCIAL UNIT | Solitary |
| ACTIVITY | ☾ |
| STRATUM | Terrestrial |

STRIKING LOOKS
*Smallest of the big cats, the*
*Clouded Leopard is one of the*
*most strikingly patterned*
*mammals in India.*

# ● CLOUDED LEOPARD

LOCAL NAME: *Lamchita* (Bengali), *Ghodaphutuki bagh* (Assamese), *Pungmar* (Lepcha), *Kung* (Bhotia), *Amchita* (Nepali), *Kelral* (Mizo).

THIS FELID HAS A WARM OCHRE COAT with gray elliptical clouds edged with black floating on it. These turn into black oval spots on its legs and into blurred rings on its very long tail. Its head is spotted, with two broad bars on its neck and stripes on its cheek. The back of each ear is black with a grey spot in the middle. The Clouded Leopard's short legs give it a heavy appearance but it is one of the most lithe of big cats. It can hang from tree branches by its hind legs and tail, and clamber down tree trunks head first. Among felids, it has the longest canine teeth in proportion to its skull size.
• BEHAVIOUR A very secretive cat, it is rarely seen in the wild. Unlike other leopards, it does not leave tell-tale scats and scrapes along its trails. Very arboreal, it ambushes prey from trees and then drags the kill up to eat. It also shelters its young in tree hollows.
• SIZE Total body length: 60–110 cm. Weight: 11–20 kg.
• CONSERVATION THREATS Poaching, habitat loss, and fragmentation.

N West Bengal,
Sikkim, NE India
(up to 3,000 m).

large head

elliptical grey
markings on
ochre coat

short
spotted
legs

long tail

| | |
|---|---|
| FAMILY NAME | Felidae |
| LATIN NAME | *Pardofelis marmorata* |
| IUCN STATUS/WPA | Vulnerable/I |
| LOCAL STATUS | Rare |
| POPULATION | Unknown, declining |
| DIET | 🐾 🦌 |
| SOCIAL UNIT | Solitary |
| ACTIVITY | ☾ |
| STRATUM | Terrestrial |

# ● MARBLED CAT

A MINIATURE VERSION of the Clouded Leopard, the Marbled Cat is one-third the size of the former. It has similar long canines but a shorter, rounder skull and a long tail equal to the length of its own body. The patches on its body have pale borders unlike the black-edged pattern of the Clouded Leopard. There are numerous black spots on its legs and tail. A sub-species of this cat, found in Jammu and Kashmir, has different markings and is much paler than the northeastern form; unfortunately, it is known only from skins procured in the trade.
- SIZE Total body length: 40– 60 cm. Weight: 5.5 kg.
- HABITAT Tropical, deciduous, and evergreen forests.
- CONSERVATION THREATS Poaching, habitat loss, and fragmentation.

Himalaya: J&K to
Arunachal Pradesh.
and Meghalaya.

rounded
head

marbled patches
on body

black spots
on limbs

| | |
|---|---|
| FAMILY NAME | Felidae |
| LATIN NAME | *Catopuma temmincki* |
| IUCN STATUS/WPA | Vulnerable / I |
| LOCAL STATUS | Rare |
| POPULATION | Unknown, declining |
| DIET | 🐾 🦌 🐀 |
| SOCIAL UNIT | Solitary |
| ACTIVITY | ☾ |
| STRATUM | Terrestrial |

# ● GOLDEN CAT

LOCAL NAME: *Shonali mekoori* (Assamese), *Shonali biral* (Bengali), *Tokpa* (Manipuri).

A MEDIUM-SIZED CAT with an unpatterned golden or fox-red coat, the Golden Cat resembles the North American Puma in its general appearance. The golden colour is only broken by a broad white moustache-like stripe, two white stripes lining the inner rims of the eyes, and a white line on the bottom of the tail. However, there are also melanistic cats with pure black coats or marbled patterns.
- SIZE Total body length: 120 cm. Weight: 6–11 kg.
- HABITAT Tropical and sub-tropical, moist deciduous, and evergreen forests.
- BEST SEEN AT Nowhere common.
- CONSERVATION THREATS Unknown.

NE India.

distal part of
tail black

short,
shiny fur

unpatterned
brown coat

white face
markings

| | |
|---|---|
| FAMILY NAME | Felidae |
| LATIN NAME | *Felis sylvestris* |
| IUCN STATUS/WPA | Lower risk/I |
| LOCAL STATUS | Uncommon |
| POPULATION | Unknown, declining |
| DIET | 🐀 🦎 🐜 🦗 |
| SOCIAL UNIT | Solitary |
| ACTIVITY | ☼ ☾ |
| STRATUM | Terrestrial |

# DESERT CAT

LOCAL NAME: *Jhengmeno* (Kutchhi), *Ran biladi* (Gujarati).

THE CLOSEST WILD RELATIVE of the domestic tabby, the Asiatic Wildcat is small and spotted, unlike its striped European counterpart. The Indian Desert Cat is the easternmost sub-species of the group and it inhabits arid or desert areas. This sandy-yellow cat is perhaps the most exploited for its fur among Indian small cats; at least 30 cat pelts are needed to make a single full-length coat.

• BEHAVIOUR This species often interbreeds with domestic cats and in areas where both are found, a large variety of cats may be seen with a dark greyish coat that is spotted or striped like the Desert Cat's. It is also the only cat that inhabits a burrow system like foxes.

• SIZE Total Body Length: 47–54 cm. Weight: 2–4 kg.

• HABITAT Low-lying scrub forest, semi-arid and desert areas, and cultivated tracts.

• BEST SEEN AT Desert NP (Rajasthan).

• CONSERVATION THREATS Habitat loss, hybridization, and poaching.

*sandy-yellow spotted body*

*white belly*

Maharashtra, Madhya Pradesh, Rajasthan, and Gujarat.

| | |
|---|---|
| FAMILY NAME | Felidae |
| LATIN NAME | *Caracal caracal* |
| IUCN STATUS/WPA | Lower risk/I |
| LOCAL STATUS | Rare |
| POPULATION | Unknown |
| DIET | 🐀 🐇 🐗 |
| SOCIAL UNIT | Solitary |
| ACTIVITY | ☾ |
| STRATUM | Terrestrial |

# ● CARACAL

LOCAL NAME: *Siyah ghosh* (Persian/Hindi), *Hinotro* ( Kutchhi).

TALL AND SLENDER, the brick-coloured Caracal is one of two cats with a plain coat, the other being the Golden Cat. Its short fur is pinkish-fawn on the back and buff on the undersides and limbs. It has two black bars above its eyes and at the corners of its mouth. Its most striking feature is its long, narrow black-tufted ears.

*long black, tufted ears*

• BEHAVIOUR This open-country cat relies largely on speed and agility, rather than stealth, to capture its prey. It lives and hunts in extremely hot and arid conditions.

• SIZE Total Body Length: 60–70 cm. Weight: 14–22 kg.

• HABITAT Humid forest, semi-arid woodland, and rocky areas.

• BEST SEEN AT Ranthambhor and Sariska NPs (Rajasthan).

• CONSERVATION THREATS Habitat loss and poaching.

Punjab, Rajasthan, Gujarat, Uttar Pradesh, and Central India.

| | |
|---|---|
| AMILY NAME | Felidae |
| ATIN NAME | Felis chaus |
| JCN STATUS/WPA | Lower risk/II |
| OCAL STATUS | Common |
| OPULATION | Unknown |
| ET | 🐾 🗡 |
| OCIAL UNIT | Solitary/pairs |
| CTIVITY | ☾ ☼ |
| TRATUM | Terrestrial |

# JUNGLE CAT

LOCAL NAME: *Jangli billi* (Hindi), *Bano biral* (Bengali), *Jongli mekuri* (Assamese), *Baul* (Marathi), *Junka pilli* (Telegu), *Kattu poonai* (Tamil), *Bana bhua* (Oriya), *Kaadu bekku* (Kannada), *Lesh* (Kashmiri), *Lam houdong* (Manipuri), *Jungli biladi* (Gujarati).

THE MOST COMMON WILD CAT in India, the Jungle Cat is buff or grey-brown with reddish ears that have short black tufts. It has two black stripes on its lanky forelegs, and its tail, which is shorter than that of a domestic cat, is black-tipped. Its coat is unmarked except for faint red stripes running across the forehead and on the outer surface of the legs. Its eyes are ringed with white, with a dark tear stripe running down each cheek. The Jungle Cats found in southern India are greyer and lightly speckled on the back.
• **BEHAVIOUR** The Jungle Cat frequents human habitation. It can hunt animals much larger than itself, such as porcupines.
• **SIZE** Total body length: 60 cm. Weight: 5 – 6 kg.
• **HABITAT** Grassland, scrub, dry deciduous and evergreen forests, semi-urban areas and villages.
• **BEST SEEN AT** Ranthambhor NP (Rajasthan) and Kaziranga NP (Assam).
• **CONSERVATION THREATS** Poaching and habitat disturbance.

STANDING TALL
*The Jungle Cat stands tall when alarmed, pricking up its ears like all cats do.*

Throughout India, except high Himalaya (up to 2,400 m).

grizzled grey-brown coat

short black-tipped tail

black tear stripe

| | |
|---|---|
| FAMILY NAME | Felidae |
| LATIN NAME | *Prionailurus bengalensis* |
| IUCN STATUS / WPA | Lower Risk / I |
| LOCAL STATUS | Uncommon |
| POPULATION | Unknown, declining |
| DIET | 🐀 🐟 |
| SOCIAL UNIT | Solitary |
| ACTIVITY | ☾ |
| STRATUM | Terrestrial, arboreal |

# LEOPARD CAT

**LOCAL NAME:** *Cheeta billi* (Hindi), *Ban biral* (Bengali), *Lota-mekuri bagh* (Assamese), *Huli bekku* (Kannada), *Wagati* (Marathi), *Keipiri* (Mizo).

THIS LEOPARD-LIKE small cat is one of the most adaptable wild cats, similar to its larger cousin, the Common Leopard (see p.87). It lives with ease in a variety of forests and even close to human habitation across most of South and Southeast Asia and the Far East. It is also widespread in Russia, except where there is dense snow. In India, the Leopard Cat is the most common small cat after the Jungle Cat (see p.93). Unlike leopards, however, this cat does not have rosettes on its buff coat. Instead, it has solid black spots or patches throughout that merge into two broad streaks at the shoulders. Like the Rusty Spotted Cat (see p.95), Fishing Cat (see p.95) and Marbled Cat (see p.91), it has white spots on the back of its black ears. Its limbs, longer than those of other cats, give it a graceful appearance. Individuals in northern India are more furry than in the south.

- **BEHAVIOUR** An extremely versatile cat, it is arboreal by nature and is also comfortable in water.
- **SIZE** Total body length: 60 cm. Weight: 3–7 kg.
- **HABITAT** Grassland, scrub, and moist decidous forests.
- **BEST SEEN AT** Corbett NP (Uttaranchal).
- **CONSERVATION THREATS** Habitat loss and poaching.

WILD CAT CUBS
*Felid young, like domestic kittens, are rounder, plumper versions of the adults.*

All over India, except Deccan Plateau and arid W India.

*solid black spots on buff coat*

*black streaks on shoulder*

*black cheek stripes*

| | |
|---|---|
| AMILY NAME | Felidae |
| ATIN NAME | *Prionailurus rubiginosus* |
| UCN STATUS / WPA | Vulnerable / I |
| OCAL STATUS | Rare |
| OPULATION | Unknown |
| IET | |
| OCIAL UNIT | Solitary |
| CTIVITY | ☾ |
| TRATUM | Terrestrial, arboreal |

# RUSTY SPOTTED CAT

LOCAL NAME: *Bitari billi* (Gujarati), *Kaadu bekku* (Kannada), *Namali pelli* (Tamil), *Chiruta pilli* (Telegu), *Thurumban poocha* (Malayalam).

THE SMALLEST CAT in the world (half to three-quarters the size of a domestic cat), the Rusty Spotted Cat has a fawn coat with rusty brown spots arranged in neat lines on its back. Its forehead has two longitudinal black-edged white stripes. Its eyes are ringed with white, and its lips, chin and undersides are white too. This cat is not a dense-forest creature, yet it is rarely seen.

• BEHAVIOUR: It is visible after a shower when it emerges from its tree hideouts to feed. Very tolerant of human habitation, there are multiple records of it giving birth to kittens on rooftops.

• SIZE Total body length: 35–48 cm. Weight: 1–1.6 kg.

• HABITAT Rocky areas, scrub, dry and open forests, and human habitation.

• BEST SEEN AT Mundanthurai NP (Tamil Nadu).

• CONSERVATION THREATS Hybridization and road kills.

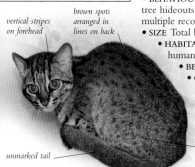

vertical stripes on forehead

brown spots arranged in lines on back

unmarked tail

light fawn coat

Peninsular India, up to Rajasthan. Isolated record in J&K.

| | |
|---|---|
| MILY NAME | Felidae |
| TIN NAME | *Prionailurus viverrinus* |
| CN STATUS / WPA | Vulnerable / I |
| OCAL STATUS | Uncommon |
| OPULATION | Unknown |
| IET | |
| OCIAL UNIT | Solitary |
| CTIVITY | ☾ |
| TRATUM | Terrestrial, semi-aquatic |

# FISHING CAT

LOCAL NAME: *Khupya bagh* (Hindi), *Meccho biral* (Bengali), *Meseka* (Assamese), *Kaattanpuli* (Malayalam).

THIS IS ONE OF the most easily recognized cats in its range, with an olive-brown coat, unlike other spotted cats that are tawny. It has short legs below a stocky body. Black elongated spots run in parallel lines over its back, merging into longitudinal stripes on its neck. Its pale cheeks have two darker stripes and there are two stripes on the inside of its forearm as in many small cats. This cat is larger than the Leopard Cat, Rusty Spotted Cat and Desert Cat (with which it could be confused) by at least a foot and it has a shorter, more muscular tail. It dens in tree trunks and ground near water.

• BEHAVIOUR The most adept Indian cat in water, it preys on fish and waterfowl. It is also a skillful hunter of small prey on land.

• SIZE Total body length: 70 cm. Weight: 5.5–8 kg.

• HABITAT Wetlands, marshes, tidal creeks, mangroves, dense jungles, and scrub.

• BEST SEEN AT Keoladeo Ghana NP (Rajasthan).

• CONSERVATION THREATS Habitat loss, poaching, and fishing activities.

N, E and NE India, south to Orissa; W. Ghats

pale cheeks with dark stripes

olive-brown patterned coat

# MUSTELIDS, VIVERRIDS AND HERPESTIDS

| AT A GLANCE | |
|---|---|
| NUMBER OF SPECIES | 31 |
| LARGEST | Hog Badger |
| SMALLEST | Small Indian Mongoose |
| MOST COMMON | Grey Mongoose |
| MOST ENDANGERED | Malabar Civet |

MUSTELID CHARACTERISTICS
• Invariable loss of fourth upper molar
• Enlarged anal sac
• Long cylindrical body
• Short limbs
VIVERRID CHARACTERISTICS
• Five toes on the hind feet
• Large ears
• External anal scent glands
HERPESTID CHARACTERISTICS
• Short ears without bursa

Mustelids, Viverrids, and Herpestids are a group of unrelated small carnivores. Of the three, mustelids are the most diverse, comprising badgers, otters, weasels, and martens. They are characterized by unique dentition (invariable loss of fourth upper molar, and no carnassial notch on the upper pre-molar), and an enlarged anal sac. They differ from wild cats in having non-retractile claws, while the presence of anal glands and a well-developed first digit on the forefeet distinguishes them from canids. Mustelids are characterized by long cylindrical bodies and short limbs. There are three sub-families of mustelids present in India: Melinae, Lutrinae and Mustelinae. The sub-family Melinae or badgers and ferret badgers are the largest of the mustelids. The sub-family Lutrinae, or otters, are adapted to an aquatic or semi-aquatic existence and to a piscivorous diet. Their thick cylindrical bodies have waterproof fur, the tail is broad and paddle-shaped, and the feet are partially webbed to aid swimming. While most other mustelids are solitary or live in pairs, otters live in close-knit families.

COMMUNAL LIFE
*Otters live in family groups, and indulge in social behaviou such as grooming and play.*

The sub-family Mustelinae includes weasels, martens, and polecats, which are all terrestrial animals that lead a partly arboreal life. Martens are relatively large in size with a thick, bushy tail and pointed ears set wide apart. Weasels and polecats, on the other hand, have round ears that do not protrude above the head.

Viverrids or civets can be distinguished from mustelids by their unique civet gland. This is a modified skin gland that is functional in true civets and vestigial in palm civets. Civets differ from cats (although many of them are called civet cats) by having five toes on the hind feet and an elongated face. Many viverrids have ringed tails while others are plain in colour.

HOME ALONE
*The Siberian Weasel is a solitary creature and is the largest weasel in India.*

Civets can be distinguished from mongooses (belonging to the Herpestidae family) in two ways: their ears are large with a well-developed bursa while mongoose ears are short and without a bursa. While mongooses are carnivorous and insectivorous, civets are more omnivorous, eating fruits as well. Most civets are nocturnal, while most mongooses are diurnal. Mongooses are the most common of the three groups and the Grey Mongoose is the best-known species among them.

DIFFERENT HUES
*The Stripe-necked Mongoose varies in colour from the bright red form in the southern part of the Western Ghats (shown here) to the yellowish grey form found in North Kanara.*

# SMALL-TOOTHED FERRET BADGER

| | |
|---|---|
| FAMILY NAME | Mustelidae |
| LATIN NAME | Melogale moschata |
| IUCN STATUS / WPA | Endangered / II |
| LOCAL STATUS | Rare |
| POPULATION | Unknown |
| DIET | 🐾 🐁 🐛 |
| SOCIAL UNIT | Solitary |
| ACTIVITY | ☾ |
| STRATUM | Terrestrial |

ALSO CALLED THE Chinese Ferret Badger, the Small-toothed Ferret Badger is a small, dark grey animal that appears silvery grey against light. It has a black bandit's mask on its face and paler or white lips, chin, throat, belly, and inner legs. Its tail is brownish-grey with a white tip. The buff-white forehead and cheeks match the white dorsal streak, which is broad at the forehead and tapers down to the shoulders. Both the ferret badgers found in India can be conclusively identified in hand only by checking their dentition. This species has small narrow crowned molars while the Large-toothed Ferret Badger has larger molars.

round ears
with white
edges

• BEHAVIOUR Both the Small- and Large-toothed Ferret Badgers have a long tail and padded feet with striations – suitable adaptations for a life in the trees. They are more arboreal than other badgers and can be seen curled up asleep on branches.

black
mask on
face

• SIZE Total body length: 35 – 45 cm. Weight: 1 – 3 kg.
• HABITAT Deciduous and evergreen forests, and grassland.
• BEST SEEN AT Nowhere common.
• CONSERVATION THREATS Habitat loss and poaching.

white
underparts

long tail
(15-20 cm)

NE India, especially Manipur, Nagaland, Arunachal Pradesh, and Assam.

# LARGE-TOOTHED FERRET BADGER

| | |
|---|---|
| FAMILY NAME | Mustelidae |
| LATIN NAME | Melogale personata |
| IUCN STATUS / WPA | Vulnerable / II |
| LOCAL STATUS | Rare |
| POPULATION | Unknown |
| DIET | 🐾 🐁 🐛 |
| SOCIAL UNIT | Solitary |
| ACTIVITY | ☾ |
| STRATUM | Terrestrial |

VERY SIMILAR TO THE Small-toothed Ferret Badger in size and colouration, this species differs only in dentition, the pattern of its facial mask, and its dorsal streak which runs all the way to its tail. It is also known as the Burmese Ferret Badger. Both Ferret Badgers are poorly studied species in the wild and very little is known about them. The two to three young that are born resemble the adults in colour and pattern at birth.

• BEHAVIOUR Like skunks, Ferret Badgers release a strong anal scent to repulse attackers, if threatened.
• SIZE Total body length: 35 – 45 cm. Weight: 1 – 3 kg.
• HABITAT Deciduous and evergreen forests, and grassland, both in the hills and plains.
• BEST SEEN AT Nowhere common.
• CONSERVATION THREATS Habitat loss and poaching.

N Bengal and throughout NE India.

| FAMILY NAME | Mustelidae |
|---|---|
| LATIN NAME | *Mellivora capensis* |
| IUCN STATUS / WPA | Lower risk / I |
| LOCAL STATUS | Uncommon |
| POPULATION | Unknown |
| DIET | 🐜🦎🐍🐾✳ |
| SOCIAL UNIT | Pairs |
| ACTIVITY | ☾ |
| STRATUM | Terrestrial, fossorial |

# ●HONEY BADGER

LOCAL NAME: *Bejoo, bajra* (Hindi), *Ghurnar* (Gujarati), *Tharaikaradi* (Tamil/Kannada), *Bigu Khawar* (Telegu), *Khakhar* (Bengali), *Gada Bhalu* (Oriya).

A BROAD STREAK of unwashed silver-grey from crown to base of tail distinguishes the Ratel or Honey Badger from a small bear. Like bears, it has a short snout, coarse yet glossy black fur, and habits such as digging large holes in the forest floor and climbing trees. The dorsal streak is more buff or rust brown in the case of juveniles. Both sexes look alike, although the males are significantly larger.

• BEHAVIOUR The Ratel is reputed to dig up graves – a local belief based on its scavenging habits. It is also a predator that feeds largely on flesh, supplemented by a small vegetarian diet. In Africa, honey guide birds are known to lead it to beehives. This symbiotic behaviour is not known in India.

• SIZE Total body length: 60–75 cm. Weight: 8–10 kg.

• HABITAT Hilly, stony arid country, and dry and moist deciduous forests.

• BEST SEEN AT Melghat NP (Maharashtra).

• CONSERVATION THREATS Habitat loss and human interference.

*short tail*

*greyish white upperside*

*jet black face and underside*

Throughout India except the Western Ghats, high Himalaya, and NE India.

| FAMILY NAME | Mustelidae |
|---|---|
| LATIN NAME | *Arctonyx collaris* |
| IUCN STATUS / WPA | Unlisted / I |
| LOCAL STATUS | Uncommon |
| POPULATION | Unknown |
| DIET | 🐾❄🐜🦎 |
| SOCIAL UNIT | Solitary |
| ACTIVITY | ☾ |
| STRATUM | Terrestrial |

# HOG BADGER

LOCAL NAME: *Bala suar* (Hindi), *Baliya suor* (Bengali).

PROBABLY THE MOST common badger of northeastern India, the Hog Badger lives in holes dug in the ground or in cracks in large rocky outcrops. It relies more on smell than sight and gambols awkwardly like a bear when running. Seen from the back, it looks like an odd cross between a wild boar and a small bear. Its coat is a uniform grizzled grey in contrast to the Honey Badger's prominent black and white colouration. The whitish face has two dark stripes as in the European badger and the white ears are prominent. This badger's legs and head are darker than the rest of its body and its claws are white unlike the Honey Badger's black ones.

• BEHAVIOUR Other than using its teeth and claws in defence, the Hog Badger, if cornered, releases a pungent odour that forces the attacker to retreat.

• SIZE Total body length: 55–70 cm. Weight: 7–14 kg.

• HABITAT Well-wooded countryside and deciduous forests.

• BEST SEEN AT Kaziranga NP (Assam).

• CONSERVATION THREATS Habitat loss.

*grey coat*

*dark legs*

*badger mask*

*whitish claws*

Sikkim, N Bengal and NE India.

# OTTERS

| | |
|---|---|
| FAMILY NAME **Mustelidae** | |
| DIET 🐟 🦐 🐸 🦆 🐀 | |
| SOCIAL UNIT Groups | |
| ACTIVITY ☽ ◑ ☼ | |
| STRATUM Aquatic, terrestrial | |
| CONSERVATION THREATS Habitat loss, poaching, siltation, and pesticides | |

Otters are carnivores that are highly specialized for an aquatic life. Three species of otters are found in India. While the Smooth-coated Otter is found mainly in standing water, the Eurasian Otter prefers running streams and the Small-clawed Otter is found at higher altitudes than the others.

**LOCAL NAME:** *Udbilao* (Hindi), *Shanamba* (Manipuri), *Neernai* (Tamil/Malayalam), *Nirukaka* (Telegu), *Neeru nai* (Kannada).

## EURASIAN OTTER *(Lutra lutra)*

THE EURASIAN OTTER *can be identified by its coarse, dusky brown coat that looks bedraggled when wet. Its underside is light grey and it often has spots on its lips and nose. This otter is not as common in India as the Smooth-coated Otter.*
• SIZE *Total body length: 60 – 80 cm. Weight: 7 – 11 kg.*
• **HABITAT AND OCCURRENCE** *Rivers, streams, and hill creeks, in the Himalaya, eastern and southern India.*
• BEST SEEN AT *Corbett NP (Uttaranchal).*

*tail 3/4 of head and body*

*coarse fur*

*w-shaped nostrils*

*webbed feet, prominent claws*

## SMOOTH-COATED OTTER *(Lutrogale perspicillata)*

*v-shaped nostrils*

*smooth fur*

THIS IS THE MOST COMMON OTTER *in India, easily identified by its well-groomed chocolate-brown coat. Its underside is lighter and its paws are dark brown but lighter than the body. It differs from the Eurasian Otter in having V-shaped nostrils and its tail is flatter towards the tip. The Smooth-coated Otter is active by day.*
• SIZE *Total body length: 65 – 79 cm. Weight: 7 – 11 kg.*
• **HABITAT AND OCCURRENCE** *Lakes and streams throughout India, except Gujarat and Rajasthan.*
• BEST SEEN AT *Chambal WLS (Uttar Pradesh), Periyar NP (Kerala).*

*webbed feet, except third digit*

*tail 1/2 of head and body*

## SMALL-CLAWED OTTER *(Amblonyx cinereus)*

THE SMALLEST OTTER, *this nocturnal species is a miniature version of the Eurasian Otter but differs in that its feet have webs and short spiky claws. Its underside is light brown to yellow and the sides of its lip, chin, and throat are almost white.*
• SIZE *Total body length: 45 – 55 cm. Weight: 3 – 6 kg.*
• **HABITAT AND OCCURRENCE** *Rivers, streams, and paddy fields in the Himalayan foothills, eastern India, and hills of southern India.*
• BEST SEEN AT *Kaziranga NP (Assam).*

*v-shaped nostrils*

*small size*

*tail 1/2 of head and body*

# MARTENS

| | |
|---|---|
| AMILY NAME | **Mustelidae** |
| DIET | 🐀 🗡 🦎 🐛 |
| OCIAL UNIT | Solitary |
| ACTIVITY | ☼ ☾ |
| TRATUM | Terrestrial, arboreal |
| CONSERVATION THREATS | Habitat loss and oaching |

Martens are mustelids found in hilly or mountainous areas. They have long limbs and tails, and are agile climbers of trees, although they are clumsy creatures when running on the ground. They den in tree hollows and sometimes behind rocks.

LOCAL NAME: *Garan* (Kashmiri), *Chitrola* (Garhwali), *Shungsam* (Bhotia), *Illingan* (Muthuvan), *Suchuyokai* (Naga).

## YELLOW-THROATED MARTEN (*Martes flavigula*)

THIS COMMON FOREST MARTEN *of the Himalaya is yellow-black above, blonde on the underside, and a deep canary yellow at the neck. Larger than the Beech Marten (below), it has a less bushy but longer tail.*
• BEHAVIOUR *A bold and agile animal, this marten hunts with equal ease on trees as well as on the ground.*
• SIZE *Total body length: 40– 60 cm. Weight: Up to 3.4 kg.*
• HABITAT AND OCCURRENCE *Moist deciduous forests through the Himalaya (160 – 2,500 m) and Northeast India.*
• BEST SEEN AT *Kedarnath WLS (Uttaranchal).*

## NILGIRI MARTEN (*Martes gwatkinsi*)

THE LARGEST AND RAREST *Indian marten, the Nilgiri Marten is considered by some to be a subspecies of the Yellow-throated Marten. It varies from dark brown to black, has a pale yellow to yellowish-orange neck, and a flat skull with a concave depression on its forehead.*
• SIZE *Total body length: 55– 65 cm. Weight: 2 kg.*
• HABITAT AND OCCURRENCE *Grassland, shola, deciduous, and ever-green forests of W Ghats.*
• BEST SEEN AT *Eravikulam NP (Kerala).*

black upperside

black head

yellow throat

tail 3/4 of head and body

## BEECH MARTEN (*Martes foina*)

ONLY SLIGHTLY BIGGER *than a large squirrel, the Beech or Stone Marten is lighter in colour than the other Indian martens, varying from chocolate to drab tawny-brown. Its throat is white to pale yellow, and there is not much distinction between the dorsal and ventral parts. The legs and tail are darker than the body. Males are larger in size.*
• BEHAVIOUR: *Less arboreal than other martens, this Marten keeps to open stony ground. It frequents human habitation and often raids hen coops.*
• SIZE *Total body length: 30– 45 cm. Weight: 1.5– 1.8 kg.*
• HABITAT AND OCCURRENCE *Temperate and alpine forests of Himalaya and near habitation (1,500 – 4,000 m).*
• BEST SEEN AT *Ladakh and J&K.*

tawny-brown coat

white throat

# WEASELS

| | |
|---|---|
| FAMILY NAME **Mustelidae** | |
| DIET 🐾 🦌 🐟 🐛 | |
| SOCIAL UNIT Solitary | |
| ACTIVITY ☼ ☾ | |
| CONSERVATION THREATS Unknown | |
| STRATUM Terrestrial, fossorial | |

Specialized predatory mustelids, weasels have a short muzzle, long, flattened skull, a slim body, and short legs. These features are adaptations for hunting prey swiftly over the ground, and for pursuit of prey underground. Most weasels specialize in hunting mice and voles, and occasionally birds. There are five species of weasels and one polecat (also of the same family) in India.

**LOCAL NAME:** *Tabo, Senai* (Nishi), *Chitrola* (Garhwali).

## PALE OR MOUNTAIN WEASEL *(Mustela altaica)*

THE PALE WEASEL *(right) is sandy-yellow above and creamish-yellow below. It has a flat, narrow skull, and a long, cylindrical body. Its long, spindly tail is the same colour as its back and its paws are conspicuously white.*

sandy-yellow back

brown tail (no black tip)

• BEHAVIOUR *It does not hibernate, but winters in deep holes in the ground.*
• SIZE *Total body length: 22–27 cm. Weight: 130–350 gm.*
• HABITAT AND OCCURRENCE *Coniferous forests and open country in the Upper Himalaya, Ladakh to Sikkim.*

white paws

## YELLOW-BELLIED WEASEL *(Mustela kathiah)*

A CHOCOLATE-BROWN *medium-sized weasel with a sulphur-yellow belly, this is one of the least-known mustelids of India. Its upper lip, chin, and upper throat are whitish and its long tail is the same colour as its back. In Nepal, this nocturnal weasel is tamed by villagers to catch rats.*
• SIZE *Total body length: 21–25 cm. Weight: 130–330gm.*
• HABITAT AND OCCURRENCE *Temperate and evergreen forests of Himalaya and Northeast India.*

chestnut-brown coat in summer

light underparts

black-tipped tail

## HIMALAYAN STOAT *(Mustela erminea)*

THE HIMALAYAN STOAT OR ERMINE *is a small chestnut-brown weasel flecked with white, with a white chin, throat, and belly. Most individuals change colour dramatically to become pure white between the winter months of October and December. The tail-tip, however, remains black all year round. This weasel is active by day.*
• BEHAVIOUR *It is known to conceive even while suckling the previous litter.*
• SIZE *Total body length: 17–22 cm. Weight: 130gm.*
• HABITAT AND OCCURRENCE *Alpine and temperate forests; prefers banks of rivers and open rock-strewn plains near lakes of Ladakh (3,200–4,200m).*

# TIBETAN POLECAT *(Mustela putorius)*

THIS CHOCOLATE-BROWN *weasel has a black mask across its eyes and forehead on a light brown face. Its chest, limbs, and tail are also black. In some individuals the tip of the tail is whitish. This species is nocturnal by nature.*
• SIZE *Total body length: 35 – 40 cm. Weight: 700 gm.*
• HABITAT AND OCCURRENCE *Dry temperate forests in open spaces of the Tibetan plateau. Its range may extend to J&K and Sikkim.*

black masked face

black tail

black legs

# SIBERIAN OR HIMALAYAN WEASEL *(Mustela sibirica)*

A UNIFORMLY COLOURED *reddish-brown species, the Siberian Weasel (see below) is the largest of its kind in India and the most widely distributed mustelid in Asia. It is the only weasel with a brown belly, although its undersides are lighter than its back. Its upper lip and chin are white, with a black stripe from its snout to the eyes, while its throat varies from white to pale brown.*
• BEHAVIOUR *It is considered to be one of the most efficient carnivores in the Himalaya, along with the Stoat, and is both diurnal and crepuscular.*
• SIZE *Total body length: 25 – 30 cm.*
• HABITAT AND OCCURRENCE *High-altitude coniferous forests of the Himalaya: J&K to the Northeast (1,500 – 4,800 m).*

# BACK-STRIPED WEASEL *(Mustela strigidorsa)*

A chocolate-brown weasel, it can be easily identified by a pale silver line running along its back from head to tail, and a corresponding yellow stripe from chin to abdomen. It has a much shorter and bushier tail than other weasels. This weasel is active at night.
• SIZE *Total body length: 28.5 cm.*
• HABITAT AND OCCURRENCE *Temperate forests of North Bengal, Sikkim, Assam, Arunachal Pradesh, and Nagaland (1,000 – 2,500 m).*

reddish-brown back

white chin and throat

| | |
|---|---|
| FAMILY NAME | **Viverridae** |
| LATIN NAME | *Viverricula indica* |
| IUCN STATUS/WPA | Lower risk/II |
| LOCAL STATUS | Common |
| POPULATION | Unknown |
| DIET | 🐀 🏹 🐛 ⚘ |
| SOCIAL UNIT | Solitary |
| ACTIVITY | ☾ |
| STRATUM | Terrestrial |

Throughout India except J&K, deserts, and high Himalaya.

# SMALL INDIAN CIVET

LOCAL NAME: *Kasturi* (Hindi), *Gandho gokul* (Bengali), *Ud manjar* (Marathi), *Punagu poonay* (Tamil), *Meru, Poo veruke* (Malayalam), *Punagina bekku* (Kannada), *Salia patini* (Oriya).

A COMMON RING-TAILED CIVET, the Small Indian Civet is buff coloured with spotting all over its body. The coat can vary from brown to grey. The black-and-white ringed tail has 8-10 dark bands. This civet lacks a spinal crest and has a cream throat with two dark bands across it. Its ears are small, rounded, and set close to each other on top of the head, more like a cat's, while its legs are dark and long.
• **BEHAVIOUR** Not very arboreal, it prefers thick grass and scrub, and dens in burrows or under rocks.
• **SIZE** Total body length: 45–60 cm. Weight: 2.5–3.5 kg.
• **HABITAT** All habitats except deserts and mountains (up to 2,500 m).
• **CONSERVATION THREATS** Habitat loss and road kills.

8–10 dark rings on tail

spots smaller on spine and larger on flanks

black marks on white throat

| | |
|---|---|
| FAMILY NAME | **Viverridae** |
| LATIN NAME | *Viverra zibetha* |
| IUCN STATUS/WPA | Vulnerable/II |
| LOCAL STATUS | Locally common |
| POPULATION | Unknown, declining |
| DIET | 🐀 🏹 🐛 ⚘ |
| SOCIAL UNIT | Solitary |
| ACTIVITY | ☾ |
| STRATUM | Terrestrial |

# LARGE INDIAN CIVET

LOCAL NAME: *Khattas* (Hindi), *Bado gokul* (Bengali), *Bhran* (Nepalese), *Kung* (Bhotia), *Moirang sathibi* (Manipuri).

A LARGE DOG-LIKE CIVET with a low-slung body accentuated by short legs, the Large Indian Civet is a greyish beast with buff overtones (but less buff than the Small Indian Civet). It has distinct black spotting on the flanks, dark limbs and a black-and-white banded tail. It has a dark dorsal crest running from shoulder to tail, the throat and fore chest are black, and the slightly large ears are widely set on the forehead. The bands on the tail are normally broader and fewer in number than in the Small Indian Civet (4-8).
• **SIZE** Total body length: 80 cm. Weight: 8–9 kg.
• **HABITAT** Low hills, moist deciduous and evergreen forests, and near human habitation.
• **CONSERVATION THREATS** Poaching and habitat loss.

dorsal crest

black-banded chest

Terai from Himachal Pradesh to NE India, Orissa, West Bengal, and Bihar up to 2,000 m.

| FAMILY NAME | Viverridae |
|---|---|
| LATIN NAME | *Viverra civettina* |
| IUCN STATUS/WPA | Crit. endangered/I |
| LOCAL STATUS | Rare |
| POPULATION | Unknown, declining |
| DIET | 🐀 🦎 🥚 🌿 |
| SOCIAL UNIT | Solitary |
| ACTIVITY | ☾ |
| STRATUM | Terrestrial |

Coastal Kerala and Karnataka.

# MALABAR CIVET

LOCAL NAME: *Jawad, Malabar veruke* (Malayalam), *Mangala Kutri, Jawadiya* (Kannada).

THE MOST ENDANGERED civet and possibly the most endangered mammal in India, the Malabar Civet was last reported from Kerala in 1990. It can be told apart from the Small Indian Civet easily by its much larger size and the dark erectile crest of hair that runs down its spine, much like that of the Large Indian Civet. Unlike in the Large Indian Civet, the dark band runs through to the tip of the tail. The underside of the tail has five black-and-white bands. The black spots on the grey coat do not form lines or patterns, but are splotched randomly. The Malabar Civet is most closely related to the Large Spotted Civet (*V. megaspila*) of Southeast Asia. In India it is close to extinction.
• BEHAVIOUR Though this behaviour is not confirmed, it probably uses fixed places for latrines.
• SIZE Total body length: 125 cm. Weight: app. 8 kg.
• HABITAT Highly degraded lowland forests. Also reported from cashew plantations.
• CONSERVATION THREATS Habitat destruction, accidental poaching, and predation (usually by dogs).

| FAMILY NAME | Viverridae |
|---|---|
| LATIN NAME | *Prionodon pardicolor* |
| IUCN STATUS/WPA | Vulnerable/II |
| LOCAL STATUS | Rare |
| POPULATION | Unknown |
| DIET | 🐀 🦎 🥚 🌿 |
| SOCIAL UNIT | Solitary |
| ACTIVITY | ☾ |
| STRATUM | Terrestrial, Arboreal |

# SPOTTED LINSANG

LOCAL NAME: *Zhik chum* (Bhotia), *Suilyu/Silu* (Lepcha).

THE SPOTTED LINSANG is the smallest viverrid in India. Its low-slung, weasel-like body and long tail are adaptations for a life in the trees. This species is richer in colouration than the other spotted civets. Its coat ranges from ochre-brown to deep buff and the spinal area is darker than the flanks. The black spots on its coat are set in lines on the spine, while the ones on the flank vary from small spots to larger patches. The legs are spotted too, and the tail has 5–6 rings.
• BEHAVIOUR The Spotted Linsang inhabits tree hollows. It is known to build nests with leaves and branches.
• SIZE Total body length: 35–40 cm. Weight: 500–600 gm.
• HABITAT Dense lowlands, temperate forests, and tropical rainforests.
• CONSERVATION THREATS Poaching.

ochre coat with black spots

banded tail

low-slung body

small size

Sikkim and NE India.

| | |
|---|---|
| FAMILY NAME | **Viverridae** |
| LATIN NAME | *Paradoxurus hermaphroditus* |
| IUCN STATUS/WPA | Lower risk/II |
| LOCAL STATUS | Common |
| POPULATION | Unknown |
| DIET | 🐦 🐀 🦎 🌿 |
| SOCIAL UNIT | Solitary |
| ACTIVITY | ☾ |
| STRATUM | Arboreal |

# COMMON PALM CIVET

**LOCAL NAME:** *Khatas* (Hindi), *Bham* (Bengali), *Tapkiri ud manjar* (Marathi), *Maranai* (Tamil), *Marappatti* (Malayalam), *Marabekku* (Kannada), *Dali odha* (Oriya), *Kehe* (Naga), *Moirang sathibi* (Manipuri).

PROBABLY THE MOST COMMON civet in India, the Palm Civet's unpatterned throat and tail distinguish it from other common plains civets. Its body colour varies from a rich cream to brownish–black or even jet black. Dark spots coalesce into stripes on the sides. It has three longitudinal stripes on its back, which are visible on close inspection.
• BEHAVIOUR An omnivore, it is very fond of the fruit of palms and honey, thus earning its reputation for having a "sweet tooth".
• SIZE Total body length: 42–69 cm. Weight: 3–4 kg.
• HABITAT Deciduous and scrub forests and well-wooded countryside.
• CONSERVATION THREATS Habitat loss and poaching.

Throughout India except Gujarat, Rajasthan, and Himalaya.

black marks on body

unringed tail

face marked with white

dark limbs

| | |
|---|---|
| FAMILY NAME | **Viverridae** |
| LATIN NAME | *Paradoxurus jerdoni* |
| IUCN STATUS/WPA | Vulnerable/II |
| LOCAL STATUS | Rare |
| POPULATION | Unknown |
| DIET | 🐦 🐀 🦎 🌿 |
| SOCIAL UNIT | Solitary |
| ACTIVITY | ☾ |
| STRATUM | Arboreal |

# BROWN PALM CIVET

A CIVET WITH a limited forest distribution, this species looks like the Palm Civet without the markings on its face and body. It is much more chocolate-brown than the Palm Civet – its head and limbs are darker, the shoulders more buff, and the flanks more grey. The tail is proportionately longer with a pale tip in many individuals. On closer examination, its neck hair can be seen growing in the opposite direction to the rest of its fur – an adaptation to deter predators.
• BEHAVIOUR Although omnivorous, it is predominantly frugivorous and is dependent on rainforest fruits to a large extent.
• SIZE Total body length: 48–59 cm. Weight: 2.4–4 kg.
• HABITAT Wet evergreen forests and coffee plantations.
• BEST SEEN AT Kalakaad-Mundanthurai NP (Tamil Nadu).
• CONSERVATION THREATS Habitat loss.

Palni, Nilgiri, Anamalai, Kodagu, and parts of southern Kerala and Tamil Nadu.

grey-brown flanks

pale tip (variable) to brown tail

plain body

| | |
|---|---|
| FAMILY NAME | **Viverridae** |
| LATIN NAME | *Paguma larvata* |
| IUCN STATUS/WPA | Lower risk/II |
| LOCAL STATUS | Common |
| POPULATION | Unknown |
| DIET | 🦎 🐀 🐦 🌾 |
| SOCIAL UNIT | Solitary |
| ACTIVITY | ☾ |
| STRATUM | Arboreal |

# HIMALAYAN PALM CIVET

LOCAL NAME: *Bichu* (Garhwali).

A LARGER PALM CIVET of hill forests, the Himalayan Palm Civet is a dark brown to black civet with greyish-buff underparts. It has a thick, black unpatterned tail and black chin and throat. The latter characteristic distinguishes it from the Yellow-throated Marten with which it shares a distribution range. Adults do not have spots on their body, though in juveniles flank spots may be present. It is also called the Masked Palm Civet because of the unique facial markings that vary a lot but commonly comprise of bands below the eye, a greyish line down the forehead and nose and markings from the ear to the cheek. The tail could be tipped a dirty grey.

- **BEHAVIOUR** Skunk-like, it ejects a foul-smelling liquid when disturbed.
- **SIZE** Total body length: 60 cm. Weight: 3–4 kg.
- **HABITAT** Near montane forests and human habitation.
- **CONSERVATION THREATS** Habitat loss.

*plain brown body*

*thick black tail*

*masked face*

Himalaya (400 – 2500 m), NE India, and Andaman Islands.

| | |
|---|---|
| FAMILY NAME | **Viverridae** |
| LATIN NAME | *Arctictis binturong* |
| IUCN STATUS/WPA | Data deficient/I |
| LOCAL STATUS | Rare |
| POPULATION | Unknown |
| DIET | 🦎 🐀 🐦 🌾 |
| SOCIAL UNIT | Solitary |
| ACTIVITY | ☾ |
| STRATUM | Arboreal |

# BINTURONG

LOCAL NAME: *Young* (Assamese).

A LARGE PALM CIVET, almost twice the size of the Common Palm Civet, the Binturong is the largest member of the civet family in India. With a characteristic thick and muscular prehensile tail, it is all black, set off by long white whiskers and a white edge to its ears. It is so large that it was mistakenly thought to be a small bear, giving it the popular name Bearcat. The head is speckled with grey, more so in the case of juveniles. Another northeastern civet species, the Small-toothed Palm Civet (*Arctogalidia trivirgata*), is a rare buff-brown forest civet with a grey head and striped back, inhabiting the south of River Brahmaputra.

- **BEHAVIOUR** Largely arboreal in nature, the Binturong can be easily identified by its prehensile tail.
- **SIZE** Total body length: 75–90 cm. Weight: 9–20 kg.
- **HABITAT** Deciduous and evergreen forests.
- **CONSERVATION THREATS** Habitat loss and poaching.

*black fur*

*grey head*

*prehensile tail*

Sikkim and NE India.

107

# MONGOOSES

| | |
|---|---|
| FAMILY NAME | **Herpestidae** |
| DIET | 🐀 🦎 🐛 🥚 🐍 |
| SOCIAL UNIT | Solitary/pairs |
| ACTIVITY | ☼ ☾ ◑ |
| CONSERVATION THREATS | Poaching and habitat loss |
| STRATUM | Terrestrial, fossorial, semi-aquatic |

The mongoose family comprises elongated, short-limbed predatory creatures related to civets, but differing from them in certain ways (see p.97). They are partly fossorial in nature.

**LOCAL NAME:** *Newala* (Hindi), *Norio* (Gujarati), *Keeree* (Tamil/Kannada/Malayalam), *Yentawa mangisa* (Telegu), *Beji* (Bengali), *Mungoos* (Marathi), *Nool* (Kashmiri), *Neula* (Oriya).

## GREY MONGOOSE *(Herpestes edwardsii)*

THE COMMON INDIAN *Grey Mongoose is the famed animal used in snake and mongoose shows and immortalized as Rikki Tikki Tavi in Rudyard Kipling's story. Its tawny-grey fur is much more grizzled and coarse than that of other mongooses and individual hairs have ten alternate dark and light bands. Its legs are darker than its body, and its tail is as long as its head and body put together. The desert sub-species is more reddish, the southern Indian one more brown, and the northern Indian one more grey. All three are distinctly more grey than the Ruddy, Small, and Stripe-necked Mongooses (see below and right).*

grizzled grey coat

- BEHAVIOUR *Very bold and inquisitive, this mongoose often lives near human habitation.*
- SIZE *Total body length: 35–45 cm. Weight: 0.8–1.4 kg.*
- HABITAT AND OCCURRENCE *Open scrub, cultivated land, rocky patches, and forest edges all over India.*

## SMALL INDIAN MONGOOSE *(Herpestes javanicus)*

THIS IS A SMALL OLIVE-BROWN *or dark-brown mongoose with golden speckles. Its fur is short and silken. An individual hair, if examined, shows three dark rings and two pale ones. Northern forms are dark brown with paler paws, while desert forms can have a pale or even whitish underside. The Marsh Mongoose of West Bengal is possibly a sub-species.*
- SIZE *Total body length: 35–50 cm. Weight: 750–900 gm.*
- HABITAT AND OCCURRENCE *Bushes, hedges, farms, human habitation, and deserts in northern plains, extending to Kolkata in the east.*

small size

gold speckled olive coat

## RUDDY MONGOOSE *(Herpestes smithii)*

A LARGE FOREST MONGOOSE *of peninsular India, the Ruddy Mongoose resembles the Grey Mongoose, but has a reddish-brown infusion, particularly on the head, neck, and shoulders. Its legs are also reddish, especially the hind ones. The tail is short with a black tip that is carried pointed upwards, a unique behavioural trait.*
- SIZE *Total body length: 39–47 cm. Weight: 950 gm –1.8 kg.*
- HABITAT AND OCCURRENCE: *Forests of central, western, and peninsular India, up to Delhi in the north and Bihar in the east.*

black-tipped tail, curved

reddish colour

## BROWN MONGOOSE *(Herpestes brachyurus)*

A LARGE, STOCKY *forest mongoose of the southern Indian hills, the fur of this dark brown creature is less coarse than that of the Grey Mongoose and is speckled yellowish-brown. The feet are black and soles of the hind feet are partially covered with hair. The tail is around two-thirds of head and body length, like the Small Indian Mongoose's, but is very bushy and tapers to a conical point – characteristic of this species.*
• BEHAVIOUR *Not much is known about this secretive animal. It breeds in burrows and below tree roots.*
• SIZE *Total body length: 38–50 cm. Weight: 1.5–2.7 kg.*
• HABITAT AND OCCURRENCE *Moist forests of the Western Ghats, south of Kodagu (12° N), 100–1,800 m.*

dark brown fur

## CRAB-EATING MONGOOSE
*(Herpestes urva)*

A LARGE MONGOOSE, *slightly smaller than the Stripe-necked Mongoose, the Crab-eating Mongoose has a broad white stripe on its neck, starting from its cheeks and progressing past its chest. Its throat is iron-grey with white hair tips giving it a speckled look. The soles of its hind feet are hairy and its tail is short and uniformly coloured with a paler tip.*
• BEHAVIOUR *Very aquatic, the Crab-eating Mongoose hunts for fish, crabs, snails, and frogs adeptly.*
• HABITAT AND OCCURRENCE *Stream banks, swamps, paddy fields, and moist deciduous forests of West Bengal, Assam, Arunachal Pradesh, and Tripura; not commonly found near human habitation.*
• SIZE *Total body length: 45 – 50 cm. Weight:1.8 – 2.3 kg.*

## STRIPE-NECKED MONGOOSE *(Herpestes vitticollis)*

A STOCKY SOUTHERN INDIAN *mongoose with a reddish tint to its body, this is the largest mongoose in Asia. Fairly variable in colour from brown to yellowish-grey to rufous, it usually has a dark stripe bordered with white from ear to shoulder. The specimens of North Kanara do not have any red on the body. The legs are short and the tail is three-fifth of the head and body length, with a black tip.*
• BEHAVIOUR: *Feeds on animals as small as a crab and as large as a mouse deer.*
• SIZE *Total body length: 40–55 cm. Weight: 2.5–3.5 kg.*
• HABITAT AND OCCURRENCE *Moist forests and swampy areas of the Western Ghats.*

black-tipped tail    large size    stripe on neck

# SCALY ANTEATERS

PANGOLINS OR SCALY ANTEATERS are elongated, armour-plated insectivores with a long tongue and no teeth. They are members of the Order Pholidota, which has an Old World distribution, and are close relatives of the sloth and armadillos of the New World. They are specialist feeders of termites and ants. Pangolins are unique in being able to curl up into a ball when threatened, and tucking away the vulnerable parts beneath the armour-plated scales. Their tongues are coated with a sticky glue-like saliva which helps them feed on ants and termites from ant hills and termite mounds. They are known to retreat into ground burrows and seal them up with loose soil, making the burrow entrance inconspicuous.

## PANGOLIN CHARACTERISTICS
- Overlapping scales all over the body
- Long, protruding, glutinous tongue
- No teeth
- Long snout
- Powerful feet with sharp claws

HOME IN A TREE
*Pangolins live in tree holes or ground burrows and emerge only after dark.*

COMPARING ARMOUR
*The Rhinoceros (left) and the Pangolin (right) are completely unrelated animals, but have evolved overlapping scales as a means of protection.*

| | |
|---|---|
| MILY NAME | Manidae |
| TIN NAME | *Manis crassicaudata* |
| CN STATUS / WPA | Lower risk / I |
| CAL STATUS | Uncommon |
| PULATION | Unknown |
| ET | 🐾 |
| CIAL UNIT | Solitary/pairs |
| TIVITY | ☾ |
| RATUM | Terrestrial, fossorial |

Throughout India but rare in NE.

# INDIAN PANGOLIN

LOCAL NAME: *Bajra keet, Bajra kapta* (Hindi), *Khavlya manjar* (Marathi), *Azhungu* (Tamil), *Eenam pechi* (Malayalam), *Kidi khau* (Gujarati).

THE INDIAN PANGOLIN has a faint pinkish-white skin that is covered dorsally by a suit of dirty yellow scales. The scales are sparsely covered with reddish-brown hair and the skin is visible only on its lower body and face. The hind legs have a calloused sole and short blunt nails in sharp contrast to its powerful forelimbs armed with very long claws.

• BEHAVIOUR Pangolins hiss sharply if confronted and then curl into a ball which is very difficult to "unroll". As they do not have teeth, curling is their primary defense mechanism.

• SIZE Total body length: 60−70 cm. Weight: 9−11 kg.

• HABITAT Scrub, urban cultivation, and mixed deciduous forest.

• BEST SEEN AT Mudumalai NP (Tamil Nadu) and Bandipur NP (Karnataka).

• CONSERVATION THREATS Poaching.

long tail

scaly, khaki-coloured body

no ear flap

| | |
|---|---|
| MILY NAME | Manidae |
| TIN NAME | *Manis pentadactyla* |
| CN STATUS / WPA | Lower risk/I |
| CAL STATUS | Uncommon |
| PULATION | Unknown |
| ET | 🐾 |
| CIAL UNIT | Solitary/pairs |
| TIVITY | ☾ |
| RATUM | Terrestrial, fossorial |

NE India excluding high Himalaya.

# CHINESE PANGOLIN

LOCAL NAME: *Bonrui* (Assamese/Bengali).

WIDESPREAD OUTSIDE INDIA in China and Southeast Asia, the Chinese Pangolin is a smaller northeastern species. A shorter tail with a naked tip and protective ear flaps are the only major external anatomical differences in relation to the peninsular Indian species.

• BEHAVIOUR The young are born with soft, not fully overlapping scales, and the mother may curl herself around the offspring to protect it. The baby and mother lie on their sides facing each other for feeding, so that the scales do not get in their way. The mother carries her young hanging from her muscular tail for the first few days.

• SIZE Total body length: 48−58 cm. Weight: 9 kg.

• HABITAT Grassland and deciduous forest.

• BEST SEEN AT Not commonly seen.

• CONSERVATION THREATS Poaching.

ear flap

naked tip on short tail

# HARES AND RABBITS

HARES AND RABBITS are small to medium-sized herbivores, which along with Pikas (see p.114) form the Order Lagomorpha. Their long limbs are built for quick flight and for jumping (the hind limbs are longer than the forelimbs), and their large ears and eyes help in quick detection of predators as well as in thermoregulation. Members of this family are known for their rapid rate of reproduction. Hares do not build nests, but "forms" or shallow depressions in the ground, as their young are born furred with open eyes. Rabbits, on the other hand, build nests as their young are born naked and blind and need to be cared for by the mother for over 2-3 weeks. Double digestion is a peculiarity of all lagomorphs – their pellet-shaped droppings are exuded wet first, then eaten and exuded again in a dry, waste form. All lagomorphs have small peg-like teeth behind the incisors, which are not found in any other animal.

## LAGOMORPH CHARACTERISTICS
• Eyes placed on top of head to enable all-round vision
• Light skull and slit-like nostrils
• Split upper lip
• Second pair of incisors in upper jaw, unlike in rodents

| | |
|---|---|
| FAMILY NAME Leporidae | |
| DIET 🌿 🥬 | |
| SOCIAL UNIT Solitary/pairs | |
| ACTIVITY ☼ | |
| CONSERVATION THREATS Poaching and habitat loss | |

## INDIAN HARE *(Lepus nigricollis)*

LOCAL NAME: *Kharghosh* (Hindi/Bengali), *Ran sassa* (Marathi), *Molla* (Kannada), *Moyal* (Malayalam), *Saslu* (Gujarati), *Thekua* (Oriya), *Musal* (Tamil), *Choura pilli* (Telegu), *Soha pohu* (Assamese).

*The characteristic hare of the Indian subcontinent, the Indian Hare is reddish-brown with black hair mixed throughout. It has 13 sub-species, of which the northern Indian form has a rufous tail and whitish underparts. In southern India it is larger, with a black patch on the back of its neck, and its tail is black on top. This sub-species is called the Blacknaped Hare. In the desert region of the west, it is more sandy-yellow in colour.*
• BEHAVIOUR *A very territorial hare, it defends up to 10 hectares of land against rival males.*
• HABITAT AND OCCURRENCE
*Open scrub, short grassy patches, and overgrazed forest land throughout India except high altitudes and mangroves (up to 2,400m).*
• SIZE *Total body length: 40–50cm. Weight: 1.8 – 3.6 kg.*
• BEST SEEN AT *All peninsular forests.*

long ears

rufous coat

black nape

MASTERS OF CAMOUFLAGE
*Hares depend on their drab colouration and ability to lie still in tall grass as means of camouflage, thus evading predators. Young hares and sub-adults (above bottom) are adept at staying still for long periods. Hares in north India have a brown nape (above top) while the southern sub-species has a black nape (left).*

## WOOLLY HARE *(Lepus oiostolus)*

*thick curly fur*

*A plump brown hare with thick, curly fur, the Woolly or Upland Hare is a creature of mountain slopes and meadows. It has a pale rump and a tail that is brown above and dirty white below. Like all lagomorphs it is susceptible to population fluctuations that sometimes makes it a very common animal in its habitat and sometimes fairly rare. Very little is known about the species.*
• BEHAVIOUR *Takes cover in marmot burrows.*
• HABITAT AND OCCURRENCE *Alpine meadows and plateaux. Upper Indus and Upper Sutlej valleys of J&K including Ladakh, and Sikkim; prefers open, rocky terrain (2,500 – 5,400 m).*
• SIZE *Total body length: 40 – 50 cm. Weight: 2.5 – 3 kg.*

## HISPID HARE *(Caprolagus hispidus)*

**LOCAL NAME:** *Khargorkata (Assamese).*
*A large grassland lagomorph of northeastern India, the Hispid Hare or Assam Rabbit is critically endangered. It has black hair mixed into its predominantly brown dorsal coat and has a rufous chest and white belly. It has shorter and more rounded ears, and smaller hind legs than the Indian Hare. It is a slow moving creature and its droppings are rounded, unlike the slightly tapered pellets of the Blacknaped Hare.*

*grizzled brown coat*

*small round ears*

• BEHAVIOUR *This hare has a characteristically smaller home range than other hares. Its pellets are normally seen near thatch cuttings.*
• HABITAT AND OCCURRENCE *Terai grassland and forests of the Himalayan foothills in Assam, West Bengal, and Uttar Pradesh.*
• SIZE *Total body length: 40– 50 cm. Weight: 2.2– 3 kg.*
• BEST SEEN AT *Manas NP (Assam).*

*long ears fringed black*

## CAPE HARE *(Lepus capensis)*

*The most common hare in the world, the Cape Hare varies in colour from sandy buff to rust-brown through its large geographical distribution that covers most of Africa and Central Asia. In India this medium-sized hare is grey overall, banded with buff and black. It has ears that are fringed black on the inside and a tail that is black. The slightly smaller Arabian Hare of Baluchistan that is also found in Jammu and Kashmir, is now thought to be a sub-species of the Cape Hare.*
HABITAT AND OCCURRENCE *Deserts and open rocky areas in J&K.*
SIZE *Total body length: 40– 50 cm. Weight: 1– 3.5 kg.*

# PIKAS

| | |
|---|---|
| FAMILY NAME Ochotonidae | |
| DIET ⬇ ✐ 🐾 ⬇ | |
| SOCIAL UNIT Family groups | |
| ACTIVITY ☼ ◑ | |
| CONSERVATION THREATS Poaching and habitat loss | |

Pikas or Mouse Hares are lagomorphs that inhabit the Himalaya. They are small (12.5 – 30 cm in length and 125 – 400 gm in weight), brownish-grey in colour, and guinea pig like in appearance. Their rounded ears and short legs give them the appearance of mice. However, they are tailless and their characteristic dentition places them in Order Lagomorph and not Rodentia. They also eat directly with their mouths and not with their hands – another characteristic of lagomorphs. Pikas live in family groups, either in burrows or under rock piles in rocky slopes or talus. Extremely inquisitive, they often sit beside their burrows or on rocks and are thus easily seen. India has seven pika species that can be told apart by careful examination of their fur colour (especially behind the ears), skull shape and size of ears. Their geographic distribution and their burrowing or non-burrowing habits are other ways of telling them apart.

LOCAL NAME: *Gumchipichi* (Bhotia), *Cumchen* (Lepcha).

## PLATEAU PIKA *(Ochotona curzoniae)*

*This small, sandy-brown pika with a distinct rust patch behind each ear, a black-tipped nose, and black lips, is also called the Black-lipped Pika. Its underparts are lighter in colour. A very social animal, it lives in a family unit in burrows. The Black-lipped Pika is highly vocal, especially while communicating with other pikas. It is currently facing an extermination programme in China where it proliferates and is believed to destroy grassland.*
• BEHAVIOUR *A family burrow usually consists of one male, one female, and offspring, but polyandry and polygyny are also known.*
• HABITAT AND OCCURRENCE *North Sikkim and Ladakh, 5,000 – 8,000 m.*

black nose and lip

rust patch behind ear

## FORREST'S PIKA *(Ochotona forresti)*

*This reddish-brown pika looks like the Moupin's Pika but has grey patches behind both ears that almost meet to form a grey nape, while the Moupin's has pale buff patches that do not meet. It has very long claws on its forefeet. The colour of its fur changes to grey-brown in winter.*
• HABITAT AND OCCURRENCE *Forested slopes in the Sikkim Himalaya, and Tushar Valley, Dhaphaboom in Arunachal Pradesh (2,600 – 4,400 m).*

## MOUPIN'S PIKA *(Ochotona thibetana)*

*The Moupin's Pika (below) is a small, rich russet-brown pika with buff underparts. Its fur is lightly speckled and the brown on the backside continues across the throat like a collar. In winters, its overall colour pales to buff-brown. On an average it weighs 80 – 85 g.*
• BEHAVIOUR *A burrowing species, it can be found in rocky areas under forested canopies.*
• HABITAT AND OCCURRENCE *Medium-altitude rhododendron and bamboo forests (1,800 – 4,100 m) of Sikkim.*

reddish-brown fur

### ROYLE'S PIKA *(Ochotona roylei)*

*The most common pika of the Himalaya, the Indian or Royle's Pika is a moderately large (17– 22.5 cm), richly coloured species. It has a rufous grey body, a chestnut head, shoulders, and upper back; reddish-purple throat and greyish-white to dark grey underparts. The reddish colouration fades in winter but the distinction between the upper and lower parts remains. It has moderately sized ears with sparse hair and its skull is only slightly arched.*
• BEHAVIOUR *It does not burrow, but moves underground through existing burrow systems in rocky and scree slopes. It constructs hay piles, hoards limited food for winter and is crepuscular.*
• HABITAT AND OCCURRENCE *Open rocky or broken ground, pine, deodar or rhododendron forests, and rock walls in human habitation: J&K to Kumaon (2,400– 4,300 m).*

chestnut brown
coat

### LARGE-EARED PIKA *(Ochotona macrotis)*

brownish-
grey coat

large ears

*This small pika is often confused with the more common Royle's Pika. It is pale brownish-grey with an ochre tinge. Its head and front are a paler russet compared to the Indian Pika's chestnut. Its ears are slightly broader, as its name suggests, and are made conspicuous by the long hairs inside them. The Large-eared Pika is found in higher altitudes than the Indian Pika almost throughout its range. Like the Indian Pika, it does not make burrows.*
• BEHAVIOUR: *This species has a weak vocalization that it normally uses when alarmed. It also uses whistles to communicate with others of its kind.*
• HABITAT AND OCCURRENCE *Alpine areas (2,500– 6,100 m) through the Himalaya: Ladakh to Arunachal Pradesh.*

### LADAKH PIKA *(Ochotona ladacensis)*

*A large, orangish, sandy-brown or grey pika with dirty white underparts, the Ladakh Pika has distinctive rust-coloured exteriors of ears.*
• BEHAVIOUR *It lives in scattered family groups, and digs large holes into which it retreats with a squeak when disturbed.*
• HABITAT AND OCCURRENCE *Ladakh (4,300– 5,450 m).*

sandy-brown
coat

### NUBRA PIKA *(Ochotona nubrica)*

*The Nubra Pika is the third species that has a distribution spanning the Himalayan range. In Sikkim its range could overlap with both the Black-lipped and the Moupin's Pikas. The Nubra Pika is pale sandy-brown with pale grey underparts and, on closer inspection, a buff midline is visible on its belly. Its feet are brownish-grey instead of the dull brown of the Moupin's Pika. This pika digs shallow burrows among root systems of bushes.*
• HABITAT AND OCCURRENCE *Sub-alpine and alpine shrubby areas in Ladakh, Sikkim, and Arunachal Pradesh.*

# MOLES

| | |
|---|---|
| FAMILY NAME | **Talpidae** |
| DIET | 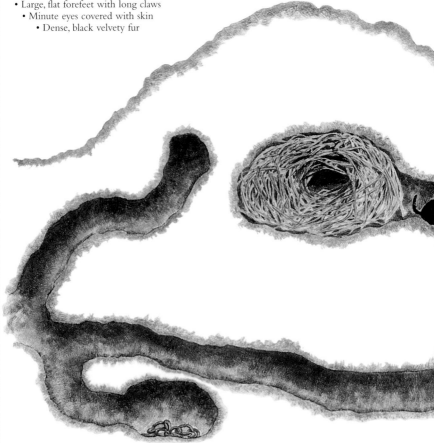 |
| SOCIAL UNIT | Solitary |
| ACTIVITY | ☾ ☼ |
| STRATUM | Fossorial |

MOLES, ALONG WITH hedgehogs (see p.122–23) and shrews (see p.118–21), belong to the Order Insectivora. All of them are small-built, ancient mammalian forms that hunt voraciously, aided chiefly by their sense of smell. They share the common characteristic of plantigrade locomotion (placing the entire palm or sole on the ground while walking) and have five digits on each foot. Moles are subterranean and rarely come above ground. Their bodies are therefore adapted to existence underground. They have extemely small or vestigial eyes, a streamlined shape, reversible hair, and powerful digging limbs. Moles have short life cycles, with the young gestating for only 35 days in the womb. Once they are born they attain adulthood in a mere 6−9 months and live to about three years of age.

### MOLE CHARACTERISTICS
- Cylindrical body
- Short neck • Short tail
- Large, flat forefeet with long claws
- Minute eyes covered with skin
- Dense, black velvety fur

## SHORT-TAILED MOLE
*(Euroscaptor micrura)*

**LOCAL NAME:** *Uk muk* (Assamese),
*Cheeka* (Bengali).

THE COMMON INDIAN *mole is also called the
Eastern or Himalayan Mole. However, the name
"Himalayan Mole" is a misnomer; it was once
thought to be found only in the hills but is, in fact, a
forest creature. This mole is covered with dense black,
velvety fur with the only exposed parts being its
pinkish nose-pad and large shovel-like forefeet. Its fur
is pliable and can lie in any direction, helping it to
scurry backwards and forwards in low burrows. The
glossy fur does not allow earth to stick to it. The tail is
short and wholly black.*
•**BEHAVIOUR** *Unlike European moles, this
species does not shovel earth out of its burrows and
thus does not leave telltale molehills on the surface
of the earth. It is territorial by nature.*
•**SIZE** *HBL: 10–16 cm.*
•**HABITAT AND OCCURRENCE** *Black vegetable
mould areas where the original forest cover has been
destroyed, in Central and Eastern Himalaya,
including Assam, Arunachal Pradesh, and Sikkim
(up to 2,040 m).*

## WHITE-TAILED MOLE
*(Parascaptor leucura)*

A RARE, LITTLE-KNOWN *mole, the White-tailed
Mole looks very much like the Short-tailed Mole
except for its tail, which is longer, narrower at the
base and widens slightly into a club shape towards
the tip. The tip is covered with white hair, thus
giving it the name "White-tailed Mole".*
•**BEHAVIOUR** *This forest species spends time
outside its burrow during the night, foraging on
the forest floor. It establishes territories of 100–
200 sq. m.*
•**SIZE** *HBL: 10 cm.*
•**HABITAT AND OCCURRENCE** *Hilly areas as
well as plains up to 2,500 m. Distributed through
Assam and Meghalaya, particularly Khasi and
Jaintia Hills.*

# SHREWS

SHREW CHARACTERISTICS
- Long snout
- Small eyes and inconspicuous ears, almost hidden in the fur
- Short five-toed limbs and plantigrade locomotion

Shrews (Soricidae) belong to Order Insectivora and are small, mouse-like mammals with long, pointed snouts, small eyes, and inconspicuous ears. The family Soricidae is divided into two sub-families: the red-toothed shrews (Soricinae) and the white-toothed shrews (Crocidurinae). Shrews, like moles and hedgehogs, are predatory, feeding mainly on small invertebrates. Sometimes, larger prey such as amphibians, reptiles, fish, and even small rodents are taken. Occasionally, shrews feed on small mammal carcasses and vegetable matter.

Shrews are mainly nocturnal, but their high metabolic rates can lead to a daily food intake of up to their body weight or more, so they show a polyphasic activity rhythm in constant search for food. Food-hoarding has been reported for several species. Shrews do not hibernate, but several species within the Crocidurinae exhibit short-term torpor. They do not actively burrow, but use the burrows of rodents, sometimes extending them. Their world is the sub-leaf stratum, logs, or crevices, where they build their nests. Some species are adapted to a semi-aquatic environment and forage under water.

A special feature exhibited by the white-toothed shrews is the "caravan". When the mother leads her young out of the nest, one or more of them latch onto her fur (or another sibling's), and the others do the same. The grip of the tiny shrews' teeth is so strong that it is possible to pick up a mother and her entire caravan off the ground. A shrew is not even remotely related to a rodent but is often mistaken for one and killed by humans when it enters houses. A shrew has a long pointed snout (compared to the short muzzle of mice) and depressed conch-shaped ears (compared to the perky triangular ears of mice). It also has characteristic front teeth that are adapted to break the cuticula of their arthropod prey. Territorial by nature, shrews tend to keep away rats and mice, sometimes even attacking them or raiding their nests.

# RED-TOOTHED SHREWS

| | |
|---|---|
| FAMILY NAME | Soricidae |
| DIET | 🌿 🐛 |
| SOCIAL UNIT | Solitary |
| ACTIVITY | ☾ (polyphasic) |
| STRATUM | Semi-fossorial, semi-aquatic, terrestrial |
| CONSERVATION THREATS | Habitat loss |

The red-toothed shrews belong to the sub-family Soricinae and in India include the genera *Sorex*, *Soriculus*, *Nectogale*, *Chimarrogale*, and *Anourosorex*. They all have a reddish pigmentation in their teeth, caused by iron deposits in the enamel, and are thus set apart from the white-toothed Crociduriane.

## TIBETAN SHREW
### (Sorex thibetanus)

THIS IS A MEDIUM-SIZED *shrew that is grey-brown all over, including the ventral side. It has a long and well-furred tail. The Tibetan Shrew is much smaller than the white-toothed shrew species (see p.120–21) that share the same distribution. A similar shrew found in Kashmir has been named the Kashmir Shrew (*Sorex planiceps*) by some taxonomists. However, many biologists consider it to be a sub-species of the Tibetan Shrew.*
• SIZE *HBL: 5.7–7.4 cm; tail: 3.7–4.8 cm.*
• HABITAT AND OCCURRENCE *High mountainous regions in J&K.*

## HIMALAYAN WATER SHREW
### (Chimarrogale himalayica)

*The Himalayan Water Shrew is a large bluish-grey water shrew with small eyes and reduced ears, which are closed by a flap when diving. It has dense, waterproof fur, darker at the back and with silvery guard hair towards the rump. To aid swimming, it has long white bristles on its feet. The whiskers on the nose have a swollen base. It has a long black tail with white hair fringes.*
• BEHAVIOUR *This shrew swims well under water and has a diet of insects, crustaceans, and small fish. It is active by night and day.*
• SIZE *HBL: 8–13 cm; tail: 8–10 cm.*
• HABITAT AND OCCURRENCE *Mountain streams up to 3,300 m in the Himalaya, from J&K to Sikkim and North Bengal.*

| SIMILAR SPECIES | | | |
|---|---|---|---|
| COMMON NAME | LATIN NAME | OCCURRENCE | IDENTIFICATION TIPS |
| TINY SHREW | *Sorex minutus* | J&K | Clearly bi-coloured and thus easy to recognize; dark grey-brown above and dull grey below. HBL: 4.6–7.4 cm; tail: 3.7–5.2 cm. |
| ARBOREAL BROWN-TOOTHED SHREW | *Soriculus macrurus* | Wet bamboo and scrub forests of Sikkim and northern Bengal | Large grey shrew (HBL: 4.7–6.8 cm) with a tail around the same size (7.7–10.3 cm). |
| INDIAN LONG-TAILED SHREW | *Soriculus leucops* | Northeastern Himalaya, Sikkim, and Manipur | Small, dark brown common shrew. Tail (9–10.5 cm) much longer than body. HBL (5.5–7.1 cm). |
| SIKKIM LARGE-CLAWED SHREW | *Soriculus nigrescens* | Sikkim | Large brown shrew (7–9.4 cm) with a short tail (3.4–4.8 cm). Has large feet and claws. |
| HODGSON'S BROWN-TOOTHED SHREW | *Soriculus caudatus* | Coniferous forests in J&K, northern Bengal, Sikkim, and Manipur (1,800–3,600 m) | Small, grey-brown common shrew. HBL: 4.7–7.4 cm; tail: 4.5–6.9 cm. |
| MOLE SHREW | *Anourosorex squamipes* | Northeast India | Different from all the above species; large shrew with truncated tail, minute ears and eyes. Has velvety, olive-grey fur and short, broad, naked feet. HBL: 8–11 cm; tail: 0.8–1.5 cm. |
| TIBETAN WATER SHREW | *Nectogale elegans* | Mountain streams of Sikkim, northern Bengal, NE Himalaya (900–2,300 m) | Slate-grey back with silver underparts, more brown in Sikkim. Unique tail with four fringes and a long tuft of white hair, that helps it to swim. HBL: 9.9–12.5 cm; tail: 9.6–12.3 cm. |

# WHITE-TOOTHED SHREWS

| | |
|---|---|
| FAMILY NAME | Soricidae |
| DIET | ✳ ⌇ |
| SOCIAL UNIT | Solitary |
| ACTIVITY | ☾ (polyphasic) |
| STRATUM | Terrestrial, semi-fossorial |
| CONSERVATION THREATS | Habitat loss |

THE CROCIDURANAE OR White-toothed Shrews are distinguished from *Soriculus* and water shrews by their white or unpigmented teeth; long, randomly scattered hair on long slim tails and prominent ears. In India, the group comprises three genera: *Crocidura, Feroculus,* and *Suncus.* Shrews of the genus *Suncus* have four upper unicuspid teeth compared to the three of *Crocidura.*

### HOUSE SHREW *(Suncus murinus)*
LOCAL NAME: *Chuchundar* (Hindi).
THE COMMON SHREW *of India, it is also called the Grey Musk Shrew because of the characteristic odour that it leaves about the house. It is greyish-brown, has a short, thick tail with a few bristles and large, pink ears. It varies in size and colour throughout India: the southern form is smaller, the western arid form is paler, and the Himalayan and Northeast form is smaller and darker.*
• BEHAVIOUR *This shrew is very aggressive, vocal, and odorous, and keeps away insects from the home. Active just after dusk, it has acute hearing but poor eyesight.*
• SIZE *HBL: 10−16 cm; tail: 4.5−9 cm.*
• HABITAT AND OCCURRENCE *Throughout India. It burrows near homes, and lives in and around sewers.*

| SIMILAR SPECIES | | | |
|---|---|---|---|
| COMMON NAME | LATIN NAME | OCCURRENCE | IDENTIFICATION TIPS |
| ANDERSON'S YELLOW-THROATED SHREW | *Suncus stoliczkanus* | Rajasthan, south to Madras | Silvery grey dorsal fur, paler venter, yellowish fur on throat that is not always evident. HBL:6–8 cm. |

## PYGMY SHREW *(Suncus etruscus)*

This is one of the smallest terrestrial mammals in the world, weighing a little over two grams. It has a velvety dark greyish-brown coat dorsally, with silvery-brown below, very short hind limbs compared to its forelimbs, conspicuous pink ears, and a long tail.
• SIZE *HBL: 3 cm − 5.5 cm; tail: 2.5−3.5 cm.*
• HABITAT AND OCCURRENCE *Throughout India, except arid regions of Gujarat and Rajasthan, and J&K.*

small size

pink ears

### HILL SHREW *(Suncus montanus)*
*A dark brown, almost black species, considerably smaller than the House Shrew.*
• SIZE *HBL: 8−10.5 cm; tail: 4.5−6.5 cm.*
• HABITAT AND OCCURRENCE *Humid forests of South Indian hills, mainly Nilgiri and Palni hills.*
• BEST SEEN AT *Eravikulam NP (Kerala).*

| SIMILAR SPECIES | | | |
|---|---|---|---|
| COMMON NAME | LATIN NAME | OCCURRENCE | IDENTIFICATION TIPS |
| DAY'S SHREW | *Suncus dayii* | Palni, Anamalai and Nilgiri hills, Tamil Nadu and Kerala | Does not have the bristles on its tail that other family members have. Small (7cm) and brownish, with tail as big as body. |

# WHITE-TOOTHED SHREWS

SHREWS OF THE genera *Crocidura* and *Feroculus* differ from *Suncus* shrews in their longer, slimmer tails and three upper unicuspids, the presence of which can only be seen in hand. These shrews have musk glands on either flank and release a putrid odour that keeps mammalian predators away. Owls are the only predators that feed on these shrews. Other than the Grey Woodland Shrew, all shrews of genus *Crocidura* are restricted-range species (see box below).

## GREY WOODLAND SHREW
*(Crocidura attenuata )*

A MEDIUM-SIZED *shrew with a greyish-brown back and pale yellowish-grey underside, the Grey Woodland Shrew is the most widely distributed white-toothed shrew in India. It has a dark brown tail, which is paler below, and its feet have short pale hairs on the back.*
• SIZE *HBL 6.8 – 8.9 cm; tail: 4.3 – 6 cm.*
• HABITAT AND OCCURRENCE *Fields, secondary forests, farmland and open land of the Himalayan foothills of North and Northeast India: Himachal Pradesh, Punjab, Uttar Pradesh, Uttaranchal, Assam, West Bengal, and Arunachal Pradesh.*

## KELAART'S LONG-CLAWED SHREW
*(Feroculus feroculus)*

AN ASHY-BLACK *shrew with paler underparts, the Kelaart's Long-Clawed Shrew was thought to be endemic to Sri Lanka before its discovery in southern India. It has characteristic large, whitish forefeet with long claws. The smaller hind feet are also pale. Its tail is grey with some whitish hairs near the tip.*
• SIZE *HBL: 10 – 12 cm; tail: 5.6 – 7.3 cm.*
• HABITAT AND OCCURRENCE *Montane swamps and marshes of southern India, especially Palni and Nilgiri hills.*
• BEST SEEN AT *Eravikulam NP (Kerala).*

## SIMILAR SPECIES

| COMMON NAME | LATIN NAME | OCCURRENCE | IDENTIFICATION TIPS |
|---|---|---|---|
| KASHMIR WHITE-TOOTHED SHREW | *Crocidura pullata* | J&K | Uniformly mousy grey-brown with longish fur. HBL: 8.3 cm; tail: 4.4 cm. |
| PALE GREY SHREW | *Crocidura pergrisea* | J&K | Pale grey on top and creamy grey undersides. HBL: 5.6 cm; tail: 4.5 cm. |
| GUELDENSTAEDT'S WHITE-TOOTHED SHREW | *Crocidura gueldenstaedtii* | J&K | Brown-grey on top and lighter below, with a shorter tail. HBL: 10.7–12 cm; tail: 9–9.5 cm. |
| NICOBAR SPINY SHREW | *Crocidura nicobarica* | Great Nicobar Islands | Sooty brown, bristly dorsal fur. HBL: 10.7–12 cm; tail: 9–9.5 cm. |
| JENKIN'S ANDAMAN SPINY SHREW | *Crocidura jenkinsii* | South Andaman Islands | Brown bristly fur. HBL: 10.7 cm; tail: 9.5 cm. |
| ANDAMAN SPINY SHREW | *Crocidura hispida* | Middle Andaman Islands | Greyish-brown bristly fur with a tail longer than head and body. HBL: 8.5 cm; tail: 10.3 cm. |
| MILLER'S ANDAMAN SPINY SHREW | *Crocidura andamanensis* | South Andaman Islands | Dorsal pelage bluish-grey washed with brown, ventral lighter brown, yellowish brown feet, dark brown tail and ears. HBL: 11.4 cm; tail: 8 cm. |
| HORSFIELDS SHREW | *Crocidura horsfieldi* | J&K, montane forests of southern India | Greyish-brown v/s neutral grey above with brown basal hairs and dark grey below tail with silver hair on top. HBL: 5.7 cm; tail: 3–4.8 cm. |
| SOUTHEAST ASIAN WHITE-TOOTHED SHREW | *Crocidura fulginosa* | Northeast India | Dark grey with lighter underparts; silver gloss on top. HBL: 7–10 cm; tail: 6.2–8.9 cm. |

# HEDGEHOGS

Though they are insectivores, hedgehogs differ from other members of their Order such as moles (see p.116) and shrews (see p.118-21). They have large external ears, quadrate low-cusped teeth, spines covering their back, and a different skeletal structure. Ecologically they are both fossorial (burrow dwelling) and terrestrial, while shrews are terrestrial and moles are fossorial. They hunt by using their sense of smell. The hedgehog seizes its prey with its teeth, half curled into a ball, with its spines erect. When the prey tries to strike back it gets impaled further on the spines. If disturbed, the hedgehog moves away rapidly, but if cornered it hisses and arches its back while erecting its spines. The defensive ability of a hedgehog to "curl up" is caused by thick muscles attached to loose skin. The hedgehog's spines are small and do not shed like those of the porcupine.

### HEDGEHOG CHARACTERISTICS
- Small, round body
- Long tubular snout
- Back covered by short, stiff spines
- Short stumpy tail
- Visible, bat-like ears
- Five digits, plantigrade locomotion

| | |
|---|---|
| FAMILY NAME | Erinaceidae |
| LATIN NAME | *Hemiechinus collaris* |
| IUCN STATUS/WPA | Lower risk/IV |
| LOCAL STATUS | Locally common |
| POPULATION | Unknown |
| DIET | 🐜 🦗 🐛 ● |
| SOCIAL UNIT | Solitary |
| ACTIVITY | ☾ |
| STRATUM | Terrestrial, fossorial |

Rajasthan, Gujarat (Kutch), up to Agra in UP. Isolated population around Pune (up to 1,000 m).

## COLLARED HEDGEHOG
LOCAL NAME: *Sharo* (Gujarati).

A SMALL DARK HEDGEHOG with long legs and ears, this species is also known as the Desert, Hardwick's, or Long-eared Hedgehog. Its belly and tail are black, and its legs have sharp, visible claws. It lives in a burrow that it also uses to aestivate during very hot summers or hibernate during very cold winters.
- BEHAVIOUR Males are known to eat other male hedgehogs and females sometimes cannibalize their young.
- SIZE *HBL*: Total body length: 14 – 18 cm. Weight: 400 – 500 g.
- HABITAT Arid plains and desert.
- BEST SEEN AT Desert NP (Rajasthan).
- CONSERVATION THREATS Habitat loss and poaching.

black spines

dark brown or black face

| | |
|---|---|
| FAMILY NAME | Erinaceidae |
| LATIN NAME | Hemiechinus micropus |
| IUCN STATUS / WPA | Lower risk /IV |
| LOCAL STATUS | Uncommon |
| POPULATION | Unknown |
| DIET | 🌾 🐛 🐀 ● 🐍 ↖ |
| SOCIAL UNIT | Solitary |
| ACTIVITY | ☾ |
| STRATUM | Terrestrial |

# INDIAN HEDGEHOG

LOCAL NAME: *Sharo* (Gujarati), *Kooram* (Kannada).

ALSO CALLED THE PALE HEDGEHOG, this species has a masked face because of greyish-white hairs on its forehead and cheeks (see picture on opposite page), and a neat parting of its spines along the top of its forehead. Its fur is pale rufous and it has smaller ears, limbs, and claws, making it more compact than the Collared Hedgehog.
• BEHAVIOUR This hedgehog is less inclined to burrow as compared to the Collared Hedgehog, probably because it does not aestivate. It can often be found curled up under a *Ziziphus* bush, the fruit of which it also eats. However, if food or water is scarce, it curls up in a burrow in a torpor for several days.
• SIZE *HBL*: Total body length: 14–23 cm. Weight: 300–450 gm.
• HABITAT Rocky areas and grassland.
• BEST SEEN AT Sariska NP (Rajasthan).
• CONSERVATION THREATS Habitat loss and poaching.

cream-tipped spines

central parting

red-brown face

short claws

Gujarat (Kutch), Rajasthan, Andhra Pradesh, Karnataka, Tamil Nadu, and Kerala.

| | |
|---|---|
| FAMILY NAME | Erinaceidae |
| LATIN NAME | Hemiechinus nudiventris |
| IUCN STATUS / WPA | Vulnerable /IV |
| LOCAL STATUS | Uncommon |
| POPULATION | Unknown |
| DIET | 🌾 🐛 🐀 ● 🐍 ↖ |
| SOCIAL UNIT | Solitary |
| ACTIVITY | ☾ |
| STRATUM | Terrestrial |

# MADRAS HEDGEHOG

LOCAL NAME: *Mulleli* (Malayalam).

PREVIOUSLY CONSIDERED to be a sub-species of the Indian Hedgehog, the Madras Hedgehog was recently described as a separate species. Little research has been done on it. This hedgehog is more reddish in appearance than the Indian Hedgehog.
• SIZE *HBL*: 14–23 cm. Weight: 250–400 gm.
• HABITAT Rocky hills.
• BEST SEEN AT Nowhere common.
• CONSERVATION THREATS Habitat loss and poaching.

Tamil Nadu and Kerala.

rufous spines

# PORCUPINES

PORCUPINES ARE THE LARGEST rodents of the subcontinent and among the largest in the world. Their dorsal hair is modified into thick, stiff spines or quills. These are usually banded black and white or deep brown and white and are easily shed if damaged or during a struggle. Quills are found commonly shed on forest floors throughout India and along with the cigar-like droppings, give away the presence of the animal. Porcupines need calcium to grow quills, so they eat bones and shed antlers from the forest floor.

**PORCUPINE CHARACTERISTICS**
- Blunt, wedge-shaped head
- Thickset, stumpy body
- Upper body and tail covered with armour of quills
- Short tail
- Powerful feet with large claws
- Strong, large incisors

| | |
|---|---|
| FAMILY NAME | Hystricidae |
| LATIN NAME | *Hystrix indica* |
| IUCN STATUS/WPA | Lower risk/IV |
| LOCAL STATUS | Locally common |
| POPULATION | Unknown |
| DIET | 🍃🐛🦴 |
| SOCIAL UNIT | Solitary/groups of 2–4 |
| ACTIVITY | ☾ |
| STRATUM | Fossorial, terrestrial |

## INDIAN PORCUPINE

LOCAL NAME: *Sayal, Sahi* (Hindi), *Sheval* (Marathi), *Yedu pandi* (Telegu), *Mullan panni* (Malayalam/Tamil), *Shojaru* (Bengali), *Khar-pusht* (Kashmiri), *Mullu handi* (Kannada), *Jhinka* (Oriya).

THE MOST COMMON AND LARGEST porcupine of India, this thickset rodent is covered with long black and white quills with a long crest of spines flowing from the forehead to the middle of the back. Its tail ends in a bunch of thick white quills. In southern India (around the common border of Karnataka, Tamil Nadu, and Kerala) a sub-species often referred to as the "Red Porcupine" (see below) has quills with a rusty tinge on its back. The Indian Porcupine is known to destroy crops near forest margins and eat up the bark of trees at ground level.

• **BEHAVIOUR** When the porcupine senses danger it erects the quills on its back and rattles its tail quills menacingly. If the danger persists, it rushes backwards into its attacker, leaving its quills embedded in the victim's flesh. In the case of leopards and tigers this can lead to serious wounds. Porcupines do not shoot quills at animals, despite common belief.

• **SIZE** *HBL*: 60–90 cm. Weight: 11–18 kg.

• **HABITAT AND OCCURRENCE** Rocky hillsides, open countryside, and deciduous forests throughout India. Inhabits burrows, thick bush, and tall grass.

• **BEST SEEN AT** Sariska NP (Rajasthan), Bandipur and Nagarahole NPs (Karnataka).

• **CONSERVATION THREATS** Poaching.

*multi-banded black-and-white quills*

*long crest on head*

*pointed muzzle*

*off-white collar*

| FAMILY NAME | Hystricidae |
|---|---|
| LATIN NAME | *Atherurus macrourus* |
| IUCN STATUS/WPA | Endangered/II |
| LOCAL STATUS | Rare |
| POPULATION | Unknown |
| DIET | 🍃🐚🦴 |
| SOCIAL UNIT | Groups of 6–8 |
| ACTIVITY | ☽ |
| STRATUM | Fossorial, terrestrial |

# ASIATIC BRUSH-TAILED PORCUPINE

LOCAL NAME: *Ketela pohu* (Assamese), *Shojaru* (Bengali).

THIS SPECIES IS THE SMALLEST and most endangered of the three Indian porcupines. It lacks the characteristic long quills of the others. Its quills are short and spiny like those of a hedgehog. The first third of its long scaly tail is spineless and the rest is covered in a swatch of quills. Each tail quill has a rice-grain sized round enlargement at the tip. Little research has been carried out on this rare species that is not easily spotted in the wild. Interestingly, the Asiatic Brush-tailed Porcupine has a distribution in West Africa and in peninsular South Asia—perhaps indicative of a time when the two continents were connected by an unbroken stretch of forests.
- **SIZE** *HBL:* 36.5–57 cm.
Weight: 1.5 – 4kg.
- **HABITAT AND OCCURRENCE** Evergreen forests, especially hilly areas of Northeast India.
- **CONSERVATION THREATS** Habitat loss.

| FAMILY NAME | Hystricidae |
|---|---|
| LATIN NAME | *Hystrix brachyura* |
| IUCN STATUS / WPA | Vulnerable / II |
| LOCAL STATUS | Locally common |
| POPULATION | Unknown, declining |
| DIET | 🍃🐚🦴 |
| SOCIAL UNIT | Solitary/groups of 2–4 |
| ACTIVITY | ☽ |
| STRATUM | Fossorial, terrestrial |

# HIMALAYAN CRESTLESS PORCUPINE

LOCAL NAME: *Ketela pohu* (Assamese), *Sakhu* (Mizo), *Suku* (Naga).

A LARGE, STOCKY RODENT with a short tail and a very short or rudimentary dorsal crest, the Crestless Porcupine is also called the Hodgson's Porcupine. This is the common porcupine of Northeast India. Like others of its kind, this species craves calcium and seeks out antlers of deer and bones to gnaw at. It can be distinguished from the Indian Porcupine by its shorter dorsal crest (15 cm instead of up to 30 cm); small tail instead of a visible tail with white quills; thinner quills on the body and smaller size. On comparing the long dorsal quills at close range, it is seen that the Indian Porcupine's quills have more than two dark bands on it while the Crestless Porcupine's quills have only one.
- **SIZE** *HBL:* 45–75 cm. Weight: 8 kg.
- **HABITAT AND OCCURRENCE** Forests and grasslands of eastern Himalaya, especially in and around cultivated land.
- **BEST SEEN AT** Orang NP (Assam).
- **CONSERVATION THREATS** Habitat loss and poaching.

thin quills
with single
black band

small size

short crest
on head

blunt
muzzle

# SQUIRRELS

| INDIAN SQUIRRELS AT A GLANCE | |
|---|---|
| NUMBER OF SPECIES | 27 |
| LARGEST | Indian Giant Squirrel |
| SMALLEST | Himalayan Striped Squirrel |
| MOST COMMON | Three- and Five-striped Palm Squirrels |
| MOST ENDANGERED | Layard's Striped Squirrel |

## SQUIRREL CHARACTERISTICS
- Thick, bushy tail
- Short muzzle
- Large incisors
- Arboreal lifestyle

A squirrel is a medium- to large-sized rodent with a long, bushy tail. There are several variations in form, behaviour, and appearance within this large family of rodents. Currently, taxonomists divide the family into two sub-families: Sciurinae and Petauristinae. Within Sciurinae, the Ratufini tribe comprises giant squirrels that live in the tropical forests of southern and eastern India. The Funambulini tribe comprises the striped squirrels. The Callosciurini tribe contains all the non-striped diurnal squirrels, including the northeastern species such as the Pallas's, the Hoary-bellied, and the Orange-bellied squirrels. The squirrels in the Petauristinae sub-family are nocturnal and include the flying squirrels. In reality, these do not fly but merely glide with the aid of flaps of skin that connect their limbs. The two ground-dwelling marmots are also considered to be members of the Sciuridae family. Squirrels build nests or dreys in tree branches or occupy tree holes.

LIFE AMONG TREES
*The highly arboreal* **Giant Squirrel** *stretches and makes spectacular leaps among tree branches while foraging for food.*

ENDEARING RODENTS
**Striped Squirrels** *are often found in pairs and make a pretty sight grooming each other on branches of trees.*

# GIANT SQUIRRELS

| | |
|---|---|
| **AMILY NAME** | Sciuridae |
| **IET** 🐿 🌿 🐛 | |
| **OCIAL UNIT** | Solitary |
| **CTIVITY** ☼ | |
| **TRATUM** | Arboreal |
| **ONSERVATION THREATS** | Habitat loss, oaching |

There are four species of giant squirrels (the largest squirrels in the world) in S and SE Asia, of which three are found in India. These forest canopy-dwellers rarely come down to the forest floor. They build multiple globe-shaped nests and use some for sleeping and at least one as a nursery. They make shrill sounds and their high-pitched alarm calls rival those of monkeys.

## MALAYAN GIANT SQUIRREL *(Ratufa bicolor)*
**LOCAL NAME:** *Ram kota (Bengali).*

A BLACK AND BUFF *eastern Indian forest squirrel, the Malayan or Black Giant Squirrel is deep brown or black on the back and buff beneath. It has*

*black back and ears*

*large black ears with hairy tufts, a black tail, and black marks on its chin. The forelegs are black in front and buff on the back.*
• **HABITAT AND OCCURRENCE** *Montane moist deciduous, semi-evergreen and evergreen forests in Sikkim, North Bengal, and Northeast India.*
• **SIZE** *HBL: 35–58 cm; tail: 60 cm.*
• **BEST SEEN AT** *Kaziranga NP (Assam).*

## INDIAN GIANT SQUIRREL *(Ratufa indica)*
**LOCAL NAME:** *Karat, Rasu (Hindi), Shekra (Marathi), Anil (Tamil), Malayannan (Malayalam), Keshalilu (Kannada).*
ALSO CALLED THE *Malabar Giant Squirrel, this is an endemic squirrel of varying bright pelages. The back is a mixture of maroon and black and the underparts are cream or buff. In the northern Western Ghats this squirrel is brownish-maroon in appearance, with an all-brown or brown and white tail. In the south it is black and dark maroon with a black and brown tail. Central and southeastern Indian forms are brown on the back with black on the forelegs, and have a black tail with a pale tip.*

• **BEHAVIOUR** *It often sleeps draped over a branch, with its tail falling over.*
• **HABITAT AND OCCURRENCE** *Mixed deciduous and evergreen forests south of 22°N.*
• **BEST SEEN AT** *Periyar NP (Kerala).*
• **SIZE** *HBL: 35–51 cm; tail: 60 cm.*

*maroon back and ears*

## GRIZZLED GIANT SQUIRREL *(Ratufa macroura)*

THIS ENDANGERED *squirrel is comparatively smaller and brownish-grey in colour, with pale hair tips giving it a grizzled look. Its underside is dirty white, while its tail has white bands. Both its ears and head are dark brown or black.*
• **HABITAT AND OCCURRENCE** *Riverine forests, with a highly restricted range of ten locations in the eastern slopes of the Western Ghats.*
• **BEST SEEN AT** *Chinnar WLS (Kerala).*
• **SIZE** *HBL: 28–41 cm; tail: 30–40 cm.*

# STRIPED SQUIRRELS

| | |
|---|---|
| **FAMILY NAME** | Sciuridae |
| **DIET** | 🐛🥬🌾🍂🌰 |
| **SOCIAL UNIT** | Solitary/pairs |
| **ACTIVITY** | ☼ |
| **STRATUM** | Arboreal, terrestrial |
| **CONSERVATION THREATS** | Habitat loss, poaching |

There are six striped squirrels in India, two of which are common in cities while the other four are rarer forest forms of the Western Ghats and eastern Himalaya.

**LOCAL NAME:** *Gileheri (Hindi), Kath beral (Bengali), Khadi khar (Marathi) Annarakannan (Malayalam), Anna pilli (Tamil).*

three pale stripes on back

bottle-brush tail

### THREE-STRIPED PALM SQUIRREL
### (Funambulus palmarum)

A SMALL, COMMON SQUIRREL *of peninsular India, the Three-striped or Indian Palm Squirrel is greyish-brown or olive-brown with pale underparts. It has three pale parallel lines on its back from head to tail. Its legs are short, and its bushy, black-and-white peppered tail has a bold, reddish-brown mid-ventral line running through it.*
• **BEHAVIOUR** *This squirrel builds conspicuous dreys in tree branches.*
• **HABITAT AND OCCURRENCE** *Urban and rural areas of southern Madhya Pradesh, Bihar, Andhra Pradesh, Orissa, Karnataka, Tamil Nadu, and Kerala.*
• **SIZE** *HBL: 12–15 cm; tail: 14–16 cm.*
• **BEST SEEN AT** *Southern Indian towns and cities.*

### FIVE-STRIPED PALM SQUIRREL
### (Funambulus pennantii)

AN UBIQUITOUS SQUIRREL *of North India, the Five-striped or Northern Squirrel is almost a replica of its South Indian cousin except that it has five pale stripes (instead of three) on its greyish-brown or olive-brown body. The tail does not have a mid-ventral line.*
• **BEHAVIOUR** *Bold and inquisitive, it has shrill, bird-like calls that it repeats up to 10 times, accompanied by frenzied tail jerks.*
• **HABITAT AND OCCURRENCE** *Urban, rural, and forested areas all over northern India (south to Dharwar, east to Meghalaya).*
• **SIZE** *HBL: 13–16 cm; tail: 14–16 cm.*
• **BEST SEEN AT** *Northern Indian towns and cities.*

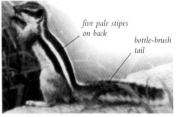

five pale stripes on back

bottle-brush tail

DUSKY STRIPED SQUIRREL
*A rare forest squirrel of the Western Ghats.*

| SIMILAR SPECIES | | | |
|---|---|---|---|
| **COMMON NAME** | **LATIN NAME** | **OCCURRENCE** | **IDENTIFICATION TIPS** |
| JUNGLE STRIPED SQUIRREL | Funambulus tristriatus | Western Ghats, north to Mumbai | Indistinguishable from Three-striped Squirrel except for jungle distribution. |
| LAYARD'S STRIPED SQUIRREL | Funambulus layardi | Kerala, southern Kodagu | Rufous head, cheeks, and underparts. Three stripes on back, mid-stripe is orange. |
| DUSKY STRIPED SQUIRREL | Funambulus sublineatus | Western Ghats south of Kodagu | Obscure or pale stripes on back, drab underparts. No stripe on tail. |
| HIMALAYAN STRIPED SQUIRREL | Tamiops macclellandi | North Bengal, Sikkim, and Northeast | Smaller, greyish-brown back with four black brown and buff stripes. |

# NORTHEASTERN FOREST SQUIRRELS

| | |
|---|---|
| FAMILY NAME | Sciuridae |
| DIET | 🐾 🍃 |
| SOCIAL UNIT | Solitary |
| ACTIVITY | ☼ |
| STRATUM | Arboreal, terrestrial |
| CONSERVATION THREATS | Poaching, habitat loss |

The six unstriped forest squirrels of Northeast India range from common Oriental Tree squirrels such as the Hoary-bellied Squirrel to the rarer Red-cheeked squirrels.

**LOCAL NAME:** *Kerketua (Assamese), Kath beral, Kotha (Bengali).*

## ORANGE-BELLIED HIMALAYAN SQUIRREL
*(Dremomys lokriah)*

THIS MEDIUM-SIZED *forest squirrel has a bright orange throat, chest, and belly. The hairs of the dorsal coat are brown at the base, yellow in the middle, and black at the tip. A shy yet common species, it has a chunky body, short limbs, small ears, and a pointed snout.*
* **HABITAT AND OCCURRENCE** *Forested hills and foothills (1,500 – 2,700 m) in Sikkim and NE India.*
* **SIZE** *HBL: 20 cm; tail: 22 cm.*

*reddish-brown upperparts*

*orange underparts*

## HOARY-BELLIED HIMALAYAN SQUIRREL
*(Callosciurus pygerythrus)*

A SMALL, BROWN AND BLACK *squirrel, the Hoary-bellied Squirrel has a pale grey or white belly and a rufous tinge at the base of its limbs. It is smaller than the Pallas's Squirrel and its muzzle is blunter than the Orange-bellied Squirrel's. Its dorsal hairs have two light rings of yellow, giving it a hoary or grizzled look. In summers and the wet season, there is a pale buff patch on the hips that fades when the winter coat appears. It has a long tail without a dark tip.*
* **HABITAT AND OCCURRENCE** *Riverine and mixed forests, and near villages in Sikkim, N Bengal and NE India (200–2,000 m).*
* **SIZE** *HBL: 18–23 cm; tail: 17–19 cm.*

*pale tip*

*drab underparts*

## PALLAS'S SQUIRREL *(Callosciurus erythraeus)*

*dark tail*

*reddish underside*

A MEDIUM-SIZED, OLIVE-BROWN *or black and buff grizzled squirrel, the Pallas's Squirrel has reddish or orange-brown undersides that may turn almost black in certain races found in Assam, and may be speckled in Sikkim. In most races the paws are coloured agouti on the dorsal side. The long tail, similar in colour to the upper coat, may have a reddish, black, or pale tip.*
* **HABITAT AND OCCURRENCE** *Mixed moist deciduous and temperate forests in Sikkim and NE India (500–2,000 m). Not found near human habitation.*
* **SIZE** *HBL: 20–26 cm; tail: 18–22 cm.*

| SIMILAR SPECIES | | | |
|---|---|---|---|
| COMMON NAME | LATIN NAME | OCCURRENCE | IDENTIFICATION TIPS |
| PERNY'S LONG-NOSED SQUIRREL | *Dremomys pernyi* | Assam, Manipur | Similar to Orange-bellied Himalayan Squirrel, with longer snout. |
| ASIAN RED-CHEEKED SQUIRREL | *Dremomys rufigenis* | Assam | Similar to Orange-bellied Himalayan Squirrel, with red cheeks. |

# LARGE FLYING SQUIRRELS

| | |
|---|---|
| FAMILY NAME | Sciuridae |
| DIET | 🐿 🌿 🍂 |
| SOCIAL UNIT | Solitary |
| ACTIVITY | ☾ |
| STRATUM | Arboreal, aerial |
| CONSERVATION THREATS | Habitat loss |

FLYING SQUIRRELS do not actually fly but are master gliders that launch themselves from high branches and glide down (see opposite page), aided by elastic membranes, to lower branches. Large flying squirrels can be distinguished from all other flying squirrels by the presence of an additional flap of skin that connects the heel and tail.

— large black eyes

### RED GIANT FLYING SQUIRREL
### (*Petaurista petaurista*)

THIS DARK RED *species is also called the Indian Flying Squirrel. Its elastic skin, which it uses to glide, is attached from wrist to ankle. It has large black-ringed, liquid brown eyes. The long slender tail is furred but not bushy and is carried curved on the back, a posture commonly adopted by most squirrels. It has a rounded head and flesh-coloured nostrils. Its belly is buff and its feet are black and furred although the soles are naked.*

• BEHAVIOUR *This squirrel runs up to the top-most branches of a tree before launching into a glide that can easily extend up to 100 m. While passing overhead it makes a noise like rushing wind. It has a monotonous call, which sounds like someone exhaling sharply. At dusk this can be heard repeated over 30–40 times.*

• HABITAT AND OCCURRENCE *Restricted to forests only, this squirrel is not found near human habitation. It inhabits the Himalayan foothills from J&K to Assam, and Manipur.*

• SIZE *HBL: 32–49 cm; tail: 38–44 cm.*

LONE RANGER
*The Namdapha Flying Squirrel is a rare, white-ventered flying squirrel of NE India.*

| SIMILAR SPECIES | | | |
|---|---|---|---|
| COMMON NAME | LATIN NAME | OCCURRENCE | IDENTIFICATION TIPS |
| | | Hills of Sikkim and Darjeeling, West Bengal | |
| GRAY'S GIANT FLYING SQUIRREL | *Petaurista nobilis* | Hills of Sikkim and Darjeeling, West Bengal | Larger and darker than Hodgson's; light shoulder patch up to sides; dark saddle patch on back; underparts salmon pink. Could have yellow line on back. |
| GREY-HEADED (SPOTTED) GIANT FLYING SQUIRREL | *Petaurista elegans* | Assam, Sikkim, and Darjeeling, West Bengal | Has a distinct grey head. Smaller than other *Petauristas*. |

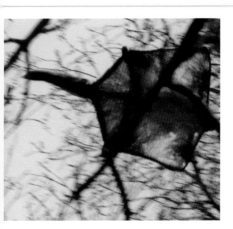

## INDIAN GIANT FLYING SQUIRREL
*(Petaurista philippensis)*

THIS IS THE COMMON *large flying squirrel found over most of peninsular India – all other flying squirrels are restricted to the Himalaya and the Northeast and one is restricted to the Western Ghats. The Indian Giant Flying Squirrel is a drabber cousin of the Red Giant Flying Squirrel. Its coat varies from coffee-brown to a predominantly grey colour. It has pale grey undersides and a speckled back. Its head is the same colour as the rest of its body and its ears have reddish-brown margins. The tail is uniformly brown-grey with the tip being noticeably darker in some individuals.*
• HABITAT AND OCCURRENCE *Deciduous, semi-evergreen, and evergreen forests of Goa, Maharashtra, parts of Rajasthan, Madhya Pradesh, Andhra Pradesh, Orissa, West Bengal, Karnataka, Tamil Nadu, and Kerala (up to 1,800 m).*
• SIZE *HBL: 30–45 cm; tail: 35–60 cm.*

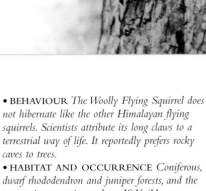

## WOOLLY FLYING SQUIRREL
*(Eupetaurus cinereus)*

THIS HIGH ALTITUDE *flying squirrel has long silken hair, rather than woolly hair as its name suggests. Larger than the genus* **Petaurista,** *it also looks bulkier because of its dense fur. Its blue-grey coat is uniformly coloured, except for a paler tip on its long, heavily furred tail. It is paler grey at the belly and creamy on the throat. Its feet are well furred and have pink soles. Its small ears are covered with buff hair and its elongated muzzle has black whiskers. A unique dentition pattern places it in a single species genus.*

• BEHAVIOUR *The Woolly Flying Squirrel does not hibernate like the other Himalayan flying squirrels. Scientists attribute its long claws to a terrestrial way of life. It reportedly prefers rocky caves to trees.*
• HABITAT AND OCCURRENCE *Coniferous, dwarf rhododendron and juniper forests, and the mountain steppe in northern J&K (Hunza, Gilgit) and Sikkim (2,800 m and above).*
• SIZE *HBL: 51–61 cm; tail: 38–48 cm.*

131

# SMALL FLYING SQUIRRELS

| | |
|---|---|
| FAMILY NAME **Sciuridae** | |
| DIET ❄ ♥ 🥜 🐦 | |
| SOCIAL UNIT Solitary | |
| ACTIVITY ☾ | |
| STRATUM Arboreal, aerial | |
| CONSERVATION THREATS Habitat loss, human interference | |

THE SMALL FLYING SQUIRRELS differ from the large flying squirrels not only in size but also in not having a flap connecting their two hind limbs together. All of them have very limited distribution; while two are found only in J&K, another is found only in a pocket of the Western Ghats. Two others are restricted to Northeast India.

## KASHMIR FLYING SQUIRREL
### (Hylopetes fimbriatus)

*black v-shaped patch on shoulders*

*feathery tail with black tip*

THIS SMALL, DARK *flying squirrel appears grizzled because of short black hairs interspersed with longer, pinkish buff ones. Its underside is cream, turning to grey-buff beneath the wing flaps. This squirrel can be distinguished from the large flying squirrels by its shorter feathery brown tail, broad at the base and narrowing to a black tip. Its muzzle is elongated and its upright pink ears are hairless.*

*Some taxonomists feel that the very similar Large Kashmir Flying Squirrel* (**Hylopetes barberi**) *is a separate species, based on the larger size of its skull and pre-molars.*

• BEHAVIOUR *Often shelters in roofs of village houses. When eating nuts, it bores a neat square hole in them—a telltale sign of this squirrel.*

• SIZE *HBL: 23.5–30 cm; tail: 25–35.5 cm.*

• HABITAT AND OCCURRENCE *Deciduous and coniferous forests of J&K (2,000– 3,500 m) east to Himachal Pradesh, and Sikkim. It is tolerant of drier areas as well as of human presence.*

*The Parti-coloured Flying Squirrel is a small flying squirrel of NE India.*

| SIMILAR SPECIES | | | |
|---|---|---|---|
| COMMON NAME | LATIN NAME | OCCURRENCE | IDENTIFICATION TIPS |
| HAIRY-FOOTED FLYING SQUIRREL | *Belomys pearsonii* | Sikkim, N Bengal, and NE India | Long chestnut hair growing out from the base of the ears. |
| PARTI-COLOURED FLYING SQUIRREL | *Hylopetes alboniger* | Sikkim, N Bengal, and NE India | Black and white squirrel, hoary upper parts. |

## TRAVANCORE FLYING SQUIRREL
### (Petinomys fuscocapillus)

*long, feather-shaped tail*

*small size*

A RARE SPECIES, *the Travancore Squirrel has yellowish-white undersides, with this colour extending to the cheeks, and white hairs fringing its wing membrane. The seven species of* **Petinomys** *found in South and Southeast Asia are placed in a separate genus due to the peculiar honeycombed bones in their ears.*

• SIZE *HBL: 30 cm; tail: 25 cm*

• HABITAT AND OCCURRENCE *Evergreen forests along Western Ghats: Tamil Nadu, Kerala, Karnataka, and possibly Goa.*

• BEST SEEN AT *Anamalai NP (Tamil Nadu), Periyar NP (Kerala).*

# MARMOTS AND HAMSTERS

MARMOTS ARE THE LARGEST rodents in India after porcupines. Belonging to the Sciuridae family, like squirrels, they are heavy-set, with a flat head, a prominent sagittal crest and a long tail. There are two species of marmots in India, both restricted to the northern Himalaya. Hamsters

**MARMOT CHARACTERISTICS**
• Thickset body • Flat head, long tail
• Small ears • Powerful incisors
**HAMSTER CHARACTERISTICS**
• Short limbs • Short tail
• Well-developed cheek pouches

belong to the Muridae family. They are small rodents with short tails and limbs. They survive in the wild in arid and steppe ecosystems of Central and South Asia, with India being the southernmost limit. There are two hamster species found in India. While marmots live in colonies in complex underground tunnel systems and are diurnal, hamsters live solitarily or in small groups in burrows in the sand and are nocturnal.

black back

black eye ring

orange undersides

### LONG-TAILED MARMOT *(Marmota caudata)*

*A MARMOT WITH a long and bushy tail, it varies in colour. While a sub-species, the Golden Marmot, is golden all over, others have varying amounts of coarse black hair spread dorsally over a base of yellow-buff or rich gold. The underparts of most are rich orange-gold, while the tip of the tail is black.*
• SIZE *HBL: 45.5–55.5 cm; tail: 21.5–27.5 cm.*
• HABITAT AND OCCURRENCE *Above the tree line in alpine meadows north of the Kashmir Valley, in Ladakh and Gilgit (2,300–2,400 m).*

## HIMALAYAN MARMOT
*(Marmota himalayana)*

THE COMMON *marmot of the Himalaya, it has short, coarse buff-grey fur on its body, with some black hair on its back. Its face is dark brown, with a buff eye ring. The short tail, which is black or brown, is a third of its body length.*
• SIZE *HBL: 45–61 cm; tail: 13–17.8 cm.*
• HABITAT AND OCCURRENCE *W and C Himalaya, Ladakh, and Sikkim (4,000–5,500 m).*

buff eye ring

buff coat

short tail

### GREY HAMSTER *(Cricetulus migratorius)*

*A BOLD AND INQUISITIVE rodent that frequents human habitation, the Grey Hamster is pale grey with white underparts and a short, blunt tail. Its face is squarish with a blunt muzzle and it has large eyes and funnel-shaped ears. The cheek pouches can distend several times when filled with food. A similar species, the Ladakh Hamster (C. alticola), is found in high altitudes of Ladakh and Himachal Pradesh. It resembles the Grey Hamster, except that its belly is light grey instead of white.*
• BEHAVIOUR *It rolls over on its back, exposing its teeth, as a defensive reaction.*
• SIZE *HBL: 9.4–12.2 cm; tail 2–4.5 cm.*
• HABITAT AND OCCURRENCE *Pasture or cultivation in Gilgit, J&K (1,500 – 4,000 m).*

# MICE AND RATS

THE MURIDS INCLUDING, rats, mice, hamsters, voles, lemmings, and gerbils comprise 281 genera and 1,326 species worldwide. They are the most widely distributed family and are found across the world, with the exception of certain islands and Antarctica. They are mostly small (10–80 cm), with long tails and short limbs. All of them are terrestrial but some live in trees and caves. They can be diurnal or nocturnal and while most of them are graminivorous (grain-eating) and feed on vegetable matter, some feed on invertebrates and small vertebrates. Rats and mice breed prodigiously almost throughout the year, when temperatures are favourable, and they usually have large litters. This is offset by their very short lives, averaging less than two years. Many species, especially the ones that live near human habitation, are considered to be vermin due to their diet and propensity of spreading diseases such as plague. However, the family also includes many non-threatening and rare forest forms that rarely come into contact with humans.

## MOUSE AND RAT CHARACTERISTICS
- Small size
- Long tail
- Sharp eyesight, smell, and hearing
- Thickly furred body
- Large incisor teeth

RARE FOREST DWELLER
*The Spiny Dormouse is a rare and unique rodent species of the Western Ghats.*

FAMILIAR FACE
*Mice and rats are the most common rodents and live alongside humans in almost all types of habitation.*

thickly furred coat

long whiskers

# BANDICOOTS

| | |
|---|---|
| FAMILY NAME | **Muridae** |
| DIET | 🐾 ⌀ ⍦ |
| SOCIAL UNIT | Groups of 2-3 |
| STRATUM | Fossorial |
| ACTIVITY | ☾ |
| CONSERVATION THREATS | Unknown |

### LARGE BANDICOOT-RAT
*(Bandicota indica)*

A LARGE, DARK BROWN, *nearly black rat with coarse fur, the large Indian Bandicoot at first sight provokes revulsion in most people. It is dark overall, as both the feet and tail are black and the underside is only slightly greyer in comparison to the rest of the body.*

• BEHAVIOUR *It lives in a single burrow system which has large openings on the surface.*
• SIZE *HBL: 21–34 cm; tail:16.7–34 cm.*
• HABITAT AND OCCURRENCE *Throughout India alongside human habitation and farms, except in deserts and mountains.*

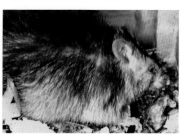

### LESSER BANDICOOT-RAT
*(Bandicota bengalensis)*

ONLY SLIGHTLY SMALLER *than **Bandicota indica**, the Indian Mole Rat or Lesser Bandicoot-Rat can be identified by its more brown than black colouration and a dark tail which is shorter than its head and body length. Its undersides are grayish and its face is more rounded, with a broad muzzle and round pinkish ears. In hand, it is observed that it can have up to 18 mammae, while the Large Bandicoot only has 12 mammae.*

coarse dark brown fur

• BEHAVIOUR *Its burrow system has up to a dozen openings, normally plugged with loose soil. It grunts often and is a very aggressive rat.*
• SIZE *HBL:14–25.5 cm; tail: 11.3–20.2 cm.*
•HABITAT AND OCCURRENCE *Near human habitation and crop fields throughout India.*

tail shorter than body

### SHORT-TAILED BANDICOOT-RAT *(Nesokia indica)*

THIS IS A SMALLER, DULL BROWN *or pale brown rat with a lighter, grey underside. Its chunky body is emphasized by a short dark tail. In hand one can see that it has only 8 mammae.*
• SIZE *HBL: 15.3–21 cm; tail: 9.7–13 cm.*
• HABITAT AND OCCURRENCE
*Cultivated fields and gardens in urban areas in the North Indian plains (Punjab, Delhi, Rajasthan, Haryana, Bihar, W Bengal, and Uttar Pradesh).*

very short tail

pink feet

# VOLES

| FAMILY NAME | **Muridae** |
|---|---|
| DIET | 🌿 |
| SOCIAL UNIT | Solitary |
| ACTIVITY | ☼ |
| STRATUM | Fossorial, terrestrial |
| CONSERVATION THREATS | Unknown |

### VOLE CHARACTERISTICS
• Rounded head • Short muzzle
• Small ears • Short thumbs, clawless or
with compressed claws
• Cylindrical body
• Tail approximately half of body length
• High altitude inhabitant

VOLES ARE SMALL, cylindrical rodents that are anatomically adapted to a fossorial or burrowing lifestyle. Limited to colder climates, in India they are only found in the Himalaya. Like elephants, they have rootless teeth that grow through their life – an adaptation for a diet of coarse vegetable matter. Voles constitute a successful group of rodents that has evolved into a number of very similar looking species. Conservative taxonomists split the family into three or four species, but others split it into over 140. All the species found across the world are characterized by hypsodont molars that have a characteristic triangular pattern on their worn surfaces.

## STOLICZKA'S MOUNTAIN VOLE *(Alticola stoliczkanus)*

A BRIGHT RUFOUS BROWN VOLE *with white or slaty-grey underparts, the Stoliczka's Vole is similar in appearance to the Silvery Mountain Vole. A plateau dweller, it constructs burrow systems which are not very deep. The Karakoram Vole is a sub-species that has a shorter tail and paler colouration.*
• SIZE *HBL: 10 – 12 cm; tail 3.9 – 5.8 cm.*
• HABITAT AND OCCURRENCE *Alpine meadows and rocky screes above 3,000 m in Northern Ladakh (J&K) and Sikkim; prefers areas near wetlands.*

rufous coat

### SIMILAR SPECIES

| COMMON NAME | LATIN NAME | OCCURRENCE | IDENTIFICATION TIPS |
|---|---|---|---|
| THOMAS'S MOUNTAIN VOLE | *Alticola stracheyi* | E Kashmir to N Sikkim | Very similar to Stoliczka's Vole, considered to be a sub-species by some. |
| ROYLE'S MOUNTAIN VOLE | *Alticola roylei* | J&K, N Kumaon, N Himachal Pradesh | Similar to the Silvery Mountain Vole but darker in colour. Brown upperparts and grey venter. |
| BALTISTAN MOUNTAIN VOLE | *Alticola albicauda* | Steep, rocky areas of N Kashmir | Similar to but duller than *A. roylei* with no rufous or fawn. Shorter tail, a third of its body length. |
| KASHMIR MOUNTAIN VOLE | *Alticola montosa* | J&K, 2,400 – 3,600 m | Identical to the Royle's Mountain Vole, except for cranial and dental differences. |

# SILVERY MOUNTAIN VOLE *(Alticola argentatus)*

LIKE ALL **ALTICOLA** VOLES, *the Silvery Mountain Vole is a resident of high altitudes, and has a longer tail and larger ears than most other voles. A silvery grey vole with dense velvet fur, it has a long bi-coloured tail – grey above and white below – and prominent rounded ears. Its feet are whitish. This vole was earlier thought to be a sub-species of* **Alticola roylei** *(see box on p.136), which it closely resembles.*

• **BEHAVIOUR** This bold rodent visits homes and camp sites. It is often seen with the Royle's Pika and Long-tailed marmots. Its small banana-shaped droppings are easy to distinguish from the round droppings of pikas.

• **SIZE:** *HBL: 10–12 cm; tail: 3.9–5.8 cm.*

• **HABITAT AND OCCURRENCE** *Alpine meadows and rocky screes above the tree line throughout the Himalaya.*

• **BEST SEEN AT** *Eastern Ladakh (J&K).*

silvery coat

large ears

# TRUE'S VOLE *(Hyperacrius fertilis)*

A DARK ALPINE VOLE with short brown dorsal fur and grey and buff underparts, the True's Vole has a short, bi-coloured tail, grey above and paler below. It is smaller than the **Alticola** voles and its ears are small as well, though larger than in the Muree Vole.

• **BEHAVIOUR** Excavates deep burrows but not as fossorial as the Muree Vole.

• **SIZE** *HBL: 9–11 cm; tail: 2.4–4 cm.*

• **HABITAT AND OCCURRENCE** *Lives in alpine meadows well above the tree line in J&K (3,000 m upwards).*

# MUREE VOLE *(Hyperacrius wynnei)*

A LARGE DARK BROWN FOREST vole with grey undersides and soft velvet fur, the Muree Vole appears black at first glance. Belly fur is dark grey with no rufous tinges.

• **BEHAVIOUR** Is known to excavate long stretches of shallow horizontal and deeper, near-vertical tunnels.

• **SIZE** *HBL: 8–12 cm; tail: 2.4–4.5 cm.*

• **HABITAT AND OCCURRENCE** *Moist temperate forests of J&K (1,850–3,050 m).*

| SIMILAR SPECIES | | | |
|---|---|---|---|
| **COMMON NAME** | **LATIN NAME** | **OCCURRENCE** | **IDENTIFICATION TIPS** |
| BLYTH'S VOLE | *Microtus leucurus* | J&K and Himachal Pradesh, high mountain steppe over 3,500 m | Long, thick grey coat, lighter below and darker above; fur is tipped ochre. |
| SIKKIM VOLE | *Microtus sikimensis* | Sikkim and Darjeeling, W Bengal, 2,100–3,700 m | Small, dark brown forest vole; hair on back tinged yellow and paler brown below. |
| PERE DAVID'S VOLE | *Eothenomys melanogaster* | Mishmi Hills, Arunachal Pradesh. | Forest-dwelling vole. Does not make tunnels. |

# GERBILS

| | |
|---|---|
| FAMILY NAME **Muridae** | |
| DIET ✳ ⁂ ⩘ ⌀ ♥ | |
| SOCIAL UNIT Colonies | |
| ACTIVITY ☾ (Gerbils) ☼ (Jirds) | |
| STRATUM Terrestrial | |
| CONSERVATION THREATS Pesticides, habitat loss | |

**GERBIL CHARACTERISTICS**
- Arid zone rodent
- Long, hairy tail ending in a tuft
- Grooved incisors
- Long legs
- Large eyes

GERBILS AND JIRDS comprise a large group of over 90 species of long-tailed rodents that are specially adapted to survive in semi-arid regions and deserts. They are found from Africa to Central and South Asia. Gerbils have characteristic tails that are furry and end in a tuft of hairs. Many gerbil species have long legs and a rabbit-like hopping locomotion. Members of this family are almost always social animals that live together in colonies. A total of four species of gerbils are distributed in the arid regions of western India.

THE ANTELOPE-RAT
*This Indian Gerbil is a common dry area rodent. Seen below with newborns.*

## INDIAN GERBIL *(Tatera indica)*

THIS GERBIL IS A *large, erect, nocturnal rodent that is biscuit-coloured with a white chest, throat, and belly. It has a peculiar long tail that is bi-coloured, cream along the sides and grey on top and bottom, ending in a tuft of blackish-brown hairs. It is distinguished from other gerbils by its long, naked ears and naked soles. It has long well-developed hind feet that are pale in front.*
- **BEHAVIOUR** *It is a very territorial animal; individuals live in separate burrow systems, within a loose colony. Due to its aggressive territorial instincts, it can turn cannibalistic and juveniles often fall prey to such attacks from adults.*
  - **SIZE** *HBL:14.3 – 18.8 cm; tail 20.5 cm.*
    - **HABITAT AND OCCURRENCE** *Drier and arid areas of sub-Himalayan northern India, east to the Ganges delta, western and peninsular India.*

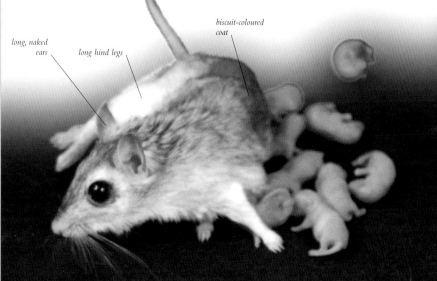

long, naked ears

long hind legs

biscuit-coloured coat

## INDIAN DESERT JIRD *(Meriones hurrianae)*

ALSO CALLED THE *Desert Gerbil, this species is more accurately described as a jird as it does not have the long hind feet and erect stature of a gerbil. The tail is shorter than head and body and it has much smaller ears than a gerbil. Its diurnal nature also distinguishes it from the three nocturnal gerbils. The jird is greyish-brown with a peppering of black on the backside and yellowish-grey on the belly. It has long black claws and its incisors are a characteristic orange.*

short ears

greyish-brown coat

long black claws

yellowish-grey belly

• BEHAVIOUR *Jirds are less aggressive than gerbils and live in colonies close to each other, their burrows honeycombing the habitat.*
• SIZE *HBL:11.5-14.3 cm; tail:10−15 cm.*
• HABITAT AND OCCURRENCE *Uncultivated, barren land with firm soil, in Rajasthan and Gujarat. This rodent is not present in extensive sand dunes or rocky areas.*
• BEST SEEN AT *Desert NP (Rajasthan).*

## PYGMY GERBIL *(Gerbillus nanus)*

A SMALL RODENT, *the Pygmy or Baluchistan Gerbil resembles the Indian Gerbil, but is half its size. Its fully furred tail is buff on top and cream below, ending in a brown tuft. Its upperparts are sandy buff and the lower parts pure white. There is a clear white spot behind the eye, which extends till the back of the ear, distinguishing it from other small rats of the area. The soles of its feet are naked and so are its pinkish ears.*
• BEHAVIOUR *This is not a colonial species although it lives in close proximity with others. The burrows are normally occupied by a single individual.*
• SIZE *HBL 6.5−8.7 cm; tail: 9.5−12.7 cm.*
• HABITAT AND OCCURRENCE *Arid areas of Rajasthan and Gujarat, including rocky zones.*
• BEST SEEN AT *Desert NP (Rajasthan).*

## INDIAN HAIRY-FOOTED GERBIL *(Gerbillus gleadowi)*

THIS GERBIL *(see below) is smaller than the Pygmy Gerbil and can be told apart by its reddish-buff fur. Its eyes look wide open because of the stiff hair surrounding them and the soles of its feet are hairy. Both these characteristics are adaptations for existence in sand dunes. Similarly, in its diet, it is more tolerant of salty vegetation, though it eats insects and seeds as well.*
• SIZE *HBL:7.5−10 cm; tail:12−14.5 cm.*
• HABITAT AND OCCURRENCE *Sand dunes of Rajasthan and Gujarat.*
• BEST SEEN AT *Desert NP (Rajasthan).*

white hair around eye

long brown-tipped tail

white underparts

# HOUSE RATS

| | |
|---|---|
| FAMILY NAME | **Muridae** |
| DIET | 🌿 ✷ |
| SOCIAL UNIT | Groups of 2-3 |
| ACTIVITY | ☾ |
| STRATUM | Terrestrial, fossorial |
| CONSERVATION THREATS | Pesticides, human interference |

FOREST RAT
*R.r. wroughtoni, the forest sub-species, with newborns.*

## HOUSE RAT *(Rattus rattus)*

**LOCAL NAME:** *Uchi* (Manipuri), *Eli* (Malayalam), *Chooha* (Hindi), *Indur* (Bengali), *Undir* (Marathi/Gujarati).

THE MOST COMMON RAT *in the world, the House or Black Rat, variously known as the Roof or Ship Rat, is a medium-sized dark brown rat with many distinct sub-species. The two most common sub-species are a grayish-buff ventered form that occurs in homes and urban areas (**R.r.rufescens**) (see below) and a white ventered forest form (**R.r.wroughtoni**). Darker forms that almost verge on black are also found, like **R.r.rattus**. Some forms in the hills such as **R.r.tistae** and **R.r.gangutrianus** have longer, softer fur in winter, while the common village rat of the Kashmir Valley (**R.r.vicerex**) has a tail that is shorter than its head and body. **R.r.satarae** is the sub-species with the longest tail of them all. The House Rat is characterized by flat spines in its dorsal fur, a feature shared by five other species (see box below).*
• SIZE *HBL: 14–20 cm; tail: 12.6–30 cm.*
• HABITAT AND OCCURRENCE *Homes and forests throughout India.*

dark brown or black coat

coarse fur with spines

tail as long as or longer than body

| SIMILAR SPECIES | | | |
|---|---|---|---|
| **COMMON NAME** | **LATIN NAME** | **OCCURRENCE** | **IDENTIFICATION TIPS** |
| MALAYSIAN WOOD RAT | *Rattus tiomanicus* | Andaman & Nicobar Islands | Similar to, but smaller than House Rat, has less coarse fur. White/buff venters; smaller hind feet. |
| MILLER'S RAT | *Rattus burrus* | Endemic to Little and Great Nicobars, and Trinket Islands | Similar to Malaysian Wood Rat. |
| NICOBAR RAT | *Rattus palmarum* | Endemic to Nicobar Islands | Very large rat – around 27.5 cm. Undersides are pale grey, tail is two-thirds the body size. |
| ANDAMAN RAT | *Rattus stoicus* | Endemic to Andaman Islands | Large rat; tail slightly longer than in the Nicobar Rat. Underside of tail lighter. |
| RANJINI'S RAT | *Rattus ranjiniae* | Endemic to Thiruvanan-thapuram district, Kerala | Can be distinguished by its large, pale hind feet and shorter palate. |

## BROWN RAT
### (Rattus norvegicus)

ALSO CALLED THE NORWAY RAT *or Sewer Rat, this is a large dark brown rat with lighter underparts and feet, small ears, and a tail that is always shorter than its head and body. It has a blunter muzzle in comparison to the common Black Rat and, like the Himalayan rats, does not have spines in its fur. The Brown Rat is more terrestrial and less of a climber than the House Rat and frequents wet areas as well.*
- SIZE *HBL:17−25 cm; tail:15.5−20 cm.*
- HABITAT AND OCCURRENCE *Sewers, ports along the coast, and banks of rivers.*
- BEST SEEN AT *Sewers in Mumbai and Kolkata.*

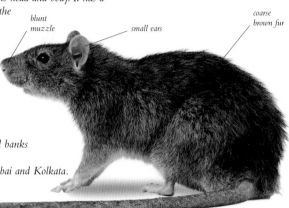

blunt muzzle

small ears

coarse brown fur

## HIMALAYAN RAT
### (Rattus nitidus)

THIS SMALL, COMMENSAL *hill rat is dark grey-brown above and dull grey or pale below. Its back has a dark mid-dorsal patch or line. The short guard hairs do not protrude out of the contour hairs, giving it a much sleeker look than other rats. Its feet are yellowish or white and its dark tail is naked and longer than the head and body. It has six pairs of mammae, which distinguishes it from* **Rattus rattus**.
- SIZE *HBL: 13−20 cm; tail: 14−19.8 cm.*
- HABITAT AND OCCURRENCE *Himalaya, from Kumaon eastwards through the Northeast, in urban and forest settings.*

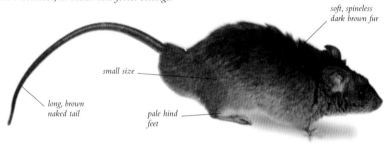

soft, spineless dark brown fur

small size

long, brown naked tail

pale hind feet

| SIMILAR SPECIES | | | |
|---|---|---|---|
| COMMON NAME | LATIN NAME | OCCURRENCE | IDENTIFICATION TIPS |
| SIKKIM RAT | *Rattus sikkimensis* | Sikkim, Arunachal Pradesh, and Meghalaya | Can be distinguished from the Himalayan Rat by its pure white ventral parts. |
| TURKESTAN RAT | *Rattus turkestanicus* | Himalayan foothills, from J&K to Arunachal Pradesh | Whitish belly and feet, pale underside of tail. |

# FIELD RATS

| | |
|---|---|
| FAMILY NAME **Muridae** | |
| DIET ∷ 🐛 ✏ | |
| SOCIAL UNIT Groups of 2–3 | |
| ACTIVITY ☾ | |
| STRATUM Terrestrial | |
| CONSERVATION THREATS Pesticides, habitat loss | |

METADS OR SOFT, FURRED field rats are medium-sized South Asian species that have characteristics of both house rats and wood rats. They are similar in having a very soft pelage, semi-naked tails and large ears, and they are not found in human habitation. Three out of the four species that exist in the world are found in India and two of these can be told apart by their having less than six soft pads (plantar pads) under their feet.

## SOFT-FURRED FIELD RAT *(Millardia meltada)*

THIS IS A MEDIUM-SIZED *field rat, smaller than the House Rat, with soft grey fur that is pale but grizzled. It has a pale grey throat, undersides, and feet. Its tail is dark grey on top and paler, almost white below, with clear annular rings, and is equal to, or shorter than, the head and body in length. It has very prominently rounded ears and eyes. On close observation, this rat has eight mammae and four or five pads on its feet (other rats have six).*
- **BEHAVIOUR** *It is a poor burrower and makes its home in cracks in the soil or embankments.*
- **SIZE** *HBL: 10–15.5 cm; tail: 9.2–14.4 cm.*
- **HABITAT AND OCCURRENCE** *Fields and open country (both rocky ground and alluvial plains) throughout India except the Himalaya and the Northeast. It prefers cultivated areas or grassy embankments.*

large round ears

grey soft fur

bi-coloured tail

| SIMILAR SPECIES | | | |
|---|---|---|---|
| **COMMON NAME** | **LATIN NAME** | **OCCURRENCE** | **IDENTIFICATION TIPS** |
| KONDANA RAT | *Millardia kondana* | Endemic to Pune district, Maharashtra | Very similar to, but larger than *M. meltada*. Has six plantar pads on soles of feet. |

## SAND-COLOURED RAT *(Millardia gleadowi)*

A SMALLER, PALER *soft-furred rat with a shorter tail, the Sand-coloured Rat has four plantar pads and six pairs of mammae. Its underparts are strikingly white. It is similar in appearance to the Pygmy Gerbil, with which it shares a common range. The gerbil, however, can be told apart by a tuft of hair at the tail tip, much smaller ears, a white patch behind the eye, and stiffer fur.*
- **BEHAVIOUR** *As it lives in harsh terrain, it has a small litter.*
- **SIZE** *HBL: 8–11 cm; tail: 6.5–9.5 cm.*
- **HABITAT AND OCCURRENCE** *Semi-desert and arid areas, especially shifting sand dunes and saline clay flat areas in Gujarat and Rajasthan.*
- **BEST SEEN AT** *Rann of Kutch (Gujarat).*

pale sandy fur

white underparts

# WOOD AND BUSH RATS

| | |
|---|---|
| FAMILY NAME **Muridae** | |
| DIET 🌿 🐛 🐌 | |
| SOCIAL UNIT Solitary/groups of 4–5 | |
| ACTIVITY ☼ ☾ | |
| STRATUM Terrestrial, arboreal | |
| CONSERVATION THREATS Habitat loss, human interference | |

THE GENUS OF *Cremnomys* is separated from *Rattus* because of anatomical features such as longer incisive foramen. The members of this group have a long fifth toe and six plantar pads on each hind foot, but this is not visible in the field. Their incisors are reddish-orange and prominently grooved.

## WHITE-TAILED WOOD RAT *(Cremnomys blanfordi)*

THIS IS AN ADAPTABLE *forest and scrub rat that is easily told apart by its bi-coloured tail. It is brownish-grey dorsally and paler ventrally, almost approaching white, but what sets it apart from other rats is the brown tail, which two-thirds of the way down is covered with long white hairs.*
• **BEHAVIOUR** *This rat builds its nest in tree hollows in southern forests, but adapts to building its nest in boulder crevices in the drier parts of central India. It is remarkably adapted to rocky country even in forests.*
• **SIZE** *HBL: 15–19.5 cm; tail: 20.2–23.5 cm.*
• **HABITAT AND OCCURRENCE** *Deciduous and evergreen forests, scrub jungle, and open country. Found in southern India, north to Madhya Pradesh and east to Bihar and West Bengal.*
• **BEST SEEN AT** *Parambikulam and Peechi WLS (Kerala).*

*brown-grey uppers*  *brown and white tail*  *white underside*

### SIMILAR SPECIES

| COMMON NAME | LATIN NAME | OCCURRENCE | IDENTIFICATION TIPS |
|---|---|---|---|
| KUTCH ROCK RAT | *Cremnomys cutchicus* | Found discontinuously in India | Similar to *C. blanfordi* except for tail, which is brown and paler underneath. |
| ELLERMAN'S RAT | *Cremnomys elvira* | Endemic to Salem district in E Ghats | Smallest of the three *Cremnomys* rats. |

## INDIAN BUSH RAT *(Golunda ellioti)*

SLIGHTLY SMALLER THAN *the House Rat, the Indian Bush Rat differs from the former in many ways. A reddish-brown rodent, it has a long tail that is brownish above and yellowish-grey below. The head is vole-like and eyes are large. Its ears are very large and conch-like and hairy on the outside, a unique characteristic of this rat, as are its naked and black hind feet soles. It is arboreal as well as terrestrial by nature and often raids crop fields and coffee estates.*
• **BEHAVIOUR** *It burrows under thick bush and makes characteristic pathways from its burrow to its foraging ground.*
• **SIZE** *HBL:11.4–15.5 cm; tail: 9.3–12.5 cm.*
• **HABITAT AND OCCURRENCE** *Grassland and scrub forests in peninsular India, east to W Assam (north of River Brahmaputra).*

*conch-shaped ears*  *speckled brown coat*  *tail brown above, grey below*

143

# BUSH RATS AND TREE MICE

## MANIPUR RAT *(Berylmys manipulus)*

A BURROWING RAT OF HILLY FORESTS, *the Manipur Rat has a dense, coarse grey pelage with a paint-brush texture. It can be recognized at close quarters by its very white incisors, with only a trace of yellow. The tail, which is as long as the head and body, has a short white tip. It has large hind feet for burrowing. The Manipur Rat is not an agricultural pest.*
- SIZE *HBL: 13.5 –18.5 cm; tail: 14.5 –19.5 cm.*
- HABITAT AND OCCURRENCE *Hills and foothills, oak and evergreen forests, scrub, and riverine meadows, south of River Brahmaputra, with a concentration from Karbi Anglong, eastwards to Upper Assam, Nagaland, and Manipur.*

| SIMILAR SPECIES | | | |
|---|---|---|---|
| COMMON NAME | LATIN NAME | OCCURRENCE | IDENTIFICATION TIPS |
| BOWER'S RAT | *Berylmys bowersi* | Assam (S of R Brahmaputra) and Meghalaya | Large (23-30 cm). Flat spines in grey coat. Pale orange incisors and two pairs of pectoral teats. |
| KENNETH'S WHITE-TOOTHED RAT | *Berylmys mackenziei* | Assam (S of R Brahmaputra), Nagaland, and Manipur | Smaller rat (19-25 cm) with shorter tail (80 % of head and body). |
| MILLARD'S LARGE-TOOTHED RAT | *Dacnomys millardi* | Northern W Bengal, Assam, and Arunachal Pradesh | Large grey-brown rat with brown tail. Very large molar teeth. |
| HUME'S MANIPUR BUSH RAT | *Hadromys humei* | Assam and Manipur | Speckled grey-brown rat with fawn or ochraceous undersides. |
| EDWARD'S NOISY RAT | *Leopoldamys edwardsi* | Northern W Bengal, Garo Hills, Arunachal Pradesh, and Nagaland | Large rat (21-25 cm) with very long brown tail. Sleek dull brown fur. |

| FAMILY NAME **Muridae** |
|---|
| DIET 🐛 ⌀ 🍃 |
| SOCIAL UNIT Solitary ♂; small family ♀ |
| ACTIVITY ☾ |
| STRATUM Arboreal |
| CONSERVATION THREATS Habitat loss |

## LONG-TAILED TREE MOUSE *(Vandeleuria oleracea)*

A MEDIUM-SIZED *mouse that is widely distributed in forests as well as near human habitation, the Long-tailed Tree Mouse or Palm Mouse is recognizable by its extremely long tail. Its overall body colour is fawn or light brown—a brighter shade in specimens found in the north and duller in those found in southern India. It has white or off-white underparts. Long-tailed mice found in Kodagu (Karnataka) and Nilgiri (Tamil Nadu) districts have yellow underparts and a very long tail (up to 13 cm). Some taxonomists classify it as a separate species (**V. nilagirica**); others feel it is a sub-species.*

- BEHAVIOUR *It builds its nest high up in the branches of trees or in tree holes.*
- SIZE *HBL: 6– 10 cm; tail: 9.5– 13 cm.*
- HABITAT AND OCCURRENCE *Almost throughout India.*

very long tail

light brown upperparts

| SIMILAR SPECIES | | | |
|---|---|---|---|
| COMMON NAME | LATIN NAME | OCCURRENCE | IDENTIFICATION TIPS |
| PENCIL-TAILED TREE MOUSE | *Chiropodomys gliroides* | Bamboo forests of Northeast India, especially Meghalaya | Warm brown or chestnut coat with white underparts and long tail; has a claw on fifth digit of both feet that is not present in *Vandeleuria*. |

# HIMALAYAN RATS AND WOOD MICE

## CHESTNUT RAT *(Niviventer fulvescens)*

INDIA IS HOME *to half a dozen species of soft, densely furred high altitude rats that are assigned to the genus* **Niviventer**. *Nearly all of them are richly coloured on the back, while the underside is white or very pale. The tail is slightly longer than the head and body and covered with hair, with an invariably paler tip. Some of the species have spines in the fur, but none of them have guard hairs. The Chestnut Rat has chestnut-brown upperparts and white underparts. Externally, its brown back is the only thing that distinguishes it from the White-bellied Rat, which has a grey back.*
- SIZE *HBL: 12−16 cm; tail: 17.1−22.2 cm.*
- HABITAT AND OCCURRENCE *Foothills of the Himalaya, from western Himalaya to Assam and Arunachal Pradesh.*

| SIMILAR SPECIES | | | |
|---|---|---|---|
| COMMON NAME | LATIN NAME | OCCURRENCE | IDENTIFICATION TIPS |
| SMOKE-BELLIED RAT | *Niviventer eha* | Coniferous and rhododendron forests in Sikkim and West Bengal | Brownish rat with a smoky or grey belly. Long tail is lighter below. |
| MISHMI RAT | *Niviventer brahma* | High altitudes of Arunachal Pradesh | A slightly larger version of the Smoke-bellied Rat. |
| WHITE-BELLIED RAT | *Niviventer niviventer* | High altitudes of Himalaya, to Sikkim | White belly, grey back and buff flanks. Darker chest patch in Sikkim. |
| LANGBIAN RAT | *Niviventer langbianis* | Arunachal Pradesh | Resembles the Chestnut Rat, but with duller dorsal fur. |
| TENASSERIM RAT | *Niviventer tenaster* | Mizoram | Larger rat with yellowish upperside and white underside. Slight tuft at end of tail. |

## WOOD MOUSE *(Apodemes sylvaticus)*

A YELLOWISH-BROWN OR *sometimes greyish field mouse, it looks remarkably like the House Mouse except that on closer examination, the feet are white and the long tail is bi-coloured: brown on top and pale grey at the bottom. The ventral parts of the body are also grey. The ears are large, rounded and the same colour as the body. The female has three pairs of teats. Some specimens have a yellowish spot on the chest but this is not frequently seen. The orange-coated upper incisors lack the notch that all* **Mus** *species normally have.*
- BEHAVIOUR *Burrowing, gregarious creatures, they cache food in burrows that are often shared by a number of mice.*
- SIZE *HBL: 9− 10.5 cm; tail: 9.8−10 cm.*
- HABITAT AND OCCURRENCE *Very widely distributed, away from human habitation, from coniferous forests to meadows to arid rocky areas through the Himalayan foothills, and the Northeast including Assam and Arunachal Pradesh.*

| SIMILAR SPECIES | | | |
|---|---|---|---|
| COMMON NAME | LATIN NAME | OCCURRENCE | IDENTIFICATION TIPS |
| FUKIEN WOOD MOUSE | *Apodemes draco* | Arunachal Pradesh and eastern Assam | Similar to common Wood Mouse, with darker ears, four pairs of teats. Darker form with longer tail found in the Mishmi Hills (*A.d.orestes*). |
| MILLER'S WOOD MOUSE | *Apodemes rusiges* | J&K, Himachal Pradesh, and Kumaon (Uttaranchal) | Dark mid-dorsal stripe along the body. Long tail. |
| WROUGHTON'S WOOD MOUSE | *Apodemes wardi* | J&K and Ladakh | Larger and paler than Miller's Wood Mouse. May be a sub-species. |

# MICE AND BIRCH MICE

| | |
|---|---|
| FAMILY NAME **Muridae** | |
| DIET ⁂ ∥ ↯ 🐛 | |
| SOCIAL UNIT Solitary/groups of 2–3 | |
| ACTIVITY ☾ | |
| STRATUM Terrestrial/fossorial | |
| CONSERVATION THREATS Pesticides | |

MICE ARE SMALL rodents with relatively short outer toes on the hind feet and unique dentition (first molar enlarged, third molar reduced or absent). Birch mice differ in having longer tails, elongated hind feet and poorly developed cheek pouches.

brown body

long tail

## HOUSE MOUSE
### (Mus musculus)

A SMALL CREATURE, *the House Mouse comes in all shades of brown, from sandy to rufous, with slightly whitish or paler underparts. There is also considerable variation in the colouration of the different body parts. The tail, which is always longer than the head and body, may be lighter below or wholly dark, while the feet may be white, or dark with white toes.*

• SIZE *HBL: 5.2–10 cm; tail: 6–9.5 cm.*
• HABITAT AND OCCURRENCE *Homes and agricultural land throughout the country.*
• BEST SEEN AT *Homes throughout India.*

## LITTLE INDIAN FIELD MOUSE
### (Mus booduga)

THIS IS A SMALL *greyish-brown field mouse, much like a miniature House Mouse. It differs most markedly in its white underparts and lower limbs. Its eyes are large and so are the rounded ears. The muzzle is more pointed than that of the House Mouse.*
• SIZE *HBL: 5.6–6.3 cm; tail: 5.5–7.5 cm.*
• HABITAT AND OCCURRENCE *Throughout India.*

### SIMILAR SPECIES

| COMMON NAME | LATIN NAME | OCCURRENCE | IDENTIFICATION TIPS |
|---|---|---|---|
| FAWN-COLOURED MOUSE | *Mus cervicolor* | Sikkim, NE India, and Andamans | Similar to Little Indian Field Mouse, distinguishable only by distribution. |
| WROUGHTON'S MOUSE | *Mus phillipsi* | Peninsular India, north to Rajasthan | Similar to Little Indian Field Mouse, distinguishable only by distribution. |
| SIKKIM MOUSE | *Mus pahari* | Sikkim, northern W Bengal and NE India | Spiny brown coat with silvery underside and light brown feet. |
| HARVEST MOUSE | *Micromys minutus* | NE India | Small grey-brown mouse with tail longer than head and body, and grey undersides. |
| KASHMIR BIRCH MOUSE | *Sicista concolor* | Gilgit, J&K (above 3,300 m) | Drab grey fawn colour. Very long (one and a half times head and body) bi-coloured tail. |

## BONHOTE'S MOUSE *(Mus famulus)*

A MEDIUM-SIZED *brown field mouse with a tail that is shorter than head and body length, the Bonhote's Mouse has dark brown feet and a light brown ventral side. The female has three pairs of mammae.*
• SIZE *HBL: 9 cm; tail: 8 cm.*
• HABITAT AND OCCURRENCE *Endemic to W Ghats (around 1,500 m).*

## SPINY FIELD MOUSE *(Mus platythrix)*

A LARGE FOSSORIAL *mouse with short, spiny fur, the Spiny Field Mouse or Indian Brown Spiny Mouse is brown on its back and white underneath, with a clear demarcating line between the two regions. The tail is shorter than the head and body length. It has five pairs of mammae (three pectorals and two inguinal) visible only in hand.*

• BEHAVIOUR *It occasionally blocks its burrow entrances with pebbles.*
• SIZE *HBL: 7.8– 10.4 cm; tail: 5.5– 9 cm.*
• HABITAT AND OCCURRENCE *Peninsular India, up to West Bengal in the east.*

| SIMILAR SPECIES | | | |
|---|---|---|---|
| COMMON NAME | LATIN NAME | OCCURRENCE | IDENTIFICATION TIPS |
| CRUMP'S MOUSE | Diomys crumpi | Assam, Manipur, Parasnath Hills, Bihar | Dark above, pale below. HBL: up to 13 cm. |
| PYGMY FIELD MOUSE | Mus terricolor | Throughout India | Similar to Mus booduga. HBL: up to 7 cm. |
| ELLIOT'S BROWN SPINY MOUSE | Mus saxicola | Scattered locations throughout India | Grey with bi-coloured tail. Bristly hind quarters. HBL: 7.2-10 cm. |
| COOKE'S MOUSE | Mus cookii | Western Ghats, Assam, and Nagaland | Tail as long as head and body, light grey underside, grey-brown feet. HBL: 7-10 cm. |

# BAMBOO RATS AND DORMICE

| | |
|---|---|
| FAMILY NAME **Muridae** | |
| DIET :: 🌿 ↓ | |
| SOCIAL UNIT Groups of 2-3 | |
| ACTIVITY ☾ | |
| CONSERVATION THREATS Poaching | |

**B**ELONGING TO THE sub-family Rhizomynae, Bamboo Rats are large rodents with small eyes, short limbs, and long incisors. They have a short, sparsely haired tail. They are burrow dwellers that feed on roots and shoots, principally bamboo.

## BAY BAMBOO RAT
### (Cannomys badius)

A RELATIVELY LARGE *rodent with a blunt face and a short tail, the Bay or Lesser Bamboo Rat has a rufous body. It has dense, soft fur that hangs down like a cloak over the body. The chunky face is blunt and the eyes and ears are small. The female has four teats. The foot pads of this rat are smooth in comparison to the granular foot pads of the Hoary Bamboo Rat.*
• SIZE *HBL: 15 – 26 cm;*
*tail: 6 – 7.5 cm.*
• HABITAT AND OCCURRENCE *Bamboo and secondary forests of Northeast India.*

## HOARY BAMBOO RAT
### (Rhizomys pruinosus)

THE HOARY BAMBOO RAT *is much larger than the Bay Bamboo Rat and has grey fur tipped with white, giving it a grizzled or hoary appearance. It has granular foot pads and the female has two teats anteriorly and three posteriorly.*
• SIZE *HBL: 25 – 35 cm;*
*tail: up to 12 cm.*
• HABITAT AND OCCURRENCE *Like the Bay Bamboo Rat, it is found all over Northeast India, especially in the foothills and mountainous areas.*

| | |
|---|---|
| FAMILY NAME **Muridae** | |
| DIET 🐛 🌿 | |
| SOCIAL UNIT Colonies | |
| STRATUM Terrestrial | |
| ACTIVITY ☾ | |
| CONSERVATION THREATS Habitat loss | |

## MALABAR SPINY DORMOUSE (Platacanthomys lasiurus)

A UNIQUE FOREST MOUSE *with no similar species, the Malabar Spiny Dormouse is brown with a long bushy tail. Its fur is spiny and light brown and its ventral surface is cream. The eyes are large and conspicuous and the hind feet are also large. An arboreal mouse inhabiting tree hollows, it is also called the Pepper Rat because of its reputation as a pest in pepper plantations. Today it is largely an evergreen forest animal.*
• SIZE *HBL: 13 – 14 cm; tail: 8 – 10.4 cm.*
• HABITAT AND OCCURRENCE *Endemic to evergreen forests of Western Ghats, usually below 900 m, in Kerala, Tamil Nadu, and Karnataka north to Shimoga.*
• BEST SEEN AT *Kalakaad-Mundanthurai NP (Tamil Nadu).*

light brown, spiny fur

conspicuous eyes

# TREE SHREWS

| | |
|---|---|
| **FAMILY NAME** | **Tupaiidae** |
| **DIET** ◑ 🦗 ✽ | |
| **SOCIAL UNIT** | Solitary |
| **STRATUM** | Terrestrial, arboreal |
| **ACTIVITY** ☼ | |
| **CONSERVATION THREATS** | Habitat loss |

TOSSED ABOUT BY taxonomists between the families of insectivorous shrews and primates for a long time, tree shrews are today placed in an order of their own, known as Scandentia. In form and behaviour, they are more like squirrels than shrews. However, they are not as arboreal, frequently coming down to the ground, contrary to what their name suggests. There are a total of 19 tree shrew species in the world and all of them are found only in Asia.

### TREE SHREW CHARACTERISTICS
- Long snout
- Laterally placed, large eyes
- Large ears with unique ear flap
- Naked, moist nose pad
- No whiskers on face, unlike squirrels
- Bushy tail

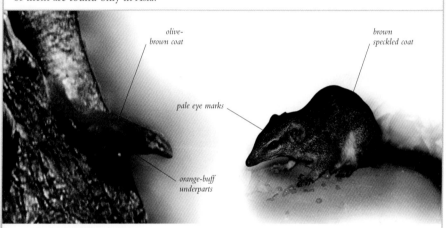

olive-brown coat

brown speckled coat

pale eye marks

orange-buff underparts

## SOUTH INDIAN TREE SHREW
### (Anathana elliotti)

ALSO CALLED THE *Madras Tree Shrew, this is a chocolate-brown tree shrew with pale markings around the eyes and a characteristic white shoulder stripe (see right above). Its upperparts are speckled yellow and brown near the shoulder and rufous red near the rump, while its underparts are greyish-white. C Indian forms have more reddish-brown upperparts (see left above) compared to the pale upper coat of southeastern forms. Those found in the northwest of the range have grizzled brown backs and grey feet. The females have three pairs of teats.*
- **BEHAVIOUR** *It displays no maternal instinct and feeds its young in a separate nest that it visits only once in two days.*
- **SIZE** *HBL: 17.5–20 cm; tail: 16–19 cm.*
- **HABITAT AND OCCURRENCE** *Forests of peninsular and southern India, to Bihar in the east and Satpuras in the west (up to 1,400 m).*
- **BEST SEEN AT** *Periyar NP (Kerala).*

## NORTHERN TREE SHREW *(Tupaia belangeri)*

ALSO KNOWN AS THE *Malay Tree Shrew, this species has an olive-brown coat that is buff or orangish ventrally. The long, furry tail is equal to its head and body length. Like all tree shrews it has naked pads below its feet and strong curved claws. The females have three pairs of teats. The Nicobar Tree Shrew (Tupaia nicobarica) which is found in the Nicobars, is very similar except that it is duller in colour, the tail is longer than the head and body and females have one pair of mammae.*
- **BEHAVIOUR** *The Northern Tree Shrew is largely a terrestrial, non-forest species, and is less wary of humans than the Indian Tree Shrew.*
- **SIZE** *HBL: 15–20 cm; tail: 15–20 cm.*
- **HABITAT AND OCCURRENCE** *Forests, plantations, gardens in NE India and E Himalaya (up to 1,830 m).*

# BATS

| INDIAN BATS AT A GLANCE | |
| --- | --- |
| NUMBER OF SPECIES | 110 + |
| LARGEST | Indian Flying Fox |
| SMALLEST | Indian Pygmy Bat |
| MOST COMMON | Several species |
| MOST ENDANGERED | Peter's Tube-nosed Bat, Wroughton's Free-tailed Bat |

**LOCAL NAME:** *Chamkadad* **(Hindi),** *Badur* **(Bengali),** *Chamachidu* **(Gujarati).**

THE ONLY MAMMALS capable of true flight, bats are found all over the world except in regions beyond the limits of tree growth. The order Chiroptera to which they all belong is divided into two sub-orders: the frugivorous, large Megachiroptera, and the insectivorous,

### STRIKING COLOURS
*The Rufous Horseshoe Bat is orange in winter and brownish-grey at other times.*

small Microchiroptera. Bats roost in caves, on trees, behind rocks or in disused buildings during the day, emerging only at night to take to the sky. When roosting, they hang upside down as a preference, although a few families cling to rocky surfaces like geckos on a wall. Most bats find their way around by echolocation, which is a technique of producing high-frequency sounds that bounce back to

them off obstacles. They have elaborate hearing aids that help them capture sounds, most spectacularly seen in the convoluted horseshoes and leaflets on the noses of two bat families. Bats fly by paddling through the air with their limbs and wings. Most bats are difficult to identify while in the air although a combination of their tail, muzzle, and ears can offer clues that can help to identify at least the family. The geographical location, time of evening or night, and the type of flight are also pointers to identification. True species identification, however, can be done only with the bat in hand, based on the length of the forearm.

**SELECTIVE DIET**
*Frugivorous bats feed by perching on trees and gnawing on fruit. Insectivorous bats hawk insects on the wing, or pick them off foliage, or the ground. A few, such as the False Vampires, are carnivorous and eat small mammals and reptiles, while others such as the Daubenton's Bat catch fish.*

## IDENTIFYING BAT FAMILIES (ADAPTED FROM BATES & HARRISON, 1997)

| FAMILY | TAIL | EARS | MUZZLE |
|---|---|---|---|
| FRUIT BATS | Small or absent | Simple, no tragus | Simple, no noseleaf. |
| MOUSE-TAILED BATS | Thin and very long, with a major part free of membrane | Membrane joins the ears above forehead, tragus present | Naked, with a small ridge. |
| TOMB BATS | Tip emerges from middle of membrane | Variable, tragus present | Simple, no noseleaf. |
| FALSE VAMPIRES | Absent | Large, joined over forehead, tragus bifid | Long, erect noseleaf. |
| HORSESHOE BATS | Enclosed in membrane | Large, no tragus | Complex noseleaf (anterior horseshoe sella, posterior lancet). |
| LEAF-NOSED BATS | Enclosed in membrane | Large, no tragus | Complex noseleaf, no sella and lancet. |
| FREE-TAILED BATS | Thick, free of membrane | Thick and fleshy, small tragus | Broad, no noseleaf, wrinkled lips. |
| EVENING BATS | Long, enclosed in membrane | Simple, tragus present | Simple, no noseleaf. |

# FRUIT BATS

| | |
|---|---|
| FAMILY NAME **Pteropodidae** | |
| DIET 🐾 🌿 📄 | |
| SOCIAL UNIT Colonies | |
| STRATUM Aerial, arboreal, cave-dwelling | |
| CONSERVATION THREATS Habitat loss, poaching | |

A LL FRUIT BATS are medium to large in size; have furred bodies, long snouts, simple nose and ears and no tail (or a small tail). The genus *Pteropus* comprises five large fruit bats of which the Indian Flying Fox is found throughout the mainland and the other four are seen in Andaman and Nicobar Islands. Eight other fruit bats are also found in India.

## INDIAN FLYING FOX *(Pteropus giganteus)*

POSSIBLY THE BEST-KNOWN BAT *in India, the Indian Flying Fox or Indian Fruit Bat is often seen roosting in hundreds on large trees. It is chestnut-brown with large black ears and huge black wings that it often folds over its tan or orange belly. Its back is blackish-brown with scattered pale hair.*
• **BEHAVIOUR** *The Indian Flying Fox constantly grooms itself. It hangs upside-down to defecate and sprinkles urine on itself to keep cool in summer. It usually flies out about half an hour after sunset to feed. It takes in only the juice and discards chewed fruit; citrus fruits are not part of its diet. The bat flies over water and drinks before feeding.*
• **SIZE** *FA: 15.2 – 18.3 cm. HBL: 19.8 – 30 cm.*
• **HABITAT AND OCCURRENCE** *Large trees in avenues, near cropland, and human habitation.*
• **BEST SEEN AT** *All over India, for example Tughlak Road, New Delhi.*

long claw on first digit

chestnut-brown coat

long black ears

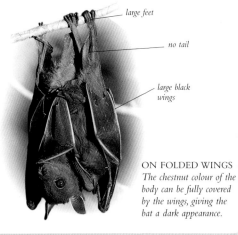

large feet

no tail

large black wings

ON FOLDED WINGS
*The chestnut colour of the body can be fully covered by the wings, giving the bat a dark appearance.*

| SIMILAR SPECIES | | | |
|---|---|---|---|
| **COMMON NAME** | **LATIN NAME** | **OCCURRENCE** | **IDENTIFICATION TIPS** |
| LARGE FLYING FOX | *Pteropus vampyrus* | Andaman and Nicobar Islands (seasonal visitor from Southeast Asia) | Dark brown chest and throat. Ears are the same size and shape as Indian Flying Fox's. FA: 19.5–20.9 cm. HBL: 25.9–30 cm. |
| NICOBAR FLYING FOX | *Pteropus faunulus* | Endemic to the Nicobars: Car Nicobar, Camorta, and Nancowrie | Smaller than the Indian Flying Fox, with triangular ears, brown back and grey-brown chest and belly. FA: 11–11.6 cm. HBL: 17 cm. |
| ISLAND FLYING FOX | *Pteropus hypomelanus* | Andaman Islands: Narcondam and Barren Islands | Grey-brown back. Short, broad and rounded ears. Fawnish crown; darker cheeks and snout. FA: 13.5–14.5 cm. HBL: 19.9–22 cm. |
| BLYTH'S FLYING FOX | *Pteropus melanotus* | Andaman and Nicobar Islands | Large, round ears and black back. Speckled grey back and black head in Andaman forms; brown head in Nicobar. FA: 14.8–16.3 cm. |

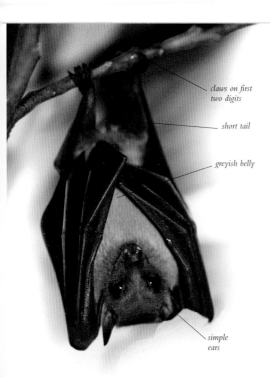

claws on first
two digits

short tail

greyish belly

simple
ears

## FULVOUS FRUIT BAT
### (Rousettus leschenaulti)

THIS BAT *is fulvous brown on the back, while its belly is grey. In older bats the flanks turn grey as well. Its fur is fine and soft and males have longer yellowish hair on the throat. It has a short tail.*

• BEHAVIOUR *Very noisy and smelling of fermented fruit, these bats roost in mixed colonies, hanging by their feet. Juveniles roost individually, while adults roost together. They can be easily disturbed and fly out en masse if disturbed.*

• SIZE *FA: 7.5 – 8.6 cm. HBL: 11.1 – 14.7 cm*

• HABITAT AND OCCURRENCE *Throughout India except deserts and high mountains (up to 1,400 m). Roosts in caves, tunnels, disused buildings, and rarely on trees.*

• BEST SEEN AT *Siju Caves, Meghalaya, and Kanheri Caves, Mumbai.*

## DAWN BAT *(Eonycteris spelaea)*

SLIGHTLY SMALLER THAN *the Fulvous Fruit Bat, the Dawn Bat has a claw only on its thumb and not on the second digit as in the former. Unlike Cynopteran bats, with which it shares roosts in the Northeast, it does not have "finger" markings on its uniform brown wings nor the pale borders on the ears.*

• BEHAVIOUR *It makes a clapping noise with its wings as it flies.*

• SIZE *FA: 6.6 – 7.8 cm. HBL: 9.2 – 13 cm.*

• HABITAT AND OCCURRENCE *Patchy distribution in dark caves of Karnataka, Uttar Pradesh, and Northeast India.*

## HILL LONG-TONGUED FRUIT BAT
### (Macroglossus sobrinus)

THIS BAT HAS A SLENDER *muzzle, upward pointing nostrils, and a long protrusible tongue with papillae at the tip–an adaptation for nectar feeding. It has a clay-brown back and buff sides, and brown rounded ears. It has no tail or a very short rod-like tail, and is smaller than the Fulvous Fruit Bat and Dawn Bat.*

• SIZE *FA: 4.4 – 5.2 cm. HBL: 7.8 – 8.9 cm.*

• HABITAT AND OCCURRENCE *Sikkim, North Bengal, and Northeast India. A forest dweller, it roosts on treetops and on the roofs of jungle dwellings.*

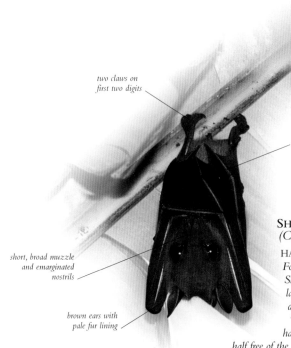

two claws on
first two digits

brown wings
with pale
fingers

short, broad muzzle
and emarginated
nostrils

brown ears with
pale fur lining

## SHORT-NOSED FRUIT BAT
### (Cynopterus sphinx)

HALF THE SIZE *of the Indian Flying
Fox, the soft and silky, brown-furred
Short-nosed Fruit Bat (see left) has
large, fur-lined coffee-brown ears and
dark brown wings marked by pale
"fingers". The first and second digits
have two distinct claws. A small tail,
half free of the membrane between the thighs, is
characteristic. Males are orangish on the chin, sides of
the chest, belly, and thighs, whereas females have a
paler grey belly and
a tawny brown collar. The bats found in northern
India are larger than those found in the south.*
• BEHAVIOUR *The male constructs a tent from
stems to shelter itself, females, and pups during the
breeding season. Active around half an hour after
sunset and through the night, these bats fly with
a low, fast wing beat like insect-eating bats. They
favour banana and guava fruits and are considered
useful pollinators.*
• SIZE *FA: 6.4–7.9 cm. HBL: 7.6–11.3 cm.*
• HABITAT AND OCCURRENCE *Throughout
India except deserts and the high Himalaya.
Favours palm and* **Ficus** *trees in gardens,
farmland, and forests, although it roosts on roofs
as well.*
• BEST SEEN AT *Throughout India.*

## LESSER DOG-FACED FRUIT BAT
### (Cynopterus brachyotis)

VERY SIMILAR IN *appearance to its slightly larger
cousin, the Short-nosed Fruit Bat, this species can
be easily identified by its much shorter ears (never
more than 1.8 cm long) without a pale border and
wings without the pale "fingers".*
• SIZE *FA: 5.7–6.3 cm. HBL: 8–9.6 cm.*
• HABITAT AND OCCURRENCE *Throughout
India (up to 1,500 m). It favours dense vegetation
and roosts on palm trees as well as in houses
and dimly lit caves. It is known to be partial to
guava trees.*
• BEST SEEN AT *Chinnamannur,
Tamil Nadu.*

## BLANFORD'S FRUIT BAT
### (Sphaerias blanfordi)

A UNIFORMLY BROWN BAT *which superficially resembles the **Cynopterus** and **Megaerops** genera, the Blanford's Fruit Bat differs from the former in not having a tail and from the latter in having pale fringes on its brown ears, two buff spots on its chin, and unique triangular incisors (visible only with the bat in hand). Its wings are uniformly brown.*
- SIZE *FA: 5.1–5.6 cm. HBL: 8.4–8.9 cm.*
- HABITAT AND OCCURRENCE *Restricted to the hills of Uttaranchal (Pithoragarh and Almora), Darjeeling in West Bengal, Sikkim, and Arunachal Pradesh. Prefers pine and oak forests in interior valleys.*

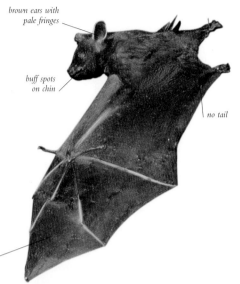

brown ears with pale fringes

buff spots on chin

no tail

grey brown colour

## SALIM ALI'S FRUIT BAT
### (Latidens salimalii)

THE ENDANGERED *Salim Ali's Fruit Bat has a highly restricted range in the southern Western Ghats. Its wings and short, soft dorsal fur is dark brown to black. While the fur on the back is dense, it becomes sparse on the belly and throat. There is a marked grizzling on the shoulders, back, and between the eyes and cheek. The lower back, elbows, and forearms are chestnut-brown. Its ears are brown ovals without a hairy or pale fringe.*
- SIZE *FA: 6.6–6.9 cm. HBL: 10.2–10.9 cm.*
- HABITAT AND OCCURRENCE *High altitude, broad-leaved montane forests interspersed with plantations in the High Wavy Mountains and Kalakaad WLS, Tamil Nadu.*
- BEST SEEN AT *Chinnamannur, Tamil Nadu.*

## RATANAWORABHAN'S FRUIT BAT
### (Megaerops niphanae)

THIS BAT SUPERFICIALLY *resembles the Lesser Dog-faced Fruit Bat, but is tailless.*
*Its coat is finer and less luxurious than in the **Cynopterus** species. It is greyish in colour and appears less brown than other fruit bats.*
*It has an olive belly and a paler grey-brown patch across the shoulders. One record of **Megaerops ecaudatus** from Namdapha NP is today believed to be of this species.*
- SIZE *FA: 5.2–6.3 cm. HBL: 8.1–9 cm.*
- HABITAT AND OCCURRENCE *Dense forests of Darjeeling in West Bengal, Manipur, Mizoram, and Arunachal Pradesh.*

# MOUSE-TAILED BATS

| | |
|---|---|
| FAMILY NAME **Rhinopomatidae** | |
| DIET 🍖 | |
| SOCIAL UNIT Groups of 1-10, at times up to 1500 | |
| STRATUM Aerial, arboreal, cave-dwelling | |
| CONSERVATION THREATS Human disturbance | |

TWO SMALL INSECTIVOROUS bats are found in the arid parts of India. A long and slender mouse-like tail that hangs partially free from the thigh membrane characterizes them. Unlike the Fruit Bats, these bats have ears that are joined at the forehead by a membrane and a nose with a pad and the beginnings of a noseleaf.

### GREATER MOUSE-TAILED BAT *(Rhinopoma microphyllum)*

GREY-BROWN IN COLOUR, *the Greater Mouse-tailed Bat has short fur on its head and on the upper part of its body. Its face, ears, membranes, wings, and the lower part of the body are naked. It has a long tail that is shorter than its forearm, unlike the Lesser Mouse-tailed Bat (see below), which has a tail that is longer than the forearm. The two have a range that overlaps. A third species,* **Rhinopoma muscatellum**, *the Small Mouse-tailed Bat, is known from two doubtful records in Rajasthan and Tamil Nadu.*
• BEHAVIOUR *Lives in sexually segregated colonies and despite being used to bright light, if disturbed, crawls along the roof in a crab-like fashion before taking flight. Flights are usually weak and fluttering, with frequent glides. A late-evening bat, it stays in large congregations of up to 1,500.*
• SIZE *FA: 5.9 − 7.4 cm. HBL: 6 − 8.4 cm.*
• HABITAT AND OCCURRENCE *Dry, arid parts of India, predominantly in Gujarat, Rajasthan, parts of Madhya Pradesh, and Maharashtra, including deserts. It lives in caves, tunnels, disused buildings, and crevices.*
• BEST SEEN AT *Tughlaqabad Fort, Delhi.*

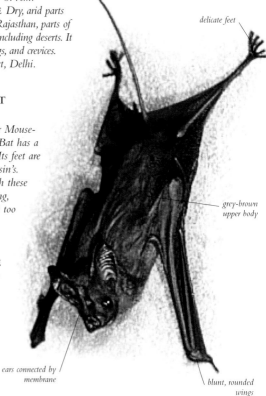

long, rat-like tail without membrane

delicate feet

### LESSER MOUSE-TAILED BAT
*(Rhinopoma hardwickii)*

A SMALLER VERSION *of the Greater Mouse-tailed Bat, the Lesser Mouse-tailed Bat has a longer tail and a distinct grey belly. Its feet are also more delicate than its larger cousin's.*
• BEHAVIOUR *The colonies of both these bats are characterized by a very strong, pungent odour. This late-evening bat too has a weak flight.*
• SIZE *FA: 5.2 − 6.4 cm. HBL: 5.5 − 7.3 cm.*
• HABITAT AND OCCURRENCE *This species has a wider distribution than* **R.microphyllum**, *which is more adapted to desert conditions. It lives in caves, tunnels, disused buildings, and crevices. Recorded in Arunachal Pradesh, Karnataka, Orissa, Bihar, and W Bengal.*
• BEST SEEN AT *Qutab Minar environs, New Delhi.*

grey-brown upper body

ears connected by membrane

blunt, rounded wings

# TOMB BATS

| | |
|---|---|
| ΛMILY NAME | Emballonuridae |
| ΙΕΤ | ✳ |
| ΟCIAL UNIT | Colonies of 100–1,000s |
| ΓRATUM | Aerial, fossorial, cave-dwelling |
| ONSERVATION THREATS | Human disturbance |

CHARACTERIZED BY A TAIL that is loosely attached to the thigh membrane but emergent at the tip, the six tomb or sheath-tailed bats are found all over India. These small, strong-smelling bats have dog-like heads, with squarish muzzles, no noseleaf, simple ears and eyes that shine in the dark. Most species have a wing spur and callosities on the feet that help them crawl up walls and stay suspended like geckos.

bare wings

### THEOBALD'S TOMB BAT
### (Taphozous theobaldi)

THE THEOBALD'S TOMB BAT *has dark beards in males (probably only in older males) and no gular sack. Unlike the Black-bearded Tomb Bat (see below), its fur is more grey and is restricted only to the body, while the wings and membranes are bare.*
• SIZE *FA: 7.1–7.6 cm. HBL: 8.8–8.9 cm.*
• HABITAT AND OCCURRENCE *Forested caves in Madhya Pradesh and Karnataka.*

### NAKED-RUMPED TOMB BAT
### (Taphozous nudiventris)

THIS IS A *dark brown bat with a naked rump. Males have a gular pouch and a circular gland on the chest but do not have a beard. The long, blackish-brown ears are widely separated.*
• SIZE *FA: 7.1–8 cm. HBL: 9–10.5 cm.*
• HABITAT AND OCCURRENCE *Arid areas of western, central, and northern India.*

### BLACK-BEARDED TOMB BAT *(Taphozous melanopogon)*

THIS BAT IS EASILY *recognized by its hairy chin (that turns black or dark brown in males). Its back is dark brown to black, or even pale buff, and the ventral side is always paler. Its hair appears grizzled because of paler hair bases. The female has a more reddish hue. Unlike other bats, its wings are attached to the shanks and not the ankles, and its ears are quite large.*
• BEHAVIOUR *Roosting in unisex colonies, this bat is easily disturbed and even flies out in daylight. The beard gets wet with secretion during the rut.*
• SIZE *FA: 6–6.8 cm. HBL: 6.7–8.6 cm.*
• HABITAT AND OCCURRENCE *Hilly terrain and well-watered forests; found in caves, ruins, and temples all over India except Northwest, Northeast, and high Himalaya.*
• BEST SEEN AT *Champa Baoli, Mandu (Madhya Pradesh).*

| SIMILAR SPECIES | | | |
|---|---|---|---|
| COMMON NAME | LATIN NAME | OCCURRENCE | IDENTIFICATION TIPS |
| LONG-WINGED TOMB BAT | *Taphozous longimanus* | Widespread in India, except extreme North and Arunachal Pradesh | Reddish-brown to black, pale patches on back. Males have a gular sack, but no beard. FA: 5.5–6.2 cm. HBL: 7.3–8.6 cm. |
| EGYPTIAN TOMB BAT | *Taphozous perforatus* | Arid thorn forests in Gujarat, MP, Rajasthan | Mousy grey with buff throat, beard and small gular pouch. FA: 5.4–6.3 cm. HBL: 7.1–8 cm. |
| POUCH-BEARING BAT | *Taphozous saccolaimus* | Scattered locations in India, including Andaman Islands | Brownish on dorsal side and greyish on ventral side. Has well-developed gular pouch and beard. FA: 6.3–6.8 cm. HBL: 8–9.3 cm. |

# HORSESHOE BATS

| | |
|---|---|
| FAMILY NAME | Rhinolophidae |
| DIET | 🕷 |
| SOCIAL UNIT | Single/colonies |
| STRATUM | Aerial |
| CONSERVATION THREATS | Human disturbance |

THE HORSESHOE BATS ARE a family of 64 species found in the Old World, of which 15 species occur in India. They have a complex noseleaf, with a horseshoe-shaped projection surrounding the nostrils. The species can be told apart by the shape of the sella (flap over the horseshoe projection) and lancet (the erect, triangular back of the noseleaf).

### GREATER HORSESHOE BAT
### (Rhinolophus ferrumequinum)

A MEDIUM-SIZED *bat with large ears and a dense, grey-brown pelage, its sella is narrow and so is the pointed lancet, which has concave sides. It can be told apart from the Intermediate and Rufous bats only by the length of the third metacarpal, once in hand.*
• BEHAVIOUR *It flies in a slow fluttering manner after dark. In the roost, these bats hang together in clusters, but once in the air they turn solitary feeders.*
• SIZE *FA: 5.4–6.2 cm. HBL: 5.6–7.9 cm.*
• HABITAT AND OCCURRENCE *Caves and ruins throughout Himalaya: J&K to Arunachal Pradesh, and Nagaland.*

### INTERMEDIATE HORSESHOE BAT
### (Rhinolophus affinis)

THIS SPECIES *is identical in colour to the Rufous Bat (see box below and p.150) but is slightly larger in size and has shorter ears.*
• SIZE *FA: 5–5.5 cm. HBL: 4.6–6.8 cm.*
• HABITAT AND OCCURRENCE *North and NE India, both in the Himalaya and plains.*

*long, soft pelage*

### WOOLLY HORSESHOE BAT
### (Rhinolophus luctus)

THIS SPECIES *has a woolly coat verging on black. Its broad horseshoe is divided into two halves and its sella has circular flaps on either side.*

• SIZE *FA: 7–8 cm. HBL: 8.5–9 cm.*
• HABITAT AND OCCURRENCE *North and NE India, south to Panchmari. A forest dweller, it is found in caves and tree hollows.*

### BIG-EARED HORSESHOE BAT
### (Rhinolophus macrotis)

THIS SMALL BAT *has a buff woolly coat and large ears. Its noseleaf differs from that of other bats of this family in having a projecting sella and a short lancet.*

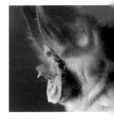

• SIZE *FA: 3.9–4.6 cm. HBL: 3.9–4.8 cm.*
• HABITAT AND OCCURRENCE *Caves and abandoned mines in hilly regions of North and NE India.*

### SIMILAR SPECIES

| COMMON NAME | LATIN NAME | OCCURRENCE | IDENTIFICATION TIPS |
|---|---|---|---|
| RUFOUS HORSESHOE BAT | Rhinolophus rouxii | Forest bat, found in southern and eastern India and Himalayan foothills | Silky fur, orangish in winter, brown-grey in summer. Lancet can be triangular or pointed, with concave sides. FA: 4.6–5.2 cm. HBL: 4.2–6.6 cm. |
| LESSER WOOLLY HORSESHOE BAT | Rhinolophus beddomei | W Ghats, in caves and tree hollows | Almost identical to Woolly Horseshoe Bat, but smaller. FA: 6.1–6.4 cm. HBL: 6.5–7.5 cm. |

## PEARSON'S HORSESHOE BAT *(Rhinolophus pearsonii)*

THIS MEDIUM-SIZED BAT *is chestnut-brown and has soft, woolly fur. Its noseleaf is broad and divided into two halves.*
• SIZE *FA: 5– 5.4 cm. HBL: 5.1 –6.4cm.*
• HABITAT AND OCCURRENCE *Mountains of northern West Bengal, Sikkim, Manipur, Meghalaya, and Uttaranchal.*

## DOBSON'S HORSESHOE BAT *(Rhinolophus yunanensis)*

THIS SPECIES IS *similar in appearance to the Pearson's Horseshoe Bat, but larger in size. Its pelage and ears resemble the Pearson's and like the former, its noseleaf is broad and bisected, and its sella does not have lappets (flaps) on either side.*
• SIZE *FA: 5.4– 5.9 cm. HBL: 6– 6.8 cm.*
• HABITAT AND OCCURRENCE *It has been recorded in two sites in Arunachal Pradesh and Mizoram.*

large size

large pointed ears

broad bisected noseleaf

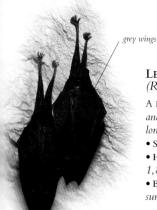

grey wings

## LESSER HORSESHOE BAT *(Rhinolophus hipposideros)*

A BUFF-BROWN OR GREY *bat, the Lesser Horseshoe Bat is small and has a unique sella with a tall, narrow, triangular lancet and a long tail in comparison to other horseshoe bats.*
• SIZE *FA: 3.5– 4 cm. HBL: 3.8– 4.8 cm.*
• HABITAT AND OCCURRENCE *Found only in J&K (1,230– 1,840 m) in caves, ruins, and outhouses.*
• BEST SEEN AT *Bumzov caves, J&K; common in Gilgit during the summer months.*

| SIMILAR SPECIES | | | |
| --- | --- | --- | --- |
| COMMON NAME | LATIN NAME | OCCURRENCE | IDENTIFICATION TIPS |
| BLYTH'S HORSESHOE BAT | *Rhinolophus lepidus* | Throughout India except J&K, Himachal Pradesh, and Gujarat | Drab brown or grey, paler on sides. Base of sella is round. FA: 3.7–4.1 cm. HBL: 3.5–5.4 cm. |
| LEAST HORSESHOE BAT | *R. pusillus* | Southern India, Himalaya, and NE India | Similar sella to *R. lepidus*, but more acute. Little known species. FA: 3.4–3.7 cm. HBL: 3–4 cm. |
| LITTLE NEPALESE HORSESHOE BAT | *R. subbadius* | Meghalaya and Arunachal Pradesh | Dark brown, short and broad lancet. FA: 3–3.5 cm. HBL: 3.5–3.7 cm. |
| ANDAMAN HORSESHOE BAT | *R. cognatus* | Endemic to Andaman Islands | Slightly larger than *R. subbadius*, horn-like sella. FA: 3.7–4 cm. |
| MITRED HORSESHOE BAT | *R. mitratus* | Endemic to Bihar | Dark brown; large ears; grooved lower lip. FA: 5.7 cm. |
| TREFOIL HORSESHOE BAT | *R. trifoliatus* | Darjeeling, W Bengal, and Assam | Woolly buff brown bat with narrow sella. FA: 5–5.3 cm. HBL: 6.2–6.5 cm. |

# LEAF-NOSED BATS

| FAMILY NAME | Hipposideridae |
|---|---|
| DIET | 🦗 |
| SOCIAL UNIT | Single/colonies |
| STRATUM | Aerial, cave-dwelling |
| CONSERVATION THREATS | Human disturbance |

CLOSELY RELATED TO horseshoe bats, leaf-nosed bats are small insect-eating cave roosters that have a complicated noseleaf comprising anterior, intermediate, and posterior layers arranged vertically above each other, and supplementary leaflets arranged below in whorls. The posterior of the noseleaf is rounded and without the horn-like projection found in horseshoe bats. The shape, size, and number of noseleafs determine which of the 13 species the bat belongs to.

## DUSKY LEAF-NOSED BAT
### (Hipposideros ater)

A SMALL BAT WITH *brownish-black wings and body fur varying from golden to dark brown to grey, the Dusky Leaf-nosed Bat has small rounded ears. Its long tail is enclosed in a membrane with only the tip sticking out. It has three clear noseleafs with no supplementary leaflets. The anterior leaf is hairy and has a triangular septum between the nostrils. The intermediate leaf is simple, with a convex upper border, and the posterior leaf is divided into four cells.*
- BEHAVIOUR *Males often live singly while females live in small unisex colonies. This late evening bat flies low with rapid wing beats.*
- SIZE *FA:3.4–3.8cm. HBL: 3.8–4.8cm.*
- HABITAT AND OCCURRENCE *Deep wells, wall crevices and abandoned mines in central, south-eastern and southern India (including Nicobars).*

3 noseleafs with no supplementary leaflets

ORNATE NOSES
*Noseleafs are complex structures developed from the skin around the nose that assist the bat in echolocation.*

## GREAT HIMALAYAN LEAF-NOSED BAT
### (Hipposideros armiger)

THE LARGEST OF THE *leaf-nosed bats, this species is clearly identified by the four supplementary leaflets on its anterior noseleaf. The intermediate leaf has wave-shaped patterns and there is a fleshy pad behind the four-celled posterior leaf. The dark brown wings and membranes stand out against a grey-brown body with soft, long fur.*
- BEHAVIOUR *It circles around trees, close to the ground or around bushes, like flying foxes, and hunts shortly after sunset. This bat is not easily disturbed by humans at its roost sites.*
- SIZE *FA: 8.5–9.5cm. HBL: 8.2–10.5cm.*
- HABITAT AND OCCURRENCE *High altitudes in central and eastern Himalaya (west as far as Mussoorie), and the Garo Hills. It roosts in caves, lofts of houses, etc.*
- BEST SEEN AT *Mussoorie.*

## SCHNEIDER'S LEAF-NOSED BAT
*(Hipposideros speoris)*

A MEDIUM-SIZED *species, the Schneider's Leaf-nosed Bat varies from grey to orange-brown, but is always palest between the shoulders and on the ventral side. It has small ears and its noseleaf is similar to the smaller leaf-nosed bats except for the three supplementary leaflets and well-developed lappets next to the nostrils.*
• BEHAVIOUR *It leaves its roost about 10 minutes after sunset and hunts in small parties of 10–15 bats. Males and females live together for most of the year.*
• SIZE *FA:4.5– 5.4 cm. HBL: 4.6– 6.2 cm.*
• HABITAT AND OCCURRENCE *Endemic to the Indian subcontinent, it is largely found in the forests and hills of southern India. Also recorded in Gujarat, Orissa, and Uttar Pradesh. It roosts in caves, tunnels, disused buildings, and hill crevices.*
• BEST SEEN AT *Elephanta Caves, Maharashtra.*

## FULVOUS LEAF-NOSED BAT
*(Hipposideros fulvus)*

SIMILAR TO *H. ater in colouration but with larger ears, it is larger and more rufous than other leaf-nosed bats. Supplementary leaflet is absent.*
• SIZE *FA: 3.8– 4.4 cm. HBL: 4– 5 cm.*
• HABITAT AND OCCURRENCE *An endemic and common bat found through the country except for the high Himalaya and NE India. It favours cool and damp places including caves and disused buildings close to water.*
• BEST SEEN AT *Elephanta Caves, Maharashtra.*

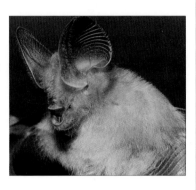

| SIMILAR SPECIES | | | |
|---|---|---|---|
| **COMMON NAME** | **LATIN NAME** | **OCCURRENCE** | **IDENTIFICATION TIPS** |
| KOLAR LEAF-NOSED BAT | *Hipposideros hypophyllus* | Caves in Kolar and Mysore. Endemic | One supplementary leaflet. Large ears. FA: 3.7–4 cm. HBL: 4.2–4.7 cm. |
| HORSFIELD'S LEAF-NOSED BAT | *Hipposideros larvatus* | Caves and mines of Northeast India | Cinnamon-brown, rounded ears; 3 supplementary leaflets. FA: 6.1–6.4 cm. HBL: 7.4–7.8 cm. |
| CANTOR'S LEAF-NOSED BAT | *Hipposideros galeritus* | Central, western and southern India. One record in Bihar | Same size as the Schneider's Bat, but with two supplementary noseleafs instead of three. FA: 4.5–5.1 cm. HBL: 4.5–5.9 cm. |
| ANDERSENS'S LEAF-NOSED BAT | *Hipposideros pomona* | Northeast and South India | Small bat similar to *H. fulvus* with noseleaf like *H. ater*. FA: 3.8–4.3 cm. HBL: 3.6–5.2 cm. |
| LEAST LEAF-NOSED BAT | *Hipposideros cineraceus* | Low Himalayan foothills, Uttaranchal to Arunachal Pradesh | Almost identical to *H. ater*, but may be paler on ventral surface. FA: 3.3–3.6 cm. HBL: 3.3–4.2 cm. |
| KHAJURIA'S LEAF-NOSED BAT | *Hipposideros durgadasi* | Endemic species found in the caves of Jabalpur | Resembles *H. ater*, but more brown than grey. Pale ventral surface, slightly longer tail. FA: 3.6–3.7 cm. |
| TAIL-LESS LEAF-NOSED BAT | *Coelops frithii* | West Bengal and Meghalaya | Funnel-shaped ears, characteristic noseleaf with two protruding flaps on anterior leaf. FA: 3.7–4.2 cm. HBL: 3.8–5 cm. |
| KELAART'S LEAF-NOSED BAT | *Hipposideros lankadiva* | Rajasthan, central and South India, W Bengal, Orissa, and Meghalaya | Similar to *H. armiger*, shorter, brighter orange fur. Fourth leaflet small or absent. FA: 7.5–9.9 cm. HBL: 8.7–10.6 cm. |
| DIADEM LEAF-NOSED BAT | *Hipposideros diadema* | Trinket Islands, Nicobar | Large bat with tri-coloured (chocolate, grey and brown) hair on back. FA: 5.8–6.4 cm. |

# FALSE VAMPIRES

| | |
|---|---|
| FAMILY NAME **Megadermatidae** | |
| DIET 🐾 🦎 🐁 🐦 | |
| SOCIAL UNIT *M. lyra*: groups of 15–20 (up to 100s); *M. spasma*: 1–25 | |
| STRATUM Aerial, arboreal, cave-dwelling | |
| CONSERVATION THREATS Unknown | |

THE MEMBERS OF THIS carnivorous family of bats are tailless, with tall oval ears that have a distinct smaller "inner ear" or tragus. They are also characterized by a simple noseleaf. Two species of False Vampires are found in India and the easiest way of telling them apart is by the shape of their noseleaf.

## LESSER FALSE VAMPIRE
### (Megaderma spasma)

AS THE NAME SUGGESTS, *the Lesser False Vampire is a smaller version of the Greater False Vampire. It is deeper grey and its tall ears are joined together at the base. Its noseleaf, by which it can be distinguished from* **M. lyra**, *is shorter and broader, and is heart-shaped at the base.*
• BEHAVIOUR *The Lesser False Vampire flies very close to the ground and may fly for the first few hours after dark without hunting, starting to feed only as the night progresses. It often rests in between its flapping flight under rocks and bushes.*
• SIZE *FA: 5.4– 6.2 cm. HBL: 5.4–8.1 cm.*
• HABITAT AND OCCURRENCE *Western coast (Goa, Maharashtra), southern India, Andaman Islands and lowland humid forests of Northeast India. Prefers a more moist habitat than the Greater False Vampire. Roosts in caves, houses, and wells.*
• BEST SEEN AT *Barapeda Caves, Karnataka.*

## GREATER FALSE VAMPIRE
### (Megaderma lyra)

THIS IS A LARGE, *well-built mouse-grey bat with paler undersides and an almost whitish belly. Its wings are broad and the membranes greyish-black. The large greyish-black ears are joined for at least two-thirds of their length. Its snout is naked and has a tall noseleaf that resembles two ovals stuck together.*
• BEHAVIOUR *A late and silent flier, it emerges an hour after sunset. The genus is unique among Indian bats in eating vertebrates (frogs, rodents, and small birds) as well as insects. Females carry the young till they are almost adult-sized.*
• SIZE *FA: 5.6– 7.1 cm. HBL: 7–9.5 cm.*
• HABITAT AND OCCURRENCE *Throughout India, except high Himalaya and deserts, in caves, forests, and human dwellings.*
• BEST SEEN AT *Kanheri Caves, Mumbai.*

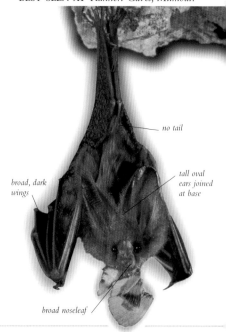

no tail

tall oval ears joined at base

broad, dark wings

broad noseleaf

# FREE-TAILED BATS

| FAMILY NAME | Molossidae |
|---|---|
| DIET | 🐛 |
| SOCIAL UNIT | Groups of 5-6 to 100s |
| STRATUM | Aerial, arboreal |
| CONSERVATION THREATS | Unknown |

## WROUGHTON'S FREE-TAILED BAT *(Otomops wroughtoni)*

A LARGE, GLOSSY BROWN, *critically endangered species, this bat has ears that meet on top of its head. It has a distinct grey collar and a small gular sac in both sexes. A small moustache is present beneath circular nostrils.*
• SIZE *FA: 6.3 – 6.7 cm. HBL: 8.7 – 9.9 cm.*
• HABITAT AND OCCURRENCE *One cave (Barapeda) in Karnataka.*

| SIMILAR SPECIES | | | |
|---|---|---|---|
| COMMON NAME | LATIN NAME | OCCURRENCE | IDENTIFICATION TIPS |
| EUROPEAN FREE-TAILED BAT | *Tadarida teniotis* | Kurseong, West Bengal | Dog-like muzzle; deeply furrowed upper lip; large ears. FA: 5.8–6.3 cm. HBL: 7.4–9 cm. |
| WRINKLE-LIPPED FREE-TAILED BAT | *Tadarida plicata* | 12 locations scattered through India | Thick ears that meet; wrinkled, over-hanging upper lip. FA: 4.3–5 cm. HBL: 6.6–7.1 cm. |
| EGYPTIAN FREE-TAILED BAT | *Tadarida aegyptiaca* | Western and southern India | Clove-brown with furrowed upper lip; clearly separated ears. FA: 4.6–5.2 cm. HBL: 6.1–7.7 cm. |

# PAINTED BATS

| FAMILY NAME | Vespertilionidae |
|---|---|
| DIET | 🐛 |
| SOCIAL UNIT | Solitary/pairs |
| STRATUM | Aerial, arboreal |
| CONSERVATION THREATS | Unknown |

DESPITE BEING AMONG the smallest bats (the size of a large moth), the Painted Bats are the easiest to recognize due to their distinctive coat. However, despite their bright colours, they are excellently camouflaged in dead banana leaves or other ingenious hiding places such as abandoned nests of weaver birds.

## PAINTED BAT *(Kerivoula picta)*

THIS SPECIES HAS *bright orange and black wings and long, dense fur which is bright orange on the back, and warm buff below. Its hairy face has no ornamentations or noseleaf. The ears are large with a transparent tragus.*
• BEHAVIOUR *It flies with an up and down flutter reminiscent of moths.*
• SIZE *FA: 3.1 – 3.7 cm. HBL: 4.5 – 4.8 cm.*
• HABITAT AND OCCURRENCE *Forest groves of Western Ghats and Assam.*

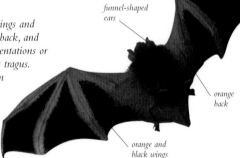

*funnel-shaped ears*

*orange back*

*orange and black wings*

| SIMILAR SPECIES | | | |
|---|---|---|---|
| COMMON NAME | LATIN NAME | OCCURRENCE | IDENTIFICATION TIPS |
| HARDWICKE'S FOREST BAT | *Kerivoula hardwickii* | Northeast India. Stray records from J&K and Karnataka | Clove-brown with a grey underside. Large ears and wings are nearly transparent. FA: 3.1–3.6 cm. HBL: 3.9–5.5 cm. |
| PAPILLOSE BAT | *Kerivoula papillosa* | Known only from Kolkata | Brownish-grey bat with unfringed wings. FA: 4–4.2 cm. HBL: 5.3–5.5 cm. |

163

# MOUSE-EARED BATS

| | |
|---|---|
| FAMILY NAME | Vespertilionidae |
| DIET | 🦟 |
| SOCIAL UNIT | Small groups |
| STRATUM | Aerial, arboreal, cave-dwelling |
| CONSERVATION THREATS | Unknown |

THE 12 SPECIES THAT are found in India are part of a genus that is distributed worldwide. These small insectivorous bats have tall and narrow ears with an equally long and slender tragus. The nostrils are simple and the tail is entirely enclosed in the inter-femoral membrane.

## HODGSON'S BAT *(Myotis formosus)*

THIS RARE MEDIUM-SIZED *tree bat of striking colouration has a ginger-brown back, orangish flanks and undersides, and a cinnamon throat. Its oval, orange-coloured ears stick out of its hairy head, and its wings are orange with triangular black markings.*
• BEHAVIOUR *The Hodgson's Bat roosts in trees, often camouflaged amongst decaying leaves or flowers of the same colour as itself.*
• SIZE *FA: 4.4–4.9 cm.*
• HABITAT AND OCCURRENCE *Throughout northern India, south to Nagpur and east to Goalpara, Assam.*

*black and orange wings*

| SIMILAR SPECIES | | | |
|---|---|---|---|
| COMMON NAME | LATIN NAME | OCCURRENCE | IDENTIFICATION TIPS |
| BURMESE WHISKERED BAT | *M. montivagus* | South India (Jog Falls) | Dark brown. FA: 4–4.6 cm. HBL: 5.6–6.2 cm. |
| HAIRY-FACED BAT | *M. annectans* | West Bengal and Nagaland | Furry face. FA: 4.5–4.6cm. HBL: 4.5–4.8 cm. |
| WATER BAT | *M. daubentonii* | Meghalaya | Sooty coat, hairy face. FA: 3.4 cm. HBL: 4.1 cm. |
| HORSFIELD'S BAT | *M. horsfieldii* | South India (Venniar Estate), once in Meghalaya | Brown bat with chocolate wings. FA: 3.6–4.1 cm. HBL: 4.9–5.9 cm. |
| VAN HASSELT'S BAT | *M. hasseltii* | Extralimital (Sri Lanka), once in Kolkata | Dark brown bat with extremely long feet. FA: 3.7–4 cm. HBL: 5.2–5.8 cm. |
| LESSER MOUSE-EARED BAT | *M. blythii* | Scrubland of N India | Largest of the family – woolly buff coat, tall ears. FA: 5.5–5.8 cm. HBL: 6.5–8 cm. |

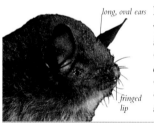

*long, oval ears*

*fringed lip*

## NEPALESE WHISKERED BAT *(Myotis muricola)*

THIS SMALL BAT *has a lip with a hairy whisker-like fringe. Its hair is russet-brown with dark bases and it has small ears and feet.*
• BEHAVIOUR *Often roosts in rolled-up banana leaves at the centre of the plant.*
• SIZE *FA: 3.1–3.7cm. HBL: 4.1–4.7cm.*
• HABITAT AND OCCURRENCE *Valleys and mountains of northern and eastern India (up to 3,000m).*

| SIMILAR SPECIES | | | |
|---|---|---|---|
| COMMON NAME | LATIN NAME | OCCURRENCE | IDENTIFICATION TIPS |
| WHISKERED BAT | *M. mystacinus* | N and E India, sympatric to *M. mystacinus* | Brown hair on back has pale tips. FA: 3.4–3.6 cm. HBL: 3.8–4.7 cm. |
| SILIGURI BAT | *M. siligorensis* | Uttaranchal, northern W Bengal, Sikkim, Meghalaya | Dark brown. FA: 3–3.1 cm. |
| MANDELLI'S MOUSE-EARED BAT | *M. sicarius* | Sikkim and northern W Bengal | Chocolate back and ginger ventral side. FA: 4.8–5.4 cm. HBL: 5–5.6 cm. |
| KASHMIR CAVE BAT | *M. longipes* | J&K, Garo and Khasi hills (Meghalaya) | Dark grey back and creamy ventral surface. FA: 3.6–3.9 cm. HBL: 4.3–4.6 cm. |

# LONG-EARED AND HARLEQUIN BATS

| | |
|---|---|
| FAMILY NAME | Vespertilionidae |
| DIET | 🦟 |
| SOCIAL UNIT | Small groups |
| STRATUM | Aerial, arboreal, cave-dwelling |
| CONSERVATION THREATS | Unknown |

THE THREE LONG-EARED bats of the northern Indian mountains are easily identified by their long oval ears set close together on the forehead, which are as long as the head and body put together. They have a long tail enclosed in a membrane that is equally long. The fur colour of these bats is variable from dark buff to cream.

## GREY LONG-EARED BAT *(Plecotus austriacus)*

A SMALL DARK BUFF *or cream bat, it has grossly exaggerated ears, characteristic of this family. They are pale brown, translucent and ridged with twenty lines on each. It is larger than P. auritus and the pelage varies from being very pale to darker buff.*
• BEHAVIOUR *This is a slow-flying, early-evening bat that hovers in front of bushes in search of food.*
• SIZE *FA: 4.1–4.5 cm. HBL: 4.7–5.3 cm*
• HABITAT AND OCCURRENCE *Forests and mountains of J&K.*

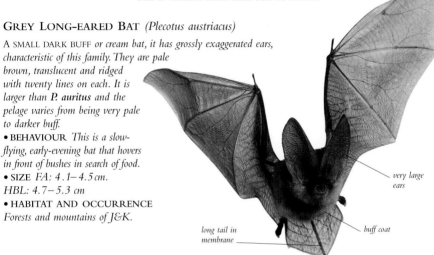

very large ears

long tail in membrane

buff coat

### SIMILAR SPECIES

| COMMON NAME | LATIN NAME | OCCURRENCE | IDENTIFICATION TIPS |
|---|---|---|---|
| BROWN LONG-EARED BAT | *Plecotus auritus* | J&K, Uttaranchal, Himachal Pradesh, W Bengal, and Meghalaya | Slightly smaller than *P. austriacus*, this species has a darker buff coat. FA: 3.6–4 cm. HBL: 4–4.5 cm. |
| HEMPRICH'S LONG-EARED BAT | *Otonycteris hemprichii* | J&K and Himachal Pradesh | Almost twice the size of the two *Plecotus* bats, its ears are yellowish-brown and not as large. Back is pale. FA: 6.4–6.5 cm. HBL: 6.1–7.6 cm. |

cream underparts

dark brown wings

naked brown ears

## HARLEQUIN BAT *(Scotomanes ornatus)*

AN ORANGE OR *orange-brown bat with an underside of brown and cream hairs, the Harlequin Bat is easy to recognize because of its unique colouration. Its wings are uniformly brown, as are its naked muzzle and small rounded ears. Its feet are black.*
• BEHAVIOUR *The Harlequin Bat emerges just before dark and twitters constantly as it flies.*
• SIZE *FA: 5.6–6.1 cm. HBL: 6.4–8.5 cm.*
• HABITAT AND OCCURRENCE *Deep valleys up to a height of 3,500 m. It prefers warmer climates and is restricted to Sikkim, northern W Bengal, and Northeast India.*

# SEROTINES AND YELLOW HOUSE BATS

| FAMILY NAME Vespertilionidae |
| --- |
| DIET 🜚 |
| SOCIAL UNIT Solitary/small groups. |
| STRATUM Aerial, arboreal, cave-dwelling |
| CONSERVATION THREATS Unknown |

THE FIVE SPECIES OF serotines found in India look very similar to the pipistrelles and cannot be distinguished from them in the field. Like pipistrelles, serotines are small or medium-sized bats with broad wings. The tragus in the ear is short and blunt. Yellow house bats are similar to serotines, with smaller ears and a pointed tragus.

## COMMON SEROTINE *(Eptesicus serotinus)*

THIS IS A LARGE, DARK BROWN BAT *with a pale brown belly and throat. It has a thick muzzle, naked except for some hair on the lip, with glandular swellings on both sides. Its ears are dark and long, with six parallel ridges on them, and it has a long tail with a small portion protruding beyond the membrane.*
• BEHAVIOUR *The Common Serotine has a straight, even, slow flight and makes constant clicks and squeaks. It hibernates in ones and twos, or small groups, in tree hollows.*
• SIZE *FA: 5.4–5.5 cm. HBL: 8 cm.*
• HABITAT AND OCCURRENCE *Hollow trees and caves in the Himalaya, from J&K to Assam, and Nagaland. It prefers foothills and is not found at high altitudes.*

## BOTTA'S SEROTINE *(Eptesicus bottae)*

A SMALLER SEROTINE, *it is pale buff with a light throat and dark brown wing membranes. The hairs on the upper body have dark hair roots.*
• BEHAVIOUR *It is an audible bat, squeaking as it flies low.*
• SIZE *FA: 4.2 cm. HBL: 5.7 cm.*
• HABITAT AND OCCURRENCE *Roofs of disused buildings in J&K.*

## THICK-EARED BAT *(Eptesicus pachyotis)*

A RARE BAT, *it resembles the common serotine and is dark brown in colour with paler undersides. It has a flat head with a short muzzle. The triangular ears have a thick and fleshy lobe that is characteristic. The tragus is short, broad and curved inwards. Very little is known of the species.*
• SIZE *FA: 3.8–4 cm. HBL: 5.5–5.6 cm.*
• HABITAT AND OCCURRENCE *Khasi hills, Meghalaya.*

### SIMILAR SPECIES

| COMMON NAME | LATIN NAME | OCCURRENCE | IDENTIFICATION TIPS |
| --- | --- | --- | --- |
| BOBRINSKII'S SEROTINE | *Eptesicus gobiensis* | J&K | Pale buff bat with a light throat and pale yellow wing membranes. FA: 4.1 cm. |
| SOMBRE BAT | *Eptesicus tatei* | Endemic to Darjeeling, W Bengal | Fully black in colour. FA: 4.3 cm. HBL: 4.8 cm. |

## ASIATIC GREATER YELLOW HOUSE BAT *(Scotophilus heathii)*

EASILY RECOGNIZABLE BY ITS *yellowish-brown back and bright yellow underside, this bat is thick-set, with a long tail that is enclosed in the membrane. The dark muzzle is naked and swollen. It has a pale nape and small ears with transverse ridges on them. The Asiatic Lesser Yellow Bat* (**Scotophilus kuhlii**) *is smaller (FA: 4.4-5.6 cm. HBL: 6-7.8 cm) and its undersides are buff, not canary yellow in colour.*
• BEHAVIOUR *It has a low, straight, silent flight and is not shy of light when roosting.*
• SIZE *FA: 5.5–6.5 cm. HBL: 6.7–9.3 cm.*
• HABITAT AND OCCURRENCE *Throughout India except J&K and the high Himalaya (up to 1,400 m). It roosts in old buildings, hollow trees, under palm fronds and even in homes.*

# FLAT-HEADED BATS

| | |
|---|---|
| FAMILY NAME | Vespertilionidae |
| DIET | 🦗 |
| SOCIAL UNIT | Groups of 3–4 |
| STRATUM | Aerial, arboreal |
| CONSERVATION THREATS | Unknown |

THE FLAT-HEADED OR Bamboo bats are two serotine-like bats with a broad and flattened head gently sloping to the nostrils. These bats have fleshy pads on the thumb and the sole of the foot, making them look club-footed.

*brown fur*

### FLAT-HEADED BAT *(Tylonycteris pachypus)*

THIS IS A VERY SMALL *bat with triangular ears and dark brown wings. It has a golden head, throat and upper back while the lower back and belly are dark brown. The Greater Flat-headed Bat (**T. robustula**) is very similar externally, except that its back is uniformly dark and the belly is paler. Unlike its smaller cousin, it is found only in Mizoram.*
- BEHAVIOUR *This bat lives in bamboos, entering the stem through slits created by insect larvae. The fleshy pads and balls on its feet help it to cling and move inside the smooth surface of the bamboo.*
- SIZE *FA: 2.6–2.9 cm. HBL: 3.4–4.6 cm.*

*flat head*

- HABITAT AND OCCURRENCE *Bamboo forests of the Western Ghats and Northeast India.*
- BEST SEEN AT *Sirsi, Karnataka.*

# TUBE-NOSED BATS

| | |
|---|---|
| FAMILY NAME | Vespertilionidae |
| DIET | 🦗 |
| SOCIAL UNIT | Groups of 3–4 |
| STRATUM | Aerial, arboreal |
| CONSERVATION THREATS | Unknown |

TUBE-NOSED BATS ARE A group of less than a dozen Southeast Asian bats, of which seven are found in India, with prominent tubular nostrils that project beyond the muzzle. They are small bats with dense woolly or wavy fur and relatively broad wings.

### ROUND-EARED TUBE-NOSED BAT *(Murina cyclotis)*

THIS IS A SMALL BAT *that is rufous on its back and paler on its ventral surface. It has rounded ears and the top of the wings have fine orange fur while the undersides are naked.*
- BEHAVIOUR *It displays slow, deliberate flight, at times skimming close to the ground.*
- SIZE *FA: 2.9 – 3.4 cm. HBL: 3.8 – 5 cm.*
- HABITAT AND OCCURRENCE *Forests and hilly plantations in northern West Bengal and the Northeast; once recorded in Andhra Pradesh.*

| SIMILAR SPECIES | | | |
|---|---|---|---|
| COMMON NAME | LATIN NAME | OCCURRENCE | IDENTIFICATION TIPS |
| SCULLY'S TUBE-NOSED BAT | *M. tubinaris* | Himalaya | Grey pelage. FA: 3–3.4 cm. HBL: 3.9–4.8 cm. |
| HUTTON'S TUBE-NOSED BAT | *M. huttonii* | Himalaya | Pointed ears, grey-brown back, whitish belly. FA: 3.2–3.5 cm. HBL: 4.8 cm. |
| GREATER TUBE-NOSED BAT | *M. leucogaster* | Darjeeling, W Bengal, and eastern Himalaya | Larger species with brownish-red and fawn hair on back. FA: 4 cm. HBL: 4.7 cm. |
| LITTLE TUBE-NOSED BAT | *M. aurata* | Sikkim and Meghalaya | Golden-brown bat with soft, thick fur. FA: 2.7–2.9 cm. HBL: 4.5 cm. |
| PETER'S TUBE-NOSED BAT | *M. grisea* | Endemic to one location in Uttar Pradesh | Dark brown bat with yellow-tipped dorsal fur and ashy grey-tipped ventral fur. FA: 3.2 cm. |
| HAIRY-WINGED BAT | *Harpiocephalus harpia* | Kerala, Tamil Nadu, and NE India | Dorsal pelage is rufous, buff and grey; pale buff-grey venter. FA: 4.4–5 cm. HBL: 6–7.5 cm. |

# PIPISTRELLES

| | |
|---|---|
| FAMILY NAME | Vespertilionidae |
| DIET | 🦟 |
| SOCIAL UNIT | Groups of 15–20 |
| STRATUM | Aerial, arboreal, cave-dwelling |
| CONSERVATION THREATS | Human disturbance |

THIS GROUP COMPRISES a dozen small bats in India, very similar to serotines. They have a simple face with a groove between the nostrils and swellings on either side of the muzzle. They lack a noseleaf and exaggerated ears. As a group they exhibit the same rapid, erratic flight and are the first bats out in the evening.

smoky brown back

black wing

## COMMON PIPISTRELLE
*(Pipistrellus pipistrellus)*

THIS IS A SMALL BAT *(see left), smoky brown on top, paler on the lower back, with narrow black opaque wings. Its ears are rounded and the tragus is pointed and slightly curved.*
• SIZE *FA: 3–3.1 cm. HBL: 4–4.8 cm.*
• HABITAT AND OCCURRENCE *Crevices in walls and rocks. Common throughout Eurasia, this bat is found in India only in J&K and in one location in Assam.*

## INDIAN PYGMY BAT
*(Pipistrellus tenuis)*

ALMOST IDENTICAL TO *the Indian Pipistrelle, the Indian Pygmy Bat is marginally smaller, darker, and with ears that appear squarish when seen in outline. It also lacks the paler wing margin of the Indian Pipistrelle. Although both species share roosts, they occupy separate spaces—probably the only way to tell them apart in the field.*
• SIZE *FA: 2.5–3 cm. HBL: 3.3–4.5 cm.*
• HABITAT AND OCCURRENCE *Common throughout India.*

## INDIAN PIPISTRELLE
*(Pipistrellus coromandra)*

A SMALL PIPISTRELLE, *this brown bat is chocolate or chestnut on top and beige below. Its wings, membranes, and tip of the muzzle are naked and black and its brown triangular ears are rounded at the tips. It has a slow, fluttering flight.*
• BEHAVIOUR *Though it inhabits dense vegetation, it is also known to fly into houses in search of insects and to roost in bamboo thatch roofs.*
• SIZE *FA: 2.5–3.4 cm. HBL: 3.4 –4.9 cm.*
• HABITAT AND OCCURRENCE *Forested areas as well as in towns and cities, almost throughout the country except Rajasthan. Found in buildings and trees alike.*

## MOUNT POPA PIPISTRELLE
*(Pipistrellus paterculus)*

A SMALL OLIVE-BROWN *bat with a deep chocolate back and ginger-brown abdomen, the Mount Popa Pipistrelle is found in eastern and NE India, and J&K. Common in Myanmar, it is little known in India. Its sloping forehead distinguishes it from P. tenuis.*
• SIZE *FA: 2.9–3.4 cm. HBL: 4.2–4.8 cm.*
• HABITAT AND OCCURRENCE *Forests, buildings, and tree stumps in J&K, Bihar and NE India.*

## KUHL'S PIPISTRELLE *(Pipistrellus kuhlii)*

THIS SPECIES WITH *its tall ears, long tail and buff-brown pelage is known from a few localities in eastern India. The ears and membranes are translucent, and there is a white border between the foot and the wing.*
• SIZE *FA: 3.3–3.6 cm.*
*HBL: 3.5–4.9 cm.*
• HABITAT AND OCCURRENCE *Open areas. It is common in Pakistan and has been recorded in West Bengal, Assam, and Meghalaya in India.*

## KELAART'S PIPISTRELLE
*(Pipistrellus ceylonicus)*

A LARGE BAT *with dark brown ears, face, and membranes, the Kelaart's Pipistrelle varies in body colour from grey-brown to chestnut, or even red-gold at times. Its ventral surface is duller and darker.*
• BEHAVIOUR *It clings to the surface of its roost with its feet and wing claws, and does not hang downward like other bats. It crawls if placed on the ground, and finds it difficult to become airborne except from a high roost.*

• SIZE *FA: 3.3–4.2 cm. HBL: 4.5–6.4 cm.*
• HABITAT AND OCCURRENCE *Forests and towns of south, central, eastern, and western India; it is not recorded north of Mount Abu or in the Northeast. Inhabits old buildings and tree hollows.*
• BEST SEEN AT *Pune and Mumbai, Maharashtra.*

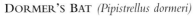

## DORMER'S BAT *(Pipistrellus dormeri)*

A MEDIUM-SIZED PIPISTRELLE *with a short tail, it has a glossy grey-brown back, sometimes yellowish-brown, and a pale front. Its face, ears, and wings are dark brown, and the veins in its inter-femoral membrane are sometimes white.*
• BEHAVIOUR *This bat is a slow flier, despite fast wing beats, and it glides occasionally.*

• SIZE *FA: 3.2–3.6 cm. HBL: 3.9–5.5 cm.*
• HABITAT AND OCCURRENCE *Throughout India, except in the high Himalaya, in towns and villages. It is especially abundant in Gujarat and Rajasthan. It roosts in disused buildings, under tiles in the roof, and tree hollows.*

| SIMILAR SPECIES | | | |
|---|---|---|---|
| COMMON NAME | LATIN NAME | OCCURRENCE | IDENTIFICATION TIPS |
| SAVI'S PIPISTRELLE | P. savii | Cherrapunji, Meghalaya | Blackish face; dark brown back, pale front; small tail. FA: 3.2–3.8 cm. HBL: 4.7–6 cm. |
| JAVAN PIPISTRELLE | P. javanicus | Scattered localities all over India | Chestnut-brown pelage. Naked wings. FA: 3–3.6 cm. HBL: 4–5.5 cm. |
| THOMAS'S PIPISTRELLE | P. cadornae | Forests of Darjeeling, West Bengal | Dark brown, with soft long fur. FA: 3.2–3.6 cm. HBL: 4.7–5.2 cm. |
| CHOCOLATE PIPISTRELLE | P. affinis | Scattered locations all over India | Grizzled, grey-brown pelage. FA: 3.8–4.1 cm. HBL: 4.3–5 cm. |
| BLACK GILDED PIPISTRELLE | Arielulus circumdatus | Shillong, Meghalaya | Totally black pelage with orange sheen created by brown hair tips; brown ears with pale margins. FA: 4.1–4.3 cm. HBL: 9.5 cm. |

# OTHER EVENING BATS

| | |
|---|---|
| FAMILY NAME | Vespertilionidae |
| DIET | 🌙 |
| SOCIAL UNIT | Colonies |
| STRATUM | Aerial, arboreal |
| CONSERVATION THREATS | Human disturbance |

*cinnamon coat*

### COMMON NOCTULE *(Nyctalus noctula)*

A LARGE, ROBUST BAT, *the Common Noctule is a mountain bat of the early evenings. It has extremely narrow and long leathery black wings and glossy cinnamon or dark brown fur. The short triangular ears have a club-shaped tragus. Its large nostrils are set above the mouth, which has a swelling on the upper lip and a yellowish buccal pad in adults.*

• BEHAVIOUR *The bats, as well as their roost, have a strong odour. Hibernating in winter in colonies, they appear only in spring.*

• SIZE *FA: 5−5.7cm. HBL: 6.8−8cm.*

• HABITAT AND OCCURRENCE *Caves, human habitation, and tree hollows in the Himalaya from J&K to Nagaland. Not a very high-altitude bat (1,000−2,000 m).*

*narrow, black wings*

| SIMILAR SPECIES | | | |
|---|---|---|---|
| COMMON NAME | LATIN NAME | OCCURRENCE | IDENTIFICATION TIPS |
| LEISLER'S BAT | *N. leisleri* | Western Himalaya | Smaller than *N. noctula*; has longer and thicker fur. FA: 4.2–4.5 cm. HBL: 6.2–7.2 cm. |
| MOUNTAIN NOCTULE | *N. montanus* | Western Himalaya | Has a bi-coloured coat due to hair being black at the roots. FA: 4.2–4.3 cm. HBL: 7 cm. |

### GREAT EVENING BAT *(Ia io)*

AMONG THE BIGGEST *of the evening bats, this species resembles a large grey-brown serotine with black wings. Its long tail sticks partially out of a dark inter-femoral membrane and its ears are broad and rounded.*

• SIZE *FA: 7−7.7cm*

• HABITAT AND OCCURRENCE *A single cave at 1,500 m, in an oak forest setting.*

• ONLY SEEN AT *Mausmai Cave near Cherrapunji, Meghalaya.*

## SCHREIBER'S LONG-FINGERED BAT *(Miniopterus schreibersii)*

THIS IS A SMALL EVENING BAT *with long, dense fur varying from russet to dark brown. It has long limbs and a highly enlarged third digit. Its ears are small, rounded, and set apart, and do not rise above the head, which has a highly domed forehead. Its tragus is slender, tall, and slightly curled at the tip, and its tail is enclosed almost fully in a membrane. It is most easily recognized by its characteristic position at rest with its wings folded back, giving it the alternate name of Bent-winged Bat. Closely resembling it but smaller and blacker is the **Nicobar Long-fingered Bat** (**M. pusillus**) found in the Nicobar Islands, Karnataka, and Tamil Nadu. A third species, the Sanborn's Long-fingered Bat (**M. magnator**), has been recorded in NE India.*

• BEHAVIOUR *Although it lives in huge colonies, it hunts solitarily. An enormous colony of bats emerging from a cave can be a spectacular sight.*
• SIZE *FA: 4.4 – 4.9 cm. HBL: 4.7 – 6.5 cm.*
• HABITAT AND OCCURRENCE *Few, but large colonies of this bat are spread sparsely over hilly and forested areas of Maharashtra, Tamil Nadu, Uttar Pradesh, West Bengal, Sikkim, Meghalaya and Arunachal Pradesh.*
• BEST SEEN AT *Robber's Cave, Mahabaleswar.*

## PARTI-COLOURED BAT
*(Vespertilio murinus)*

ALTHOUGH NOT A *serotine, this bat has some similarities with the genus. It has short, rounded ears and a very short muzzle. The fur on its back is frosted chocolate as it has dark roots and buff tips.*
• SIZE *FA: 4.2 – 4.5 cm. HBL: 5.5 – 6.6 cm.*
• HABITAT AND OCCURRENCE *Gilgit, in Kashmir.*

## YELLOW DESERT BAT
*(Scotoecus pallidus)*

THIS BAT HAS *a pale brown or fawn back and a paler grey-brown underside. It has fleshy lips on a broad, flat muzzle, and round nostrils.*
• SIZE *FA: 3.4 – 3.7 cm. HBL: 5 – 5.8 cm.*
• HABITAT AND OCCURRENCE *Found in northern and eastern India.*

## TICKELL'S BAT
*(Hesperoptenus tickelli)*

THIS IS A LARGE, PALE YELLOW BAT *with a grey head. Its ears are yellowish-brown with white hair at the base. Its wings are long and its long tail is enclosed in a membrane, except for the tip. Its muzzle is broad and swollen.*
• BEHAVIOUR *A slow flier, it emerges in the early evening.*
• SIZE *FA: 5 – 6 cm. HBL: 6.1 – 7.9 cm.*
• HABITAT AND OCCURRENCE *Lowland bat of floodplains and even low hills, it is found in southern and southeastern India with a few records in North Bengal.*

| SIMILAR SPECIES | | | |
|---|---|---|---|
| COMMON NAME | LATIN NAME | OCCURRENCE | IDENTIFICATION TIPS |
| EASTERN BARBASTELLE | *Barbastella leucomelas* | Himalaya, from J&K to Meghalaya | Squared ears joined at forehead. Ridged nostrils open upward. FA: 3.8–4.2 cm. HBL: 4.7–5.1 cm. |

# WHALES AND DOLPHINS

## CETACEAN CHARACTERISTICS

- Completely aquatic
- Torpedo-shaped body
- Front flippers, no hind limbs
- Horizontally aligned tail flukes
- No external ear, scales, or gills
- Naked, rubbery skin with few hairs
- No sweat or sebaceous glands
- Thick layer of blubber below skin
- Nostrils open on top of head
- Spongy bones

| INDIAN WHALES AND DOLPHINS AT A GLANCE | |
|---|---|
| NUMBER OF SPECIES | 29 (30) |
| LARGEST | Blue Whale |
| SMALLEST | Finless Porpoise |
| MOST COMMON | Bottle-nose/Humpbacked dolphin |
| MOST ENDANGERED | Ganges River Dolphin |

WHALES AND DOLPHINS belong to the Order Cetacea which evolved around 60 million years ago when the dinosaurs had just died out. They were considered to be fish by biologists till the eighteenth century when it was discovered that they were actually mammals as they were warm blooded, gave birth to live young, and breathed through lungs and not gills. Externally, fish and cetaceans can be easily distinguished by the horizontal tail flukes of the latter as compared to the vertically aligned tail fins of fish. Dolphins and some whales belong to a sub-order called the Odontoceti or toothed whales. They are carnivorous and eat crustaceans, small fish, and small marine mammals. The other sub-order, Mysticeti or baleen whales, are toothless and filter plankton and small copepods through large sheets that hang in their mouths like curtains. Indian cetacean species are diverse and wide-ranging. Most of them are marine, some live in estuaries and tidal creeks, and one species inhabits rivers. Some such as the Ganges River Dolphin are endemic to India, while others such as the Humpback Whale are global in their distribution. Ranging from the mammoth Blue Whale that is the largest living creature in the world, to the small dolphins, the order Cetacea encompasses some of the most enigmatic, social and intelligent creatures in our universe.

Other than the 29 species profiled in this section, the Northern or Black Right Whale (*Eubalaena glacialis*) may also be found in Indian waters. There is a single stranding report of the species from off the coast of Gujarat but no other record of the family of Right Whales (*Balaenidae*) in Indian waters.

OUT OF WATER
*Cetaceans are almost impossible to see or photograph above water. For a whale or dolphin to jump clear out of the water like the Killer Whale (left) is uncommon and for people to see it is rare. The Humpbacked Dolphin (above) is how cetaceans normally appear in their aquatic habitat. It is for this reason that illustrations rather than photographs have been used for cetaceans in this book.*

| | |
|---|---|
| FAMILY NAME | **Platanistidae** |
| LATIN NAME | *Platanista gangetica* |
| IUCN STATUS / WPA | Endangered/I |
| LOCAL STATUS | Uncommon |
| POPULATION | 4,000 – 6,000 |
| DIET | 🐟 🦐 |
| SOCIAL UNIT | 1–2, up to 10 |
| ACTIVITY | ☼ |
| STRATUM | Aquatic (freshwater) |

# GANGES RIVER DOLPHIN

LOCAL NAME: *Susu* (Hindi), *Susuk* (Bengali),
*Hiho, Seho* (Assamese), *Bhoolan, Sunsar* (Sindhi).

The only true freshwater cetacean in India, this rare dolphin is easily recognized by its long beak, bearing a row of sharp, interlocking teeth designed to trap prey. When viewed closely, its mouth curves upwards at the end of its snout, giving it a menacing leer. Its flexible neck enables it to turn its head at right angles and scan the area with echolocating pulses. Other distinguishing features are large, paddle-shaped flippers and a low hump on the back. The colour of its stocky body may vary from slate-blue to muddy-brown. The Indus River Dolphin (*Platanista minor*) appears identical to the Ganges River Dophin but genetic studies show it to be a different species inhabiting the River Indus and its tributaries.

long snout

upward curving mouth

DOLPHIN

GHARIAL

**SMOOTHER SNOUT**
*Both the Gharial and this dolphin stick their heads out of the water. However, the snout of the dolphin is without a lump at its tip.*

| | |
|---|---|
| FAMILY NAME | **Phocoenidae** |
| LATIN NAME | *Neophocaena phocaenoides* |
| IUCN STATUS / WPA | Data deficient/I |
| LOCAL STATUS | Locally common |
| POPULATION | Unknown |
| DIET | 🦐 🐟 🦑 |
| SOCIAL UNIT | 1–2, up to 80 |
| ACTIVITY | ☼ |
| STRATUM | Aquatic (marine, estuarine) |

# FINLESS PORPOISE

LOCAL NAME: *Bhulga* (Marathi), *Molagan* (Tamil).

ONE OF THE SMALLEST CETACEANS in the world, this is the only porpoise found in Indian waters. An active, yet shy creature, the Finless Porpoise, also known as Black or Little Indian Porpoise, inhabits both oceans and estuaries. Its pale blue or grey-blue body colour is like the Ganges River Dolphin's (see above), but it has a blunt melon instead of the long-toothed snout of the dolphin. As the name indicates, it has no fin on its back. Its lips, chin, and underside are pale and some individuals may have a dark chinstrap. Porpoises can be distinguished from dolphins by their spade-shaped teeth, as opposed to the dolphin's conical ones.

pointed and distinctly notched tail flukes

**BLUNT MELON**
*The **Finless Porpoise** has a bulge resembling a dolphin's on its forehead and a slightly beaked snout. Its small pointed mouth is turned up so that it appears to wear a perennial smile.*

• **BEHAVIOUR** Very active and continuously vocal, this river dolphin is highly visible as it sticks its beak out of the water. It swims a few inches above the river bed on its side, with its head bobbing sideways and its right flipper trailing in the mud. A loud, sneeze-like blow gives it its common Hindi name, Susu. This is the only cetacean without a crystalline eye lens, rendering it blind.
• **SIZE** Total body length: 1.7−2.5 m. Weight: 70−85 kg.
• **HABITAT AND OCCURRENCE** Rivers Ganga, Brahmaputra, and their tributaries.
• **BEST SEEN AT** Vikramshila WLS (Bihar) and Kaziranga NP (Assam).
• **CONSERVATION THREATS** Pollution, habitat destruction, poaching, large dams, and fishing nets.

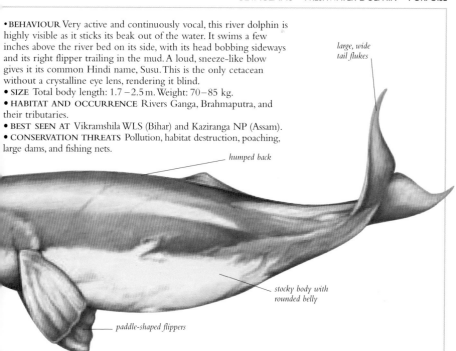

*large, wide tail flukes*

*humped back*

*stocky body with rounded belly*

*paddle-shaped flippers*

• **BEHAVIOUR** This porpoise does not normally come out of the water, but it "spyhops" − holds itself vertically and lifts its head clear of the water surface. Young calves may surface completely as they ride on the mother's back.
• **SIZE** Total body length: 1.4−1.87 m. Weight: 30−45 kg.
• **HABITAT AND OCCURRENCE** Mainly estuarine, in murky and warm waters of east and west coasts. Recorded off Kerala, Tamil Nadu, Karnataka, Goa, Orissa, and Lakshadweep.
• **CONSERVATION THREATS** Habitat destruction, fishing nets, and poaching.

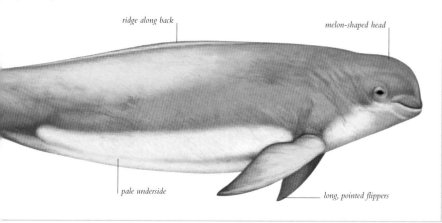

*ridge along back*

*melon-shaped head*

*pale underside*

*long, pointed flippers*

| | |
|---|---|
| FAMILY NAME | Delphinidae |
| LATIN NAME | *Orcaella brevirostris* |
| IUCN STATUS/WPA | Data deficient/I |
| LOCAL STATUS | Locally common |
| POPULATION | Unknown |
| DIET | 🐟 🦐 |
| SOCIAL UNIT | 2–10 |
| ACTIVITY | ☼ |
| STRATUM | Aquatic (marine, estuarine) |

# IRRAWADDY DOLPHIN

AN ESTUARINE SPECIES like the Finless Porpoise, the Irrawaddy Dolphin is closer in size to the Ganges River Dolphin (see p.174). Its body colour varies from dark blue-grey to pale blue, with an invariably lighter underside, and it has a small dorsal fin. It has broad flippers, broad flukes notched in the middle and its mouth is straight, lacking the familiar "smile" of the river dolphin or porpoise.

• BEHAVIOUR Though this dolphin's blow is loud, it is invisible, as it rarely comes out of the water. It usually performs a smooth, slow roll in a leisurely style and breaches occasionally.

• SIZE Total body length: 2.1–2.7 cm. Weight: 90–150 kg.

• HABITAT AND OCCURRENCE Oceans and estuaries. Recorded off Andhra Pradesh, Tamil Nadu, and Orissa, estuaries of Ganga and Krishna, and in Chilika Lake, Orissa.

• CONSERVATION THREATS Habitat destruction and fishing.

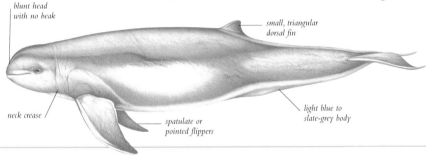

blunt head with no beak

small, triangular dorsal fin

neck crease

spatulate or pointed flippers

light blue to slate-grey body

| | |
|---|---|
| FAMILY NAME | Delphinidae |
| LATIN NAME | *Tursiops truncatus* |
| IUCN STATUS/WPA | Data deficient/II |
| LOCAL STATUS | Common |
| POPULATION | Unknown |
| DIET | 🐟 🦑 🦐 |
| SOCIAL UNIT | 1–10 inshore, 500 offshore |
| ACTIVITY | ☼ |
| STRATUM | Aquatic (marine) |

# BOTTLENOSE DOLPHIN

LOCAL NAME: *Gadamu* (Telegu).

THE TAXONOMY of this species is unclear although there is a clear distinction between a slimmer inshore form (perhaps a different species) and a bulkier offshore one. The species in Indian waters could be *Tursiops aduncus*. This dolphin appears drab grey in most waters, but the colours can vary. It has a short, distinct beak separated from the forehead by a sharp crease. The dorsal fin is darker than the rest of its body, while its flippers are slender and moderately long.

• BEHAVIOUR Friendly and active, this dolphin swims close to boats and is said to help fishermen drive shoals of fish into their nets. It shows its forehead, not the beak, when breaching.

• SIZE Total body length: 1.9–3.9 m. Weight: 90–650 kg.

• HABITAT AND OCCURRENCE In tropical waters it is more an offshore species. Found on both east and west coasts. Recorded off Kerala, Andhra Pradesh, Tamil Nadu, and West Bengal.

• CONSERVATION THREATS Habitat destruction and fishing.

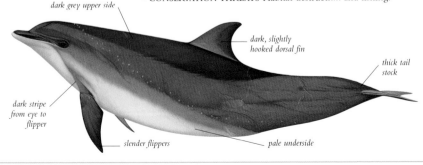

dark grey upper side

dark, slightly hooked dorsal fin

thick tail stock

dark stripe from eye to flipper

slender flippers

pale underside

| | |
|---|---|
| FAMILY NAME | Delphinidae |
| LATIN NAME | *Delphinus delphis* |
| IUCN STATUS / WPA | Data deficient/II |
| LOCAL STATUS | Common |
| POPULATION | Unknown |
| DIET | 🐟 🦑 |
| SOCIAL UNIT | 10–500 |
| ACTIVITY | ☼ |
| STRATUM | Aquatic (marine) |

# COMMON DOLPHIN

THOUGH IT VARIES WIDELY IN colour, form, and shape, the Common Dolphin is one of the easiest dolphins to identify as it has a characteristic hourglass pattern on its body. Its flanks are criss-crossed with various coloured streaks. The back, always darker, can be brownish, black, or purplish, with a yellow patch on both sides. Its undersides are white or creamy and there is a dark circle around its eyes. This dolphin has broad flippers and its dorsal fin is tall with a pointed tip. Currently, despite a debate on the species status of a long-beaked and short-beaked form, it is believed that all Common Dolphins are the same species.
• SIZE Total body length:1.7–2.4 m. Weight: 70–110 kg.
• HABITAT AND OCCURRENCE Offshore and open waters off the east and west coasts. Recorded off Goa, Kerala, Andhra Pradesh, Tamil Nadu, Orissa, Andaman and Lakshadweep Islands.
• CONSERVATION THREATS Fishing nets, poaching, human disturbance, and pollution.

white streak over eye

long black beak

dark v-shaped cape under dorsal fin

hourglass pattern on body

dark flukes

| | |
|---|---|
| FAMILY NAME | Delphinidae |
| LATIN NAME | *Stenella coeruleoalba* |
| IUCN STATUS / WPA | Lower risk/II |
| LOCAL STATUS | Uncommon |
| POPULATION | Unknown |
| DIET | 🐟 🦑 🦐 |
| SOCIAL UNIT | 10–1000 |
| ACTIVITY | ☼ |
| STRATUM | Aquatic (marine) |

# STRIPED DOLPHIN

THE STREAMLINED BODY of this dolphin is accentuated by three stripes that start at the eye and clearly delineate a pale pink or cream underside. Its upper body is uniformly bluish to brownish-grey but a lighter coloured swathe cuts across with a finger-like projection just below a prominent, strongly falcate and dark dorsal fin. The next stripe runs from the eye to the tail while the third ends at the short, stubby flippers. A dark patch encircles the eyes.
• BEHAVIOUR Very active, social, and acrobatic, this dolphin sometimes jumps to about 2 m in the air. Large pods of 50–500 dolphins can race across water close to boats.
• SIZE Total body length: 1.8-2.5 m. Weight: 90-150 kg.
• HABITAT AND OCCURRENCE Probably found off east and west coasts. Recorded off Sri Lanka and Maldives.
• CONSERVATION THREATS Fishing nets and poaching.

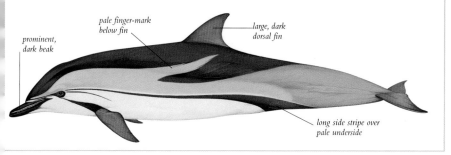

prominent, dark beak

pale finger-mark below fin

large, dark dorsal fin

long side stripe over pale underside

| | |
|---|---|
| FAMILY NAME | Delphinidae |
| LATIN NAME | *Stenella longirostris* |
| IUCN STATUS/WPA | Lower risk/II |
| LOCAL STATUS | Common |
| POPULATION | Unknown |
| DIET | 🐟 🦐 🦑 |
| SOCIAL UNIT | 50–200 |
| ACTIVITY | ☼ |
| STRATUM | Aquatic (marine) |

# LONG-SNOUTED SPINNER DOLPHIN

THIS DOLPHIN IS CONSPICUOUS due to its spectacular leaps and acrobatics. It is uniformly grey with a creamy white underside; the pale colouration can be either fairly extensive or restricted to a patch on the belly. Its streamlined body ends in a very long, dark-tipped beak with a prominent crease where it joins the forehead. Other distinguishing features are a large, erect, and triangular dorsal fin and long flippers. In males, the tail is prominently keeled on top and below.

• BEHAVIOUR This dolphin throws itself in the air up to a height of 3 m and then twists on a vertical axis up to seven times. It is the only dolphin in Indian waters that spins, while others only somersault and dive. Large schools of Spinner Dolphins can often be seen churning the water into frothy foam.

• SIZE Total body length: 1.3–2.5 m. Weight: 45–75 kg.

• HABITAT AND OCCURRENCE Warm waters off both coasts. Recorded in Gulf of Mannar, and off Maharashtra, Kerala, Karnataka, Andhra Pradesh, Orissa, and Lakshadweep.

• CONSERVATION THREATS Fishing nets and poaching.

long, slender beak

tall, erect dorsal fin

swept back flukes

slender, grey body

creamy white belly patch

| | |
|---|---|
| FAMILY NAME | Delphinidae |
| LATIN NAME | *Stenella attenuata* |
| IUCN STATUS/WPA | Lower risk/II |
| LOCAL STATUS | Uncommon |
| POPULATION | Unknown |
| DIET | 🦑 🐟 🦐 |
| SOCIAL UNIT | 5–1,000 |
| ACTIVITY | ☼ |
| STRATUM | Aquatic (marine) |

# PANTROPICAL SPOTTED DOLPHIN

THE GREY OR BLUE BODY of this dolphin is extensively spotted. Newborns are plain, but spots appear with age and older dolphins can be completely covered in bubble-like spots. The Pantropical Spotted Dolphin has three bands of grey across its body: a dark cape on its back, a medium-grey body and a pale grey underside. Other distinguishing features are a dark fin and small flippers that are strongly convex. It has a white-tipped black beak and white lips.

• BEHAVIOUR This dolphin is an active and energetic swimmer that jumps about a lot in the water. Occasionally it breaches, making high leaps in the air and falling back into the water after a moment or two of being motionless in the air.

• SIZE Total body length: 1.6–2.5 m. Weight: 90–120 kg.

• HABITAT AND OCCURRENCE Probably found off east and west coasts. Recorded off Sunderbans (West Bengal) and Tamil Nadu.

• CONSERVATION THREATS Fishing nets and poaching.

white lips

dark grey dorsal fin and cape

body covered with dark spots

distinct tail keel

dark line from flipper to beak

| | |
|---|---|
| FAMILY NAME | Delphinidae |
| LATIN NAME | *Sousa chinensis* |
| IUCN STATUS/WPA | Data deficient/II |
| LOCAL STATUS | Locally common |
| POPULATION | Unknown |
| DIET | 🐟 |
| SOCIAL UNIT | 3–25 |
| ACTIVITY | ☼ |
| STRATUM | Aquatic (marine, estuarine, freshwater) |

# INDO-PACIFIC HUMP-BACKED DOLPHIN

A CHARACTERISTIC HUMP TOPPED with a small dorsal fin is the main feature of this dolphin. It is brown-grey with a pinkish tinge on the underside, flippers, and flukes with occasional spotting on its body. The mouth line is straight while the forehead bulges slightly.
• BEHAVIOUR This dolphin breaks out of the water at an angle, arches its back, and lifts its flukes in the air before flopping back. Courtship rounds may involve high-speed circular swimming.
• SIZE Total body length: 2–2.8 m. Weight: 150–200 kg.
• HABITAT AND OCCURRENCE Mangroves, estuaries, and shallow open waters off both coasts. Recorded off Andaman Islands, Maharashtra, Gujarat, Goa, Kerala, Tamil Nadu, Andhra Pradesh, and Orissa.
• CONSERVATION THREATS Fishing, poaching, habitat destruction, and pollution.

*slightly bulging forehead*

*elongated hump on back*

*slender, long beak*

*pinkish tinge on underside*

| | |
|---|---|
| FAMILY NAME | Delphinidae |
| LATIN NAME | *Steno bredanensis* |
| IUCN STATUS/WPA | Data deficient/II |
| LOCAL STATUS | Uncommon |
| POPULATION | Unknown |
| DIET | 🐟 🦑 |
| SOCIAL UNIT | 10–50; sometimes larger |
| ACTIVITY | ☼ |
| STRATUM | Aquatic (marine) |

# ROUGH-TOOTHED DOLPHIN

UNLIKE MOST BEAKED DOLPHINS, the beak of the Rough-toothed Dolphin does not have a crease separating it from the forehead. Its head has a unique conical shape which, combined with its white lips and throat, makes it easy to recognize. Another unique feature is its almond-shaped teeth, with vertical striations. There are yellowish or pink blotches on its underbelly, while its large dorsal fin has a concave trailing edge and is set at an angle of 45° to its body.
• BEHAVIOUR This species swims fast just beneath the water surface and rarely surfaces. When it does, it pops out in a low arc. It is often seen with Bottlenose Dolphins and tuna.
• SIZE Total body length: 2.1–2.6 m. Weight: 100–150 kg.
• HABITAT AND OCCURRENCE Warm, deep offshore waters. Probably found off east and west coasts. Recorded off Nicobar Islands.
• CONSERVATION THREATS Fishing nets and poaching.

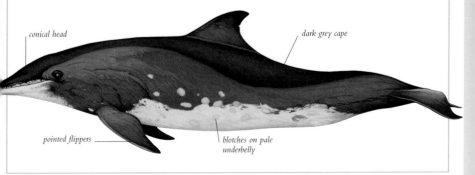

*conical head*

*dark grey cape*

*pointed flippers*

*blotches on pale underbelly*

| | |
|---|---|
| FAMILY NAME | Delphinidae |
| LATIN NAME | *Grampus griseus* |
| IUCN STATUS/WPA | Data deficient/II |
| LOCAL STATUS | Uncommon |
| POPULATION | Unknown |
| DIET | ◄═ ➡ |
| SOCIAL UNIT | 3–50, sometimes 100+ |
| ACTIVITY | ☼ |
| STRATUM | Aquatic (marine) |

# GREY OR RISSO'S DOLPHIN

AN OCEANIC DOLPHIN, LIKE Fraser's Dolphin (see below), the Grey or Risso's Dolphin is easily identified by its dome-shaped forehead with a crease that runs from the centre to the mouth-line. Its body is heavily scarred with white streaks and varies from very dark grey to almost white, while its underside is always paler. The dorsal fin of the female is almost as tall as a Killer Whale's and has a rounded edge.
• BEHAVIOUR This dolphin tends to come half out of the water before slapping its head back in. It feeds primarily on deep water squid and uses echolocation and a variety of clicks to navigate.
• SIZE Total body length: 2.6–3.8 m. Weight: 300–500 kg.
• HABITAT AND OCCURRENCE Deep offshore waters of the Indian Ocean. Recorded off Tamil Nadu and Kerala.
• CONSERVATION THREATS Poaching and fishing nets.

bulging forehead with deep crease

rounded tip to dorsal fin

notched tail

upward tilting mouth

heavily scarred body

| | |
|---|---|
| FAMILY NAME | Delphinidae |
| LATIN NAME | *Lagenodelphis hosei* |
| IUCN STATUS/WPA | Data deficient/II |
| LOCAL STATUS | Uncommon |
| POPULATION | Unknown |
| DIET | ◄═ ➡ ➡ |
| SOCIAL UNIT | 100–500, up to 1,000 |
| ACTIVITY | ☼ |
| STRATUM | Aquatic (marine) |

# FRASER'S DOLPHIN

A BLUE-GREY DOLPHIN with a creamy white underside, Fraser's Dolphin was scientifically described only in the late 1950s from the waters around Malaysia. Like the Striped Dolphin (see p.177), it has a clear dark stripe running along the length of its body. However, it is easy to distinguish this dolphin by its shorter beak, a smaller dorsal fin, and small, pointed flippers.
• BEHAVIOUR Fraser's Dolphin swims actively, splashing and spraying water, but does not approach vessels. It swims in mixed parties with other cetaceans, such as Striped and Spotted Dolphins, and Melon-headed, Sperm or Killer Whales.
• SIZE Total body length: 2–2.6 m. Weight: 160–210 kg.
• HABITAT AND OCCURRENCE Deep waters and oceanic shelf of the Indian Ocean. Recorded off Sri Lanka and Maldives.
• CONSERVATION THREATS Fishing nets and poaching.

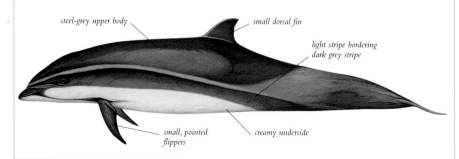

steel-grey upper body

small dorsal fin

light stripe bordering dark grey stripe

small, pointed flippers

creamy underside

| | |
|---|---|
| FAMILY NAME | Delphinidae |
| LATIN NAME | *Peponocephala electra* |
| IUCN STATUS/WPA | Data deficient/II |
| LOCAL STATUS | Uncommon |
| POPULATION | Unknown |
| DIET | ◄● ●➤ |
| SOCIAL UNIT | 100–500, up to 2,000 |
| ACTIVITY | ☼ |
| STRATUM | Aquatic (marine) |

# MELON-HEADED WHALE

A ROUNDED HEAD GIVES this dark, torpedo-shaped cetacean its name. Its face has a dark mask and white lips, while a dark cape runs across its back. Along with the Pilot and Killer Whales (see p.182), this species belongs to a group of smaller toothed whales (also known as "blackfish"). These are larger in size, but closely related to dolphins and alternately classified as whales or dolphins.
• BEHAVIOUR Little seen and shy of sailing vessels, this dolphin makes shallow leaps out of the water. It travels in large numbers and, like the Pilot Whale, can also strand in large numbers.
• SIZE Total body length: 2.1–2.7 m. Weight: 160–275 kg.
• HABITAT AND OCCURRENCE Found off both coasts. Recorded off Andhra Pradesh, Orissa, Tamil Nadu, Andaman and Nicobar and Lakshadweep Islands.
• CONSERVATION THREATS Poaching and fishing nets.

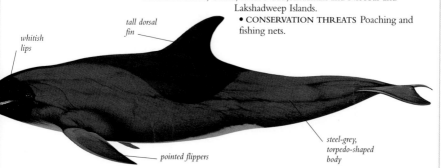

tall dorsal fin

whitish lips

pointed flippers

steel-grey, torpedo-shaped body

| | |
|---|---|
| FAMILY NAME | Delphinidae |
| LATIN NAME | *Feresa attenuata* |
| IUCN STATUS/WPA | Data deficient/II |
| LOCAL STATUS | Rare |
| POPULATION | Unknown |
| DIET | ◄● ●➤ |
| SOCIAL UNIT | 1–50 |
| ACTIVITY | ☼ |
| STRATUM | Aquatic (marine) |

# PYGMY KILLER WHALE

VERY SIMILAR TO THE Melon-headed Whale (see above), this whale is one of the lesser-known deep tropical water species. It has a large white patch on its belly, divided by a deep groove, and rounded flippers. Many individuals have a white chin. The Pygmy Killer Whale is generally seen in smaller numbers than the Melon-headed Whale.
• BEHAVIOUR An active swimmer that often vocalizes and even growls, it may be seen in large schools. More aggressive than other Killer Whales, it probably preys on small dolphins to a greater extent.
• SIZE Total body length: 2.1–2.6 m. Weight: 110–275 kg.
• HABITAT AND OCCURRENCE Deep, warm waters of the Indian Ocean. Recorded off Sri Lanka and Maldives.
• CONSERVATION THREATS Fishing nets.

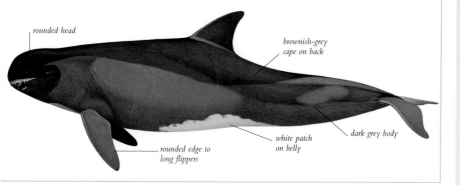

rounded head

brownish-grey cape on back

white patch on belly

dark grey body

rounded edge to long flippers

| | |
|---|---|
| FAMILY NAME | Delphinidae |
| LATIN NAME | *Orcinus orca* |
| IUCN STATUS/WPA | Lower risk/II |
| LOCAL STATUS | Uncommon |
| POPULATION | Unknown |
| DIET | 🐟 🦑 |
| SOCIAL UNIT | 3–50 |
| ACTIVITY | ☼ |
| STRATUM | Aquatic (marine) |

# KILLER WHALE

PROBABLY THE BEST-KNOWN whale in the world because of its appearance in films and marine shows, the Killer Whale is a black-and-white dolphin with a huge dorsal fin that may in males be as long as 1.8 m. Its jet black body has a white oval patch behind the eye and a grey saddle patch behind the fin. It has a white chest, white side patches, and rounded flippers. Males are larger and heavier than females and have taller, straighter dorsal fins.
• BEHAVIOUR A very inquisitive, acrobatic species, the Killer Whale often approaches boats and humans. It has a low blow but displays other whale-like behaviour such as lob tailing, breaching, flipper-slapping, and speed swimming.
• SIZE Total body length: 5.5–9.8 m. Weight: 2,600–9,000 kg.
• HABITAT AND OCCURRENCE Deep, colder waters off east and west coasts. Recorded off Gujarat, Tamil Nadu, Andaman and Nicobar and Lakshadweep Islands.
• CONSERVATION THREATS Poaching and habitat destruction.

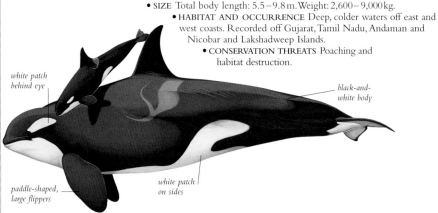

white patch behind eye

black-and-white body

paddle-shaped, large flippers

white patch on sides

| | |
|---|---|
| FAMILY NAME | Delphinidae |
| LATIN NAME | *Pseudorca crassidens* |
| IUCN STATUS/WPA | Data deficient/II |
| LOCAL STATUS | Rare |
| POPULATION | Unknown |
| DIET | 🦑 🐟 |
| SOCIAL UNIT | 10–50, sometimes 100+ |
| ACTIVITY | ☼ |
| STRATUM | Aquatic (marine) |

# FALSE KILLER WHALE

A RARE, LARGE, AND ACTIVE whale, the False Killer Whale is uniformly dark grey in colour. It has a slightly grey or off-white "W" on its chest, a large dorsal fin, and a unique flipper which is set very far forward on the body and has a clear elbow. This whale has a long slender head unlike the Pilot Whale and is larger than the Melon-headed and Pygmy Killer Whales.
• BEHAVIOUR An active swimmer, this whale is known to feed on smaller cetaceans. It frequently swims with its mouth open, exposing its sharp teeth.
• SIZE Total body length: 4–6 m. Weight: 1,100–2,200 kg.
• HABITAT AND OCCURRENCE Deep warm waters off both coasts. Recorded in Gulf of Cambay, and off Maharashtra, Kerala, Tamil Nadu, Andaman and Nicobar and Lakshadweep Islands.
• CONSERVATION THREATS Poaching and fishing nets.

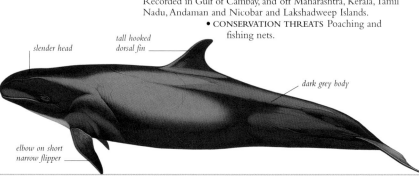

slender head

tall hooked dorsal fin

dark grey body

elbow on short narrow flipper

BUILT TO HUNT
*The **Killer Whale** is known as an
extraordinary and diverse hunter among
all the toothed whales. Its food ranges
from fish to small marine mammals,
turtles, and seabirds.*

| FAMILY NAME | Delphinidae |
|---|---|
| LATIN NAME | *Globicephala macrorhynchus* |
| IUCN STATUS/WPA | Lower risk/II |
| LOCAL STATUS | Uncommon |
| POPULATION | Unknown |
| DIET | |
| SOCIAL UNIT | 10–50 |
| ACTIVITY | ☼ ☾ |
| STRATUM | Aquatic (marine) |

## SHORT-FINNED PILOT WHALE

THIS WHALE, LIKE THE Melon-headed Whale, is known from being
stranded in large numbers. It has an off-white belly patch on a dark
grey body, a W-shaped grey patch on its throat, and a grey or white
diagonal stripe from its eye to the dorsal fin. It closely resembles the
False Killer Whale, but has a more bulbous head and a rounded dorsal
fin. Very social, this night-feeder travels in large pods and often
associates with other cetaceans, especially the Bottlenose Dolphin.
• BEHAVIOUR It has a strong blow and is one of the more easily
identified whales, since it approaches ships in large numbers.
• SIZE Total body length: 3.6–6.5 m. Weight: 1,100–1,400 kg.
• HABITAT AND OCCURRENCE Deep waters of the Bay of Bengal.
Recorded off Maharashtra, in Gulf of Mannar and Hoogly river mouth.
• CONSERVATION THREATS Poaching and fishing nets.

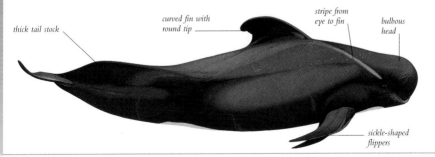

thick tail stock

curved fin with
round tip

stripe from
eye to fin

bulbous
head

sickle-shaped
flippers

183

| | |
|---|---|
| FAMILY NAME | **Physeteridae** |
| LATIN NAME | *Physeter catodon* |
| IUCN STATUS/WPA | Vulnerable/II |
| LOCAL STATUS | Uncommon |
| POPULATION | Unknown |
| DIET |  |
| SOCIAL UNIT | 1–50, sometimes 100+ |
| ACTIVITY | ☼ |
| STRATUM | Aquatic (marine) |

# SPERM WHALE

THE MOST EASILY RECOGNIZABLE large whale, the Sperm Whale has a large, square head with an inconspicuous lower jaw and small eyes. The shrivelled prune-like purple-brown body has no dorsal fin although it has a triangular hump on the back and a row of knuckles between the hump and the tail. Its flippers are short and its face, mouth, and belly may be paler or whitish. Its large conical teeth are used as an ivory substitute in Japan.

• BEHAVIOUR This whale blows an angled bushy blow of water from the left side of its nose, which is unlike any other cetacean.

• SIZE Total body length:11–18 m. Weight: 2,000–5,000 kg.

• HABITAT AND OCCURRENCE Deep waters (more than 200 m) off east and west coasts. Recorded off Gujarat, Maharashtra, Kerala, Tamil Nadu, Pondicherry, Andaman and Nicobar and Lakshadweep Islands.

• CONSERVATION THREATS Poaching and fishing.

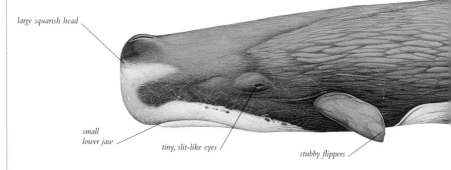

large squarish head

small
lower jaw

tiny, slit-like eyes

stubby flippers

| | |
|---|---|
| FAMILY NAME | **Kogiidae** |
| LATIN NAME | *Kogia breviceps* |
| IUCN STATUS/WPA | Data deficient/II |
| LOCAL STATUS | Uncommon |
| POPULATION | Unknown |
| DIET | |
| SOCIAL UNIT | 3–6, up to 10 |
| ACTIVITY | ☼ |
| STRATUM | Aquatic (marine) |

# PYGMY SPERM WHALE

THIS SMALL WHALE IS not related to the Sperm Whale but is probably a close cousin of the Dwarf Sperm Whale. Both the Pygmy and the Dwarf Sperm Whales are so called because of their squarish heads that resemble that of the Sperm Whale. However, this smaller species is very poorly studied. It is steel grey overall, with a pale or pinkish underside, a tiny hooked dorsal fin, a prominent false gill behind the ear, and broad flippers. The body may appear wrinkled although not as much as that of the Sperm Whale.

• BEHAVIOUR The Pygmy Sperm Whale has a low blow that is not very conspicuous. When rising to the surface, it may drop back into the water without arching out of it, a habit unique to this whale. Like the squid, it releases a red or brown ink jet if startled.

• SIZE Total body length: 2.7–3.4 m. Weight: 300–400 kg.

• HABITAT AND OCCURRENCE Recorded off east coast up to Thiruvananthapuram, including Orissa, Andhra Pradesh, and Andaman and Nicobar Islands.

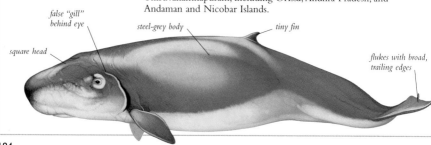

false "gill"
behind eye

steel-grey body

tiny fin

square head

flukes with broad,
trailing edges

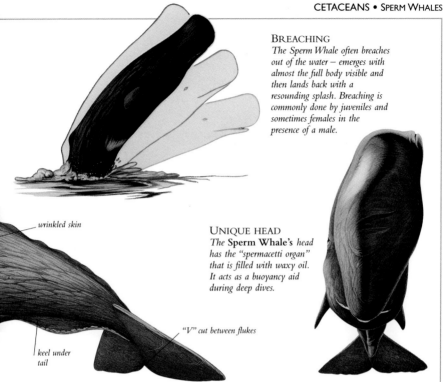

**BREACHING**
*The Sperm Whale often breaches out of the water – emerges with almost the full body visible and then lands back with a resounding splash. Breaching is commonly done by juveniles and sometimes females in the presence of a male.*

*wrinkled skin*

**UNIQUE HEAD**
*The* **Sperm Whale's** *head has the "spermacetti organ" that is filled with waxy oil. It acts as a buoyancy aid during deep dives.*

*"V" cut between flukes*

*keel under tail*

| | |
|---|---|
| FAMILY NAME | **Kogiidae** |
| LATIN NAME | *Kogia simus* |
| IUCN STATUS/WPA | Data deficient/II |
| LOCAL STATUS | Uncommon |
| POPULATION | Unknown |
| DIET | 🦐 ◀🐟 🐟 |
| SOCIAL UNIT | 1–2, up to 10 |
| ACTIVITY | ☀ |
| STRATUM | Aquatic (marine) |

# DWARF SPERM WHALE

THE DWARF SPERM WHALE is almost identical externally to the Pygmy Sperm Whale and was thought to be a sub-species until recently. The shape and size of the dorsal fin can, however, easily tell them apart. The Dwarf and Pygmy Sperm Whales can sometimes be confused with sharks because of their under-slung jaw, small sharp teeth and false gill behind the eye. However, their blowhole and bulky bodies betray the fact that they are whales. The Dwarf Sperm Whale is found in deeper waters than the Pygmy Sperm Whale.
• **SIZE** Total body length: 2.1–2.7 m. Weight: 135–275 kg.
• **HABITAT AND OCCURRENCE** Deep waters off both coasts. Recorded off Andhra Pradesh, Tamil Nadu, and Kerala.

*sickle-shaped dorsal fin*

*small, clearly notched tail*

*light blue or white underside*

| | |
|---|---|
| FAMILY NAME | Ziphidae |
| LATIN NAME | *Ziphius cavirostris* |
| IUCN STATUS/WPA | Data deficient/II |
| LOCAL STATUS | Uncommon |
| POPULATION | Unknown |
| DIET | 🐟 🦑 |
| SOCIAL UNIT | 1–25 |
| ACTIVITY | ☼ |
| STRATUM | Aquatic (marine) |

# CUVIER'S BEAKED WHALE

BEAKED WHALES ARE MEDIUM to large cetaceans that live in deep ocean trenches and are rarely seen above water. All of them have reduced number of teeth and females have no teeth at all. The most abundant of all beaked whales, the Cuvier's Beaked Whale may be recognized by its goose-beak shaped mouth and a gently sloping forehead. The colour of this species varies from pale brown to cream to purplish-black and red, thereby making identification extremely difficult. Two small conical teeth are present in the lower jaw of the male. White or cream-coloured scars are seen on the lower side and on the tail.
• BEHAVIOUR Rarely breaches and has an indistinct blow that appears in front and to the left of the whale. Head may be exposed while swimming.
• SIZE Total body length: 5.5–7 m. Weight: 2,000–3,000 kg.
• HABITAT AND OCCURRENCE Deep waters of the Indian Ocean. Recorded in the Gulf of Mannar and Lakshadweep.

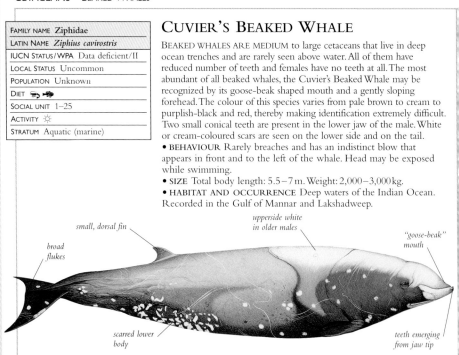

*small, dorsal fin*

*upperside white in older males*

*"goose-beak" mouth*

*broad flukes*

*scarred lower body*

*teeth emerging from jaw tip*

| | |
|---|---|
| FAMILY NAME | Ziphidae |
| LATIN NAME | *Mesoplodon ginkodens* |
| IUCN STATUS/WPA | Data deficient/II |
| LOCAL STATUS | Rare |
| POPULATION | Unknown |
| DIET | 🐟 🦑 |
| SOCIAL UNIT | Unknown |
| ACTIVITY | ☼ |
| STRATUM | Aquatic (marine) |

# GINGKO-TOOTHED BEAKED WHALE

VERY LITTLE IS KNOWN about the Gingko-toothed Beaked Whale. Unless stranded, it is difficult to distinguish from the Blainville's. Its teeth are characteristically fan shaped, like the leaf of the Gingko tree. Lack of scarring on body, a slightly larger size and a very triangular fluke with no notch can help distinguish it from the Blainville's. It has not been recorded from Indian waters thus far but this may well be because of mis-identification due to its similarity with other beaked whales.
• BEHAVIOUR Not known, though lack of scarring suggests fewer fights among males compared to the Blainville's.
• SIZE Total body length: 4.7–5.2 m. Weight: 1,500–2,000 kg.
• HABITAT AND OCCURRENCE Warm waters of the Indian Ocean. Recorded only off Sri Lanka.

**FLUKES**
*The flukes are broad, fairly triangular in shape, and have no notches between them.*

*broad flukes*

| | |
|---|---|
| FAMILY NAME | Ziphiidae |
| LATIN NAME | *Mesoplodon densirostris* |
| IUCN STATUS/WPA | Data deficient/II |
| LOCAL STATUS | Uncommon |
| POPULATION | Unknown |
| DIET | 🐟 🦑 |
| SOCIAL UNIT | 1–12 |
| ACTIVITY | ☼ |
| STRATUM | Aquatic (marine) |

# BLAINVILLE'S BEAKED WHALE

A MARGINALLY SMALLER BEAKED whale, this species can be identified only at close range by its large, single-lobed, flattened teeth. The teeth emerge in males from an arched lower jaw and protrude well over the upper jaw. Its dark bluish-grey body has a lighter patch on the underside and a large number of parasitic shark bite scars all over.
• BEHAVIOUR A series of shallow dolphin-like dives is followed by a slightly longer, deeper dive from which it emerges with its beak pointing skywards.
• SIZE Total body length: 4.5–6m. Weight: 1,000–1,500 kg.
• HABITAT AND OCCURRENCE Deep and pelagic waters. Recorded off Nicobar Islands.

*large spots all over body* — *small dorsal fin* — *arched lower jaw, with large teeth*

GINGKO TREE LEAF

WHALE TOOTH

TEETH
*The male's distinctive teeth are shaped like the leaves of the Gingko tree and are about 10cm wide.*

*dorsal fin may have a hooked tip* — *bluish-black body* — *prominent beak*

| | |
|---|---|
| FAMILY NAME | **Balaenopteridae** |
| LATIN NAME | *Balaenoptera acutorostrata* |
| IUCN STATUS/WPA | Lower risk/II |
| LOCAL STATUS | Uncommon |
| POPULATION | 5,000 in Indian Ocean |
| DIET | 🐟 🦐 |
| SOCIAL UNIT | 1–3, can reach up to 100 |
| ACTIVITY | ☼ |
| STRATUM | Aquatic (oceanic) |

# MINKE WHALE

THE SMALLEST AND MOST COMMON of the rorqual whales, the Minke is dark grey or slaty-brown above, and white or pale grey-brown on its lower side. It has a sharp triangular head with a pointed snout and a single longitudinal ridge on the head. Most Indian populations have a white band on the flipper, although this is variable.

• BEHAVIOUR The Minke can be easily spotted by the appearance of its triangular snout, with which it breaks out of the water surface. It starts blowing as soon as the snout emerges but the low, indistinct blow is almost like spray and easy to miss (it reaches only 2–3 m in height). During breaching, which it seldom does, the Minke leaves the water at 45° and then either slaps down back into water or enters head first like a dolphin.

• SIZE Total body length: 6.7–10.7 m. Weight: 500–1000 kg.

• HABITAT AND OCCURRENCE Temperate waters, rarely in tropical waters. Washed ashore in Tamil Nadu, Andhra Pradesh, and Orissa.

• CONSERVATION THREATS Commercial whaling and fishing nets.

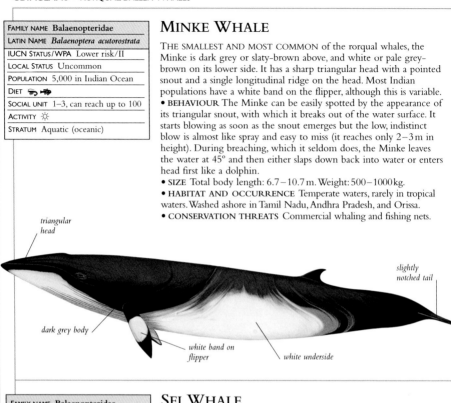

*triangular head*

*slightly notched tail*

*dark grey body*

*white band on flipper*

*white underside*

| | |
|---|---|
| FAMILY NAME | **Balaenopteridae** |
| LATIN NAME | *Balaenoptera borealis* |
| IUCN STATUS/WPA | Endangered/II |
| LOCAL STATUS | Uncommon |
| POPULATION | 40,000 in Indian Ocean |
| DIET | 🐟 🦐 |
| SOCIAL UNIT | 2–5, up to 30 |
| ACTIVITY | ☼ |
| STRATUM | Aquatic (oceanic) |

# SEI WHALE

A BLUISH-GREY WHALE, the Sei has a slender dorsal fin, dark flippers, and a small tail that is clearly notched. Its underside is mottled with white scars and there is a single ridge on its head.

• BEHAVIOUR The Sei Whale swims close to the surface at times. Its blowhole and dorsal fin are both visible during a dive. When diving and breaching, its head comes out at a much shallower angle than other rorquals', almost kissing the water surface. In a breach, its belly flops back into water and in a dive the dorsal fin and back are visible for a longer period; the fin is the last to disappear. Its short, narrow blow rises up to 3 m.

• SIZE Total body length: 13.5 m – 14.5 m. Weight: 2,000–3,000 kg.

• HABITAT AND OCCURRENCE Temperate waters; warmer waters during winter. Recorded off Tamil Nadu. Washed ashore in Kerala and Gujarat.

• CONSERVATION THREATS Fishing, collision with ships, sound pollution, and commercial whaling.

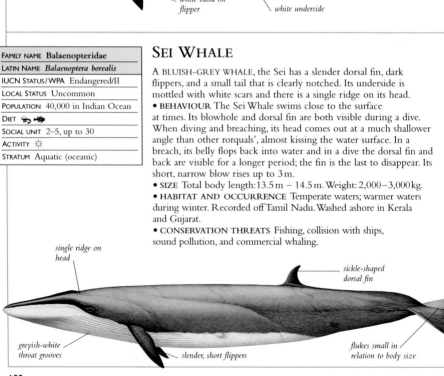

*single ridge on head*

*sickle-shaped dorsal fin*

*greyish-white throat grooves*

*slender, short flippers*

*flukes small in relation to body size*

| | |
|---|---|
| FAMILY NAME | **Balaenopteridae** |
| LATIN NAME | *Balaenoptera edeni* |
| IUCN STATUS/WPA | Data deficient/II |
| LOCAL STATUS | Uncommon |
| POPULATION | 14,000 in Indian Ocean |
| DIET | 🦐 🐟 |
| SOCIAL UNIT | 1–2, groups up to 30 |
| ACTIVITY | ☼ |
| STRATUM | Aquatic (oceanic) |

# BRYDE'S WHALE

THIS IS A SMOKY-GREY or brown tropical whale with blue-grey, purplish, or creamy grey undersides. The Bryde's Whale has three longitudinal ridges on its head – a unique feature among whales.
• **BEHAVIOUR** It breaches fairly regularly, at times leaving the water almost vertically between 70° and 90°, showing three-quarters of its body as it does. Its back arches before it flops back into water. While diving, its blowholes disappear before the dorsal fin is seen and just before the dive, the whale arches its back and tail stock clearly. Its indistinct and thin blow can rise up to 4 m.
• **SIZE** Total body length: 12.2–12.5 m. Weight: 1,200–2,000 kg.
• **HABITAT AND OCCURRENCE** Prefers warm waters (between 40° N and 40° S only) off both the east and west coasts. Washed ashore in Maharashtra, Kerala, and Tamil Nadu.
• **CONSERVATION THREATS** Fishing, collision with ships, sound pollution, and commercial whaling.

*three ridges on head*

*whitish-yellow throat grooves*

*slender, short flippers*

*mottled skin*

*notched tail flukes*

| | |
|---|---|
| FAMILY NAME | **Balaenopteridae** |
| LATIN NAME | *Balaenoptera physalus* |
| IUCN STATUS/WPA | Endangered/II |
| LOCAL STATUS | Uncommon |
| POPULATION | 500 in Indian Ocean |
| DIET | 🦐 🐟 |
| SOCIAL UNIT | 3–7, up to 100 |
| ACTIVITY | ☼ |
| STRATUM | Aquatic (oceanic) |

# FIN WHALE

THE SECOND-LARGEST whale in the world after the Blue Whale, the Fin Whale is easily recognizable because of its bi-coloured lip. The lower lip is dark grey on the left side and white on the right. Its white underside usually appears as a small patch on the belly as its throat grooves (present in all baleen whales) are exceptionally long and reach up to the navel. A distinct ridge joins the fin to the tail flukes, giving it the alternative name of Razorback.
• **BEHAVIOUR** The Fin Whale's blow is a visible tall, narrow column of spray that can reach up to 6 m in height. First its head emerges out of water, after which it rests with only its back showing and then it blows tall and loud. After the blow, it arches and dives. During breaching, its body breaks the surface at around 45° and then re-enters with a loud splash.
• **SIZE** Total body length: 19–26 m. Weight: 4,000–7,500 kg.
• **HABITAT AND OCCURRENCE** Found off east and west coasts. Washed ashore in Kerala, Tamil Nadu, Andhra Pradesh, Orissa, Goa, Gujarat, Karnataka, and Maharashtra.
• **CONSERVATION THREATS** Fishing and collision with fishing trollies.

*single ridge on head*

*small dorsal fin*

*bi-coloured lower lip*

*slender, short flippers*

*broad, triangular flukes*

189

| | |
|---|---|
| FAMILY NAME | Balaenopteridae |
| LATIN NAME | *Balaenoptera musculus* |
| IUCN STATUS/WPA | Endangered/II |
| LOCAL STATUS | Uncommon |
| POPULATION | 6,000–14,000 globally |
| DIET | 🦐 |
| SOCIAL UNIT | 1–2, more in feeding area |
| ACTIVITY | ☼ |
| STRATUM | Aquatic (oceanic) |

# BLUE WHALE

LOCAL NAME: *Hut, Raghwa* (Hindi), *Devmasa* (Marathi), *Thimingilam* (Tamil/Telegu/Malayalam), *Thimingila* (Kannada).

THE BLUE WHALE is the largest living creature on earth. The largest animal on land, the elephant, weighs only as much as its tongue. This whale is uniformly blue-grey. Its throat grooves, which are a lighter blue, like the leading edges of its flippers, extend to its belly.
• BEHAVIOUR When diving, the Blue Whale comes out of the water at a shallow angle, blows, and dives back. Its back is visible for longer, the dorsal fin emerging just before it sinks downwards. Sometimes, its tail flukes are visible in a dive.
• SIZE Total body length: 20–27 m. Weight: 8,000–12,000 kg; maximum weight recorded: 20,000 kg.
• HABITAT AND OCCURRENCE Cold waters and open seas off both coasts. Washed ashore in Karnataka, Maharashtra, Gujarat, Tamil Nadu, Kerala, and Andhra Pradesh.
• CONSERVATION THREATS Fishing and sound pollution.

tiny dorsal fin

thick tail with broad flippers

| | |
|---|---|
| FAMILY NAME | Balaenopteridae |
| LATIN NAME | *Megaptera novaeangliae* |
| IUCN STATUS/WPA | Vulnerable/II |
| LOCAL STATUS | Uncommon |
| POPULATION | 500 in Indian Ocean |
| DIET | 🦐 🐟 |
| SOCIAL UNIT | 1–3, more in feeding area |
| ACTIVITY | ☼ |
| STRATUM | Aquatic (oceanic) |

# HUMPBACK WHALE

A LARGE, ENERGETIC WHALE with very distinctive flippers, head, and tail, the Humpback Whale is one of the best-known whales in the world. It has a slender head with a single ridge and a large splashguard similar to the Blue Whale's, but it also has a number of small knobs (known as tubercles) on the head and lower jaw. Its flippers are the longest in any whale, nearly one-third of the entire body size, and they also have tubercles along the edges. The whale's body is blue-black or dark grey although there may be whitish patches on the underside, especially on the belly. The broad blue-black tail flukes are frayed along the leading edges.

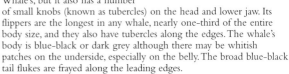

tattered edges of tail flukes

• BEHAVIOUR This whale is one of the most active and visible of all large whales. It is known to leap clear out of the water and land on its back. During a dive its tail is arched and its flukes break clear above the water. It is also one of the best-known vocalizers among aquatic mammals. Males sing uninterrupted for as long as 35 minutes and continue vocalizing all day till other whales join in.
• SIZE Total body length: 11–16 m. Weight: 2,500–3,000 kg.
• HABITAT AND OCCURRENCE Low-latitude, warm waters in winter and high-latitude, cold waters in summer. Found off east and west coasts. Washed ashore in Tamil Nadu and Kerala.
• CONSERVATION THREATS Fishing and collision with ships.

## STRAIGHT BLOW
*The most characteristic feature of this large whale is its spectacular blow that may be up to 6–10 m high and appears as a slender vertical column of spray.*

## COLOURATION
*Blue Whales are all blue-grey, but vary from a uniform dark slate-grey to light blue with extensive mottling. The underside may be white or sulphur-yellow.*

U-shaped head

whitish mottling
on body

low, stubby
dorsal fin

dark grey body

knobs on head

long blue and white
flippers with knobs

## BUSHY BLOW
*The Humpback Whale's distinctive blow is bushy, 3 m tall and wide, and bifurcates into two balloons. The blowholes and the blow are seen before the back of the whale appears.*

# DUGONG

The Order Sirenia comprises dugongs (Family Dugongidae) and manatees (Family Trichechidae) – creatures somewhat like a cross between a walrus and a dolphin – that live in marine waters. Sirenians are the only marine mammals that are completely vegetarian and are considered to be closely related to the elephant.

**DUGONG CHARACTERISTICS**
- Spindle-shaped body
- No dorsal fin, nor hind limbs
- Paddle-like forelimbs
- Fleshy pad for muzzle
- Small eyes, no external ears
- Nostrils on top of head
- Horizontally flattened tail

They have only six pairs of vertebrae while all other mammals have seven. Dugongs are found in the oceans of East Africa, Asia, and Australia, while manatees only inhabit the New World waters. Dugongs are poorly studied in India, although off Australia they have been well studied and are known to be voracious feeders of sea grass. Unlike turtles that eat only the blades of sea grass, dugongs dig up sea grass beds and eat the tubers as well. They have a long life span (70 years on record), with a very low reproductive rate – the period between two births being between three and seven years. Dugongs are known to chirp, trill and whistle.

| | |
|---|---|
| FAMILY NAME | Dugongidae |
| LATIN NAME | *Dugong dugon* |
| IUCN STATUS/WPA | Critically endangered/I |
| LOCAL STATUS | Uncommon |
| POPULATION | Unknown |
| DIET | ⱱ ⱬ |
| SOCIAL UNIT | 2–6 |
| ACTIVITY | ☼ |
| STRATUM | Aquatic (marine) |

## DUGONG
**LOCAL NAME:** *Kadal pasu* (Malayalam).

THE SEA COW or Dugong is a very large marine mammal resembling a dolphin in general body shape, with a streamlined torso, flattened and deeply notched tail flukes, and flippers for forelimbs. The face of the Dugong is more like that of a seal or walrus and ends in a fleshy pad-like lip with several bristles around the muzzle. The general body colour is brownish-grey above and whitish below. Males have a pair of protruding, tusk-like incisors.
- **BEHAVIOUR** Dugongs are secretive creatures of turbid waters, rarely displaying the familiarity with humans that their cousins, the manatees, do. Although they are normally found in small groups or in mother-calf pairs, herds of over 100 have been recorded where sea grass beds are profuse.
- **SIZE** Total body length: 2.5–3 m. Weight: 140–170 kg.
- **HABITAT** An Indian Ocean resident, found off both coasts. Recorded off Gujarat, Karnataka, Kerala, Tamil Nadu, and Andaman and Nicobar Islands.
- **BEST SEEN AT** Gulf of Mannar (Tamil Nadu).

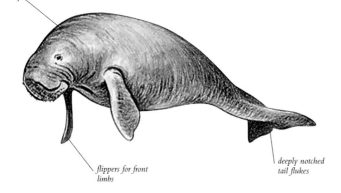

streamlined brown or grey-brown body

flippers for front limbs

deeply notched tail flukes

# ACKNOWLEDGMENTS

This book should have been written over many years by many collaborative authors. That I managed to put it together was largely due to the help of several people who gave of their time and knowledge unstintingly. I wish to thank all of them for their generosity, patience, and friendship.

The editorial board comprising five eminent naturalists and scientists – J.C. Daniel, A.J.T. Johnsingh, Ajith Kumar, Nameer P. Ommer, and Anwaruddin Choudhury – went through the manuscript and suggested ways of improving clarity and precision. It is due to their inputs that the text reads the way it does, although the fault is entirely mine for any mistakes that may have crept in.

Other than the editorial board, subject specialists commented on species or groups of species. Without their pertinent, rigorous and painstaking comments, the text would have been much poorer. Arun Venkataraman and Y.V. Jhala advised me on the subject of Canids; Ravi Chellam on Felids; George Schaller on Deer and Antelopes; Werner Haberl on Shrews; Iqbal Malik, Jayantha Das, Joydeep Bose, and Prabal Sarkar on Primates; S.S. Saha on Mustelids, Viverrids, Herpestids, Rodents and Insectivores; Otto Pfister on Mustelids, Voles, Pikas, Foxes and Equids; N.V.K. Ashraf and S.A. Hussain on Mustelids, Viverrids and Herpestids; S. Sathyakumar on Deer, Antelopes, Goat, Goat-antelope and Bears; Surendra Varma on Deer, Antelopes, Cattle, Pigs, Pangolin and Elephants; Yashveer Bhatnagar on Goat, Sheep, Goat-antelope and high-altitude Felids; Nandini Rajamani on Flying Squirrels; Nita Shah on Equids and high-altitude Antelope and Cattle; Renee Borges on Giant Squirrels; Gopinathan Maheswaran on Lagomorphs; G. Marimuthu on Bats; R.S. Tripathi on Rodents; C. Srinivasulu and Manoj Muni on Rodents and Bats; and Petra Deimer, Kumaran Sathasivam, and Dipani Sutaria on Cetaceans.

Two former colleagues, Suraj Saigal and Khalid Pasha, assisted during the formative stages of the book, in text and picture research. Towards the end, my Executive Assistant at the Wildlife Trust of India, Vinod Kumar, bore the burden of typing in parts and researching last-minute additions. To all of them, my heartfelt thanks.

Several others assisted me in the course of my work: Ambika Aiyyadurai, Anand Ramanathan, Andrew Smith, Aniruddha Mukherjee, Anish Andheria, Arvind Krishnan, Ashok Kumar, S.P. Goyal, Bharat Jethwa, Dilip Chetri, Dipanker Ghosh, Diwakar Sharma, Harry Andrews, James Zaccharias, Jihuosuo Biswas, Mohammed Idris, Mohideen Wafar, Nidhi Gureja, P.C. Bhattacharjee, P.S. Easa, Partha Chatterjee, Peter Jackson, Prabal Sarkar, Qamar Qureshi, R. Arumugam, R. Krishnamani, Riyaz Ahmed, S.C. Neginhal, B.K. Gogoi, Sally Walker, Sandeep Tiwari, Sanjay Molur, Sunil Subba Kyarong, Sujon Chatterjee, T. Ganesh, Tom Augustine, the Shrew Shrine (http://members.vienna.at/shrew//), and Yogesh Dubey.

If I have inadvertently left somebody out of this list, my sincere apologies and thank you all the same.

Dorling Kindersley and Penguin Books India, my publishers, worked through several extenuating deadlines to make the book happen. A special word of thanks to Anita Roy, Ira Pande, and Shuka Jain for setting me off and to Romi Chakraborty, Glenda Fernandes, and Bena Sareen for being there to help finish it. Thank you to the entire DK team including Sheema Mookherjee, Elizabeth Thomas, Kiran Mohan, Pallavi Narain, Aparna Sharma, Shefali Upadhyay, Kajori Aikat, Pankaj Sharma, and Suresh Kumar, who designed, mapped, and edited the book. And to David Davidar, for having faith in the book under trying circumstances.

Finally, a line in admiration for my wife V.K. Karthika who stood by me during the two years of writing frenzy with good humour, sharp editorial comments and the fervent hope that I would never write a book again! Thanks are also due to our families who allowed us the time, space, and peace of mind to concentrate on the book.

I dedicate this book to the memory of my grandmother C.P. Ambujakshi Amma, who was the first to listen to my stories about animals, and to Shiva, the newest mammal in my life.

# GLOSSARY

**Aestivate** Spend the summer or dry season in a dormant condition.

**Alpha male** The dominant male in a group.

**Anterior** Of or near the head end.

**Antitragus** A lobe developed from the basal part of the outer margin of the ear in some bats.

**Baleen** Comb-like plates hanging from the upper jaw of many large whales.

**Bifid** Of a structure, having two distal processes.

**Blow** Cloud of moisture-laden air exhaled by cetaceans.

**Brachiation** To swing by the arms from one hold to the next.

**Breaching** The act of leaping completely out of the water (or almost completely) and landing back with a splash.

**Browser** A herbivore which feeds on shoots and leaves of trees.

**Buccal** Pertaining to cheek.

**Buff** A yellowish-beige colour.

**Bursa** A fluid-filled sac or sac-like cavity.

**Canine** A single tooth, situated immediately behind the incisors in each jaw.

**Class** A taxonomic division subordinate to Phylum and superior to Order.

**Commensal** Species living in close association with man without interdependence.

**Dewclaw** Non-functional claw.

**Digitigrade** Walking so that only the toes touch the ground.

**Dimorphism** Pertaining to a population or taxon having two genetically determined, discontinuous morphological types.

**Dorsal** Towards the upper side.

**Echolocation** Determination of the position of an object by measuring the time taken for an echo to return from it, and its direction.

**Endemic** Peculiar to, or prevailing in, some specified country or area.

**Estuarine** Inhabiting or found in an inlet of the sea.

**Even-toed ungulate** Animal having horny covering at the end of the foot with an even number of toes.

**Falcate** Sickle shaped.

**Family** A taxonomic division subordinate to Order and superior to Genus.

**Flehmen** German word describing a facial expression of goats and sheep associated with smelling, when the head is lifted and nose wrinkled.

**Flipper** Paddle-shaped front limb of a cetacean.

**Flukes** Horizontally flattened tail of cetaceans.

**Foramen** A natural hole, especially in a bone, through which nerves and blood vessels pass.

**Forearm of a bat (FA)** The measurement from the extremity of the elbow to the extremity of the carpus, with the wings folded.

**Form** An individual or group of specimens with a scientific name; the nest of a hare or rabbit.

**Fossorial** Living under ground.

**Genus** A taxonomic division subordinate to Family and superior to Species.

**Grazer** A herbivore that feeds upon grasses.

**Gregarious** Animals living together in herds or flocks.

**Guard hairs** Longer, stiffer bristle-like hair that lies outside the fur.

**Gular sac** A glandular pouch in the skin of the throat of certain bats.

**Harem** A group of female animals of the same species that are the mates of a single male.

**Head & Body Length (HBL)** A measurement from the tip of the nose to the base of the tail, dorsally.

**Hibernate** Spend the winter in sleep or in a dormant condition.

**Hybridization** Production of an animal or plant from a cross between genetically unlike individuals.

**Incisor** A front, or cutting tooth.

**Inter-femoral membrane** Membrane stretching between thighbones in bats.

**Keel** Distinctive bulge on the tailstock near the flukes in cetaceans; a ridge-like part.

**Lancet** The erect, sub-triangular, posterior part of the noseleaf of bats of the Genus *Rhinolophus*.

**Lobtailing** A whale beating the water with its tail flukes to communicate with other whales.

**Melanistic** Dark coloured.

**Metacarpal** Relating to the skeleton of the hand between the wrist and the fingers, consisting of five long bones.

**New world** The western hemisphere; the Americas.

**Noseleaf** Structure developed from the skin around the nostrils in some bats.

**Ochre** A moderate yellow-orange to orange colour.

**Odd-toed ungulate** Animal having horny covering at the end of the foot with an odd number of toes.

**Old World** Palearctic, Oriental, African, and Australian regions.

**Order** A taxonomic division subordinate to Class and superior to Family.

**Pastern** Part of a horse's foot between fetlock and the hoof.

**Pectoral** Pertaining to the anterior chest region.

**Pelage** The coat of a mammal, consisting of hair, wool, fur, etc.

**Pelagic waters** Relating to the open sea.

**Plantar** Pertaining to the sole of the foot.

**Plantigrade** Walking with the entire sole of the foot touching the ground.

**Pod** Coordinated group of cetaceans; term often used in connection with larger, toothed whales; a gland in the case of musk deer.

**Posterior** Of or near the hind end.

**Prehensile** Adapted for grasping.

**Pronking** Movement where animal leaps vertically with all four feet off the ground.

**Retractile** Capable of being drawn in.

**Rhodendron** A Himalayan flowering plant.

**Rorqual** A baleen whale of the genus *Balaenoptera*; many experts include the Humpback Whale in this group.

**Ruminant** Animal having the habit of chewing partially digested food.

**Russet** Brown with a yellowish or reddish tinge.

**Sagittal crest** A variably developed median crest on the vault of the skull.

**Septum** A dividing partition between two tissues or cavities.

**Sexual dimorphism** Phenotypic difference between the males and females of a particular taxon.

**Sheaths** An enclosing or protective structure, such as a leaf base encasing the stem of a plant.

**Shola** Unique evergreen forest of the Western Ghats.

**Sounder** The collective term for a group of pigs.

**Species** A taxonomic division subordinate to Genus and superior to sub-species.

**Steppe** An extensive grassy plain usually without trees.

**Sub-species** A recognizable sub-population of a single species, typically with a distinct geographical distribution.

**Tail Length** Measurement from the tip of the tail to its base adjacent to the body.

**Tailstock** Region from just behind the dorsal fin to the flukes.

**Taxon** A group of organisms of any taxonomic rank.

**Terai** A belt of poorly drained land at the foot of mountains (the Himalaya in the Indian context).

**Thatch** A species of grass found in the Gangetic plain.

**Throat Grooves** Grooves on the throat present in some groups of whales.

**Tine** Sharp terminal branches of a deer's antler.

**Tragus** A cutaneous and cartilaginous projection found at the opening of the external ear in some bats.

**Tubercle** A small rounded elevation especially on the skin or on a bone.

**Ungulate** Mammal having horny covering at the end of the foot.

**Unicuspid** Teeth having a single cusp or prominence on top of tooth.

**Ventral** Relating to the underside.

**Vestigial** A structure that has become a more or less functionless relict.

**Wallow** To roll about in mud, water, etc., for pleasure.

**Whisker** Any of the stiff sensory hairs growing on the face of a cat, rat, or other mammal.

**Whithers** Ridge between shoulder blades especially of horses and antelopes.

# INDEX

# E

Eastern Himalayan Cats 90–91
Eco-niches 18
Edentates 110
Edward's Noisy Rat 144
Elephantidae 8, 67
Elephants 8, 66–67
*Elephas maximus* 67
Elliot's Brown Spiny Mouse 147
Emballonuridae 9, 157
*Eonycteris spelaea* 153
*Eothenomys melanogaster* 137
*Eptesicus bottae* 166
*Eptesicus pachyotis* 166
*Eptesicus serotinus* 166
Equidae 8, 69
Equids 11, 68
*Equus asinus* 68
*Equus caballus* 68
*Equus kiang* 68, 69
*Equus onager* 68, 69
Erinaceidae 9, 122–23
Ermine 15, 102
  *See also* Himalayan Stoat
*Eubalaena glacialis* 172
*Eupetaurus cinereus* 131
Eurasian Lynx 89
Eurasian Otter 100
*Euroscaptor micrura* 17
Evening Bats 9, 151, 170–71

# F

False Killer Whale 182–83
False Vampires 9, 151, 162
Fawn-coloured Mouse 146
Felidae 9, 82–95
Felids 82–95
*Felis chaus* 93
*Felis sylvestris* 92
*Feresa attenuata* 181
*Feroculus feroculus*, 121
Field Rats 142
Fin Whale 189
Finless Porpoise 174, 176
Fishing Cat 94, 95
Five-striped Palm Squirrel 126, 128
Flat-headed Bats 167
Flying Fox 11, 152
Flying Squirrels 130–32
Forest Bears 75
Forest Elephant 66
Forest Rat 140
Forrest's Pika 114
Four-horned Antelope 46, 50
Foxes 80–81
Fraser's Dolphin 180
Free-tailed Bats 9, 151, 163
Freshwater Dolphin 174–75
Frugivorous 10, 11, 150
Fruit Bats 9, 151–56
Fukien Wood Mouse 145
Fulvous Fruit Bat 153
Fulvous Leaf-nosed Bat 161
*Funambulus layardi* 128
*Funambulus macclellandi* 128

*Funambulus palmarum* 128
*Funambulus pennantii* 128
*Funambulus sublincatus* 128
*Funambulus tristriatus* 128

# G

Ganges River Dolphin 172, 174, 176
*Gazella bennettii* 50
Gazelles 46, 69
Gaur 11, 14, 60, 62
*Gerbillus gleadowi* 139
*Gerbillus nanus* 139
Gerbils 138–39
Giant Panda 72
Giant Squirrels 126–27
Gingko-toothed Beaked Whale 186
*Globicephala macrorhynchus* 183
Gnu 54
Goat 8, 11
Goat-antelopes 52, 54–55
Golden Cat 91, 92
Golden Langur 26, 36
*Golunda ellioti* 143
Goral 14, 52, 55
Graminivorous 134
*Grampus griseus* 180
Grassland Deer 45
Gray's Giant Flying Squirrel 130
Great Evening Bat 170
Great Himalayan Leaf-nosed Bat 160
Great Tibetan Sheep 58
Greater False Vampire 162
Greater Horseshoe Bat 158
Greater Mouse-tailed Bat 156
Greater One-horned Rhino 70–71
Grey Dolphin 180
Grey Hamster 133
Grey Long-eared Bat 164
Grey Mongoose 96, 108
Grey Woodland Shrew 121
Grey-headed (Spotted) Giant Flying Squirrel 130
Grizzled Giant Squirrel 127
Gueldenstaedt's White-toothed Shrew 121

# H

Habitats 16, 18
  Loss and fragmentation 23
*Hadromys humei* 144
Hamsters 133
Hanuman Langur 12, 26, 30, 37
Hares 9, 112–13
Harlequin Bats 165
Harvest Mouse 146
Hedgehogs 9, 122
*Helarctos malayanus* 75
*Hemiechinus collaris* 122
*Hemiechinus micropus* 123
*Hemiechinus nudiventris* 123

*Hemitragus hylocrius* 56
*Hemitragus jemlahicus* 56
Herbivores 10, 11
*Herpestes brachyurus* 109
*Herpestes edwardsii* 108
*Herpestes javanicus* 108
*Herpestes smithii* 108
*Herpestes urva* 109
*Herpestes vitticolis* 109
Herpestidae 9, 97, 108–09
Herpestids 96–97, 108–09
*Hesperoptenus tickelli* 171
Hill Long-tongued Fruit Bat 153
Hill Shrew 120
Himalayan Brown Bear 74
Himalayan Crestless Porcupine 125
Himalayan Marmot 133
Himalayan Musk Deer 40
Himalayan Palm Civets 107
Himalayan Rats 141
Himalayan Stoat 15, 102
  *See also* Ermine
Himalayan Striped Squirrel 126, 128
Himalayan Tahr 56
Himalayan Water Shrew 119
Himalayan Weasel 103
Hipposideridae 9, 160
*Hipposideros armiger* 160
*Hipposideros ater* 160
*Hipposideros fulvus* 161
*Hipposideros speoris* 161
Hispid Hare 113
Hoary Bamboo Rat 148
Hoary-bellied Himalayan Squirrel 127
Hodgson's Bat 164
Hodgson's Brown-toothed Shrew 119
Hodgson's Flying Squirrel 130
Hodgson's Porcupine 125
Hog Badger 96, 99
Hog Deer 45
Honey Badger 99
Hoolock Gibbon 27, 29
Horseshoe Bats 9, 151, 158
Horsfield Shrew 121
House Mouse 146
House Rat 140
House Shrew 120
Hume's Manipur Bush Rat 144
Humpback Whale 172, 190–91
Humpbacked Dolphin 172
*Hyaena hyaena* 77
Hyaenidae 9, 77
Hyenas 9, 76–77
Hylobatidae 8, 29
*Hylopetes fimbriatus* 132
*Hyperacrius fertilis* 137
*Hyperacrius wynnei* 137
Hystricidae 9, 124–25
*Hystrix brachyura* 125
*Hystrix indica* 124

# I

*Ia io* 170
Ibex 53
Indian Bush Rat 143
Indian Desert Jird 139
Indian Flying Fox 152
Indian Fox 80
Indian Gazelle 50
  *See also* Chinkara
Indian Gerbil 138
Indian Giant Flying Squirrel 131
Indian Giant Squirrel 15, 126–27
Indian Hairy-footed Gerbil 139
Indian Hare 112
Indian Hedgehog 123
Indian Long-tailed Shrew 119
Indian Muntjac 44
  *See also* Barking Deer
Indian Pangolin 111
Indian Pipistrelle 168
Indian Porcupine 124–25
Indian Pygmy Bat 168
Indian Rhinoceros 86
Indian Wild Dog 76, 79
  *See also* Dhole
Indo-Pacific Hump-backed Dolphin 179
Indus River Dolphin 174
Infanticide 12
Insectivora 9, 116, 118
Insectivores 9, 11, 116–23, 150
Intermediate Horseshoe Bat 158
Irawaddy Dolphin 176

# J

Jackal 76, 77
Javan Rhinoceros 70
Jenkin's Andaman Spiny Shrew 121
Jungle Cat 82, 93, 94
Jungle Striped Squirrel 128

# K

Kashmir Birch Mouse 146
Kashmir Flying Squirrel 132
Kashmir Fox 81
Kashmir Markhor 57
Kashmir Mountain Vole 136
Kashmir Red Deer 42
Kashmir White-toothed Shrew 121
Kelaart's Long-clawed Shrew 121
Kelaart's Pipistrelle 169
Kenneth's White-toothed Rat 144
*Kerivoula picta* 163
Killer Whale 172, 180, 182–83
*Kogia breviceps* 184
*Kogia simus* 185
Kogiidae 184–85
Kuhl's Pipistrelle 169

# PICTURE CREDITS

This book would not have been possible without the generous contribution of more than a hundred photographers, some of whose work could not be used due to constraints of space and design. Thanks are due to all of them.

A.J.T. Johnsingh, 20, 32b, 33a, 55, 60a, 71a, 72; Ajith Kumar, 3a, 12a, 34, 56b, 126a; Amrit Pal Singh, 61a, 69a, 75a, 123a; Anoop K.R., 13, 96; Arun Srivastava, 14b; Asha Jayakumar,10b; Ashok Kumar, 173; Atul Kumar Gupta, 35b; Batcom, 150a, 151, 157a, 158a, 160a, 162b, 164b, 167b, 169a; Bharat Rughani/Sanctuary, Back cover b; Bholu Abrar Khan, 95b; Chuku Loma, 28a; Claus Reuther, 100a, 100b, 100c; Dilip Chetry, 30a, 33b; Dipankar Ghose, 90a, 114b, 129c; Divya Mudappa, 104a, 106a, 106b, 109a; Dorling Kindersley Picture Library, 7b, 7c, 15c, 42b, 74a, 74b, 82a, 103a, 116–117, 125b, 141a, 146a, 156, 168, 172–173, 183a, 191a, 191b, all cetacean illustrations, Back cover a; Easa P.S., 2, 28b, 95a, 123b, 163a; Eldhose, 132c; George Schaller, 15a, 51a, 51b, 57a, 59b, 63b, 68a, 88a, 89a, 113a, 114a; Gabor Csorba, 153a, 153b, 153c, 155c, 157c, 158b, 158c, 158d, 159a, 159b, 159c, 160b, 162a, 164a, 165a, 165b, 170a, 170b, 171; G.S. Rawat, 54a; Heerak Nandy, 129b; Jayakumar M.N., 39b, 109b; Jayantha Das, 29b, 36b; Jayaprakash S.R., 97b; Jeremy Holden, 91b; Jihuosuo Biswas, 36a; Joanna Van Gruisen, Title page, 6, 27c, 37b, 42a, 45b, 48b, 49b, 50b, 58a, 58b, 59a, 70a, 85a, 93b, 108b; Joshua Barton, 41a, 66b, 83b, 86a, 94b, 108c; K.M.B. Prasad, 3b, 4, 5, 7a, 8a, 8b, 9, 11a, 12b, 44b, 73b; Kailash Sankhala, 92a; Karthik Shanker, 118, 134a, 134c, 140a, 140b, 142a, 143a 147; Karthikeyan S.R., 107b, 111a, 134b, 144, 149b, 154; Kathy Conforte, 91a; Lahiri P.S., 43b, 49a; Madhavan Arrakal, 167a; M.D. Madhusudan, 101a;

Manoj Muni, 155b, 163b; Manoj P., 150b; Marimuthu G., 157b, 161a, 161b; Mark Kostich, 104b; Mohit Aggarwal, 37a, 40b, 41b, 46, 48a, 77a, 82b, 107a, 110a; M.K.S. Pasha, 22b, 26, 27d, 43a, 60b, 62b, 75b; Nameer P. Ommer, 120c, 166, 169b; Nandini Rajamani, 131a; Otto Pfister, 56a, 63a, 69b, 81c, 86b, 88b, 89b, 101c, 102a, 102b, 112c, 113c, 115a, 115b, 115c, 115d, 122a, 126b, 127a, 129a, 136, 137, 139a; Oxford University Press, 120a, 132a, 133c, 138a, 142b, 143b; Pankaj Neginhal, 112b; Prabal Sarkar, 68b; Pramod G. Shanbhag, 31a, 65a, 67, 76, Back Cover c; Prasanta Bordoloi, 11b, 110b, 111b; Rajiv Bhartri, 94a; Ramakantha V., 27b, 44a, 98, 101b, 110c, 124; Ravi Chellam, 10a, 18; Ravi Sankaran, 122b; R. S.Tripathi, 128b, 135a, 135b, 135c, 138b, 139b, 141b, 146b; Rupin Dang, 81a, 97a, 103b, 108a; S.S. Saha, 32a, 130b, 155a; Sandeep Sharma, 90b; Saravana Kumar, 148; S. Sathyakumar, 38a, 40a, 132b, 133a; Sathyanarayana C.R., 39a, 52, 64, 79a; Sati J.P., 29a; Satish Kr. Sharma, (courtesy) 131b; Sharad Gaur, 87a; Shivanandappa, 27a, 79b, 120b, 127b; Sujon Chatterjee, 65b, 133b, 149a; Sukumar R., 14a; Sumit Sen, 112a; Suresh Elamon, 127c, 128c; Sushant Choudhary, 45a; Ullas Karanth, 99a;Vishnu Dutt Sharma, 81b;Vivek Menon, 16a, 16b, 16c, 19, 22a, 23a, 23b, 30b, 31b, 53a, 54b, 62a, 66a, 70–71, 93a, 99b, 105, 130a;Vivek R. Sinha, Front cover, 35a, 38b, 47a, 50a, 61b, 73a, 78b, 80, 83a, 84–85, 87b, 113b, 128a, 152a,152b; Yashveer Bhatnagar, 15b, 53b, 57b;Y. V. Jhala, 47b, 77b, 78a, 92b.

# SELECT BIBLIOGRAPHY

I have drawn upon a number of sources, both scientific and lay accounts, for creating this work. Although a complete bibliography is not possible because of space constraints, all major mammalian works referring to India have been consulted and a selection of these, which could form an important reference for those interested in further reading, is as follows:

Anon (2000): *ENVIS Bulletin: Wildlife & Protected Areas, Directory of Wildlife Protected Areas in India.* Vol.3, No.1. Wildlife Institute of India.

Anon (2002): *Conservation Assessment & Management Plan (CAMP) Workshop for South Asian Chiroptera.*

Anon (2002): *Conservation Assessment & Management Plan (CAMP) Workshop for South Asian Primates.*

Bates, P.J.J. & D.L. Harrison (1997): *Bats of the Indian Subcontinent.* Harrison Zoological Museum.

Blanford, W.T. (1888): *The Fauna of British India including Ceylon and Burma. Mammalia.* Part I & II. Taylor and Francis.

Brosset, A. (1962): *Bats of Central & Western India.* Part I, II & III. J. Bombay Nat. Hist. Soc., 59.

Brosset, A. (1963): *Bats of Central & Western India.* Part IV. J. Bombay Nat. Hist. Soc., 59.

Carwardine, M. (1995): *Whales, Dolphins and Porpoises: A Visual Guide to All the World's Cetaceans.* Eyewitness Handbook. Dorling Kindersley.

Chakraborty, S. (1983): 'Contribution to the Knowledge of the Mammalian Fauna of Jammu & Kashmir, India'. Miscellaneous publications. Occasional paper no.38. Records of the Zoological Survey of India.

Chakraborty, S. (1985): 'Studies on the Genus Callosciurus Gray (Rodentia Sciuridae)'. Miscellaneous publications. Occasional paper no.63. Records of the Zoological Survey of India.

Chapman, J.A. & J.E.C. Flux (1990): *Rabbits, Hares and Pikas, Status Survey & Conservation Action Plan.* IUCN/SSC Lagomorph Specialist Group.

Choudhury, Anwaruddin (1997): *Checklist of the Mammals of Assam.* Gibbon Books.

Corbet, G.B. & J.E. Hill (1992): *Mammals of Indomalayan Region: A Systematic Review.* Natural History Museum Publications, Oxford University Press.

Duncan, P. (Ed.) (1992): *Zebras, Asses & Horses: Action Plan for the Conservation of Wild Equids.* IUCN/SSC Equids Specialist Group.

Easa, P.S, J. Zacharias & P. Padmanabhan (2001): *Survey of Small Mammals in Kerala, With Special Reference to Endangered Species.* Kerala Forest Research Institute.

Ellerman, J.R. (1961): *The Fauna of British India including Ceylon and Burma. (Mammalia.* Part III. Rodentia). Zoological Survey of India. (In 2 parts).

Ellerman, J.R. and T.C.S. Morrison-Scott (1951): *Checklist of Palaearctic and Indian Mammals, 1758-1946.* Second Edition. British Museum of Natural History.

Foose, T. J. & N. van Strien (Eds.) (1997): *Asian Rhinos, Status Survey and Action Plan.* IUCN.

Gee, E.P. (1964): *The Wildlife of India.* Collins Fontana Books.

Glatston, R. A & the IUCN/SSC Mustelid, Viverrid and Procyonid Specialist Group (1994): *The Red Panda, Olingos, Coatis, Raccoons and Their Relatives.* IUCN.

Groombridge, B. (Ed.) (1993): *The IUCN Red List of Threatened Animals.* IUCN.

Gupta, A.K. (Ed.) (2002): *ENVIS Bulletin: Wildlife & Protected Areas, Non-Human Primates of India.* Vol.1, No.1. Wildlife Institute of India.

Hawkins, R.E. (1986): *Encyclopedia of Indian Natural History.* Bombay Natural History Society.

Hussain, S.A. (Ed.) (1999): *ENVIS Bulletin: Wildlife & Protected Areas, Mustelids, Viverrids and Herpestids of India.* Vol.2, No.2. Wildlife Institute of India.

Israel, S. & T. Sinclair (2001): *Indian Wildlife.* Insight Guide. APA.

Jain A.P, R.S.Tripathi & B.D. Rana (1993): *Rodent Management: The State of Art.* Technical Bulletin No.1. Central Arid Zone Research Institute.

Jerdon, T.C. (1867): *The Mammals of India.* British Museum of Natural History.

Lekagul, B. & J. A. McNeely (1977): *Mammals of Thailand.* Association of Conservation of Wildlife, Bangkok.

Macdonald, D. (Ed.) (2001): *New Encyclopedia of Mammals.* Oxford University Press.

Molur, S., N.P. Ommer & S. Walker (Eds.) (1998): *Report of the Workshop "Conservation Assessment and Management Plan for Mammals of India"* (BCCP-Endangered Species Project). Zoo Outreach Organization, Conservation Breeding Specialist Group.

Nowell, K. & P. Jackson (1996): *Wild Cats, Status Survey & Conservation Action Plan.* IUCN/SSC Cat Specialist Group.

Oliver, W.C.R. (1980): *The Pigmy Hog: The Biology and Conservation of the Pigmy Hog (Sus salvinius) and the Hispid Hare (Caprolagus hispidus).* Special Scientific Report. Jersey Wildlife Preservation Trust.

Ommer, N P. (1998): *Checklist of Indian Mammals.* Kerala Forest Department (Wildlife Wing) and Kerala Agriculture University.

Pocock, R.I. (1939). *The Fauna of British India including Ceylon and Burma; Mammalia* Vol.1, *Primates and Carnivora,* in part. Taylor and Francis.

Pocock, R.I. (1941). *The Fauna of British India including Ceylon and Burma; Mammalia* Vol.2, *Carnivora,* in part. Taylor and Francis.

Prater, S.H. (Edition 1, 1948; Edition 2, 1965; Edition 3, 1971): *The Book of Indian Animals.* Bombay Natural History Society.

Rana, B.D., A.P. Jain & R. S. Tripathi (1994): *Fifteen Years of Co-ordinated Research on Rodent Control.* Technical Bulletin No.3. Central Arid Zone Research Institute.

Roberts, T.J. (1997): *The Mammals of Pakistan.* Oxford University Press.

Sathasivam, K. (2000): 'A Catalogue of Indian Marine Mammal Records'. *Blackbuck* 16(2&3).

Schreiber, A.R., M. R. Wirth & van Rompaey (1989): *Weasels, Civets, Mongoose and Their Relatives, an Action Plan for the Conservation of Mustelids and Viverrids.* IUCN.

Sinha, Y.P. (1986): 'The Bats of Bihar: Taxonomy & Ecology'. Miscellaneous publications. Occasional paper no.77. Records of the Zoological Survey of India.

Sinha, Y.P. (1999): 'Contribution to the Knowledge of Bats (Mammalia, Chiroptera) of Northeast Hills, India'. Miscellaneous publications. Occasional paper no.174. Records of the Zoological Survey of India.

Sterndale, R.A. (1984): *Natural History of the Mammals of India and Ceylon.* Thacker, Spink and Co.

Stone, R.D. (1995): *Eurasian Insectivores & Tree Shrews, Status Survey & Conservation Action Plan.* IUCN/SSC Insectivore, Tree Shrew and Elephant Shrew Specialist Group.

Yin, Tun (1966): *Wild Mammals of Myanmar.* Forest Department, Myanmar.

In addition, I would recommend that readers look out for these publications which are slated to be out very soon (please note that titles are provisional):

Johnisngh, A.J.T. & N. Manjrekar (Eds.): *Mammals of South Asia.*

Pfister, O.: *Mammals of Ladakh.*

Sathasivam, K.: *The Marine Mammals of India.*